Smartsheet for Beginners
The Quick-Start Guide

Kiet Huynh

Table of Contents

Introduction 6
   1.1 What is Smartsheet? 6
   1.2 Why Use Smartsheet? 10
   1.3 Who This Guide is For 15
   1.4 How to Use This Book 19

CHAPTER I Getting Started with Smartsheet 24
   1.1 Setting Up Your Smartsheet Account 24
      1.1.1 Creating an Account 24
      1.1.2 Choosing a Pricing Plan 30
      1.1.3 Navigating the Dashboard 41
   1.2 Understanding the Smartsheet Interface 48
      1.2.1 Sheets, Dashboards, and Workspaces 48
      1.2.2 The Toolbar Overview 57
      1.2.3 Key Features and Their Uses 63
   1.3 Creating Your First Sheet 76
      1.3.1 Selecting a Template 76
      1.3.2 Adding and Editing Columns 84
      1.3.3 Saving and Sharing Your Sheet 92

CHAPTER II Working with Data in Smartsheet 98
   2.1 Adding and Managing Data 98
      2.1.1 Inputting Data Manually 98
      2.1.2 Importing Data from Excel and Google Sheets 103
      2.1.3 Editing and Deleting Data 109
   2.2 Organizing Your Sheet 114
      2.2.1 Sorting and Filtering Data 114

TABLE OF CONTENTS

    2.2.2 Grouping and Highlighting Key Information 119

    2.2.3 Using Conditional Formatting 125

2.3 Leveraging Formulas and Functions 131

    2.3.1 Basic Formulas (SUM, AVERAGE, COUNT, IF ...) 131

    2.3.2 Linking Data Across Sheets 145

    2.3.3 Using Advanced Functions 151

CHAPTER III Collaborating in Smartsheet **156**

3.1 Sharing Your Sheets and Workspaces 156

    3.1.1 Inviting Collaborators 156

    3.1.2 Setting Permissions 160

    3.1.3 Sharing Links and Embedding Sheets 165

3.2 Communicating with Team Members 171

    3.2.1 Using Comments and Notes 171

    3.2.2 Assigning Tasks to Team Members 177

    3.2.3 Notifications and Alerts 181

3.3 Version Control and History 186

    3.3.1 Accessing Revision History 186

    3.3.2 Restoring Previous Versions 191

    3.3.3 Best Practices for Collaboration 195

CHAPTER IV Automating Your Workflows **200**

4.1 Introduction to Automation in Smartsheet 200

    4.1.1 Why Automate? 200

    4.1.2 Automation Basics 204

4.2 Creating Automation Rules 212

    4.2.1 Setting Up Alerts and Notifications 212

    4.2.2 Automating Approvals 218

    4.2.3 Recurring Tasks and Updates 222

4.3 Workflow Optimization Tips 228

TABLE OF CONTENTS

    4.3.1 Identifying Repetitive Processes 228

    4.3.2 Using Templates for Automation 232

    4.3.3 Monitoring Automated Workflows 238

CHAPTER V Visualizing Data **243**

  5.1 Creating and Customizing Reports 243

    5.1.1 Generating a New Report 243

    5.1.2 Filtering and Grouping Data in Reports 248

    5.1.3 Sharing Reports with Stakeholders 253

  5.2 Using Dashboards 259

    5.2.1 Building a Dashboard from Scratch 260

    5.2.2 Adding Widgets (Charts, Metrics, etc.) 264

    5.2.3 Best Practices for Effective Dashboards 268

  5.3 Exporting and Presenting Data 274

    5.3.1 Exporting to Excel, PDF, and Other Formats 274

    5.3.2 Printing Sheets and Reports 279

    5.3.3 Integrating Smartsheet with Presentation Tools 284

CHAPTER VI Tips and Tricks for Beginners **289**

  6.1 Keyboard Shortcuts for Efficiency 289

  6.2 Troubleshooting Common Issues 294

    6.2.1 Resolving Login Problems 294

    6.2.2 Fixing Formatting Errors 299

    6.2.3 Handling Collaboration Conflicts 304

  6.3 Best Practices for Staying Organized 310

    6.3.1 Naming Conventions for Sheets and Workspaces 310

    6.3.2 Archiving Old Projects 315

    6.3.3 Maintaining Data Security 320

CHAPTER VII Expanding Your Smartsheet Skills **326**

  7.1 Integrating Smartsheet with Other Tools 326

7.1.1 Smartsheet and Microsoft Office 326

7.1.2 Smartsheet and Google Workspace 330

7.1.3 Smartsheet and Third-Party Applications 335

7.2 Learning from the Smartsheet Community 341

7.2.1 Accessing Tutorials and Resources 341

7.2.2 Joining Smartsheet Forums 346

7.2.3 Attending Smartsheet Events 350

7.3 Planning for Advanced Features 355

7.3.1 Exploring Premium Add-Ons 355

7.3.2 Introducing Advanced Integrations 359

7.3.3 Preparing for Enterprise-Scale Use 365

CHAPTER VIII Conclusion **371**

Recap of Key Concepts 371

Next Steps for Beginners 377

Acknowledgments 383

Introduction

1.1 What is Smartsheet?

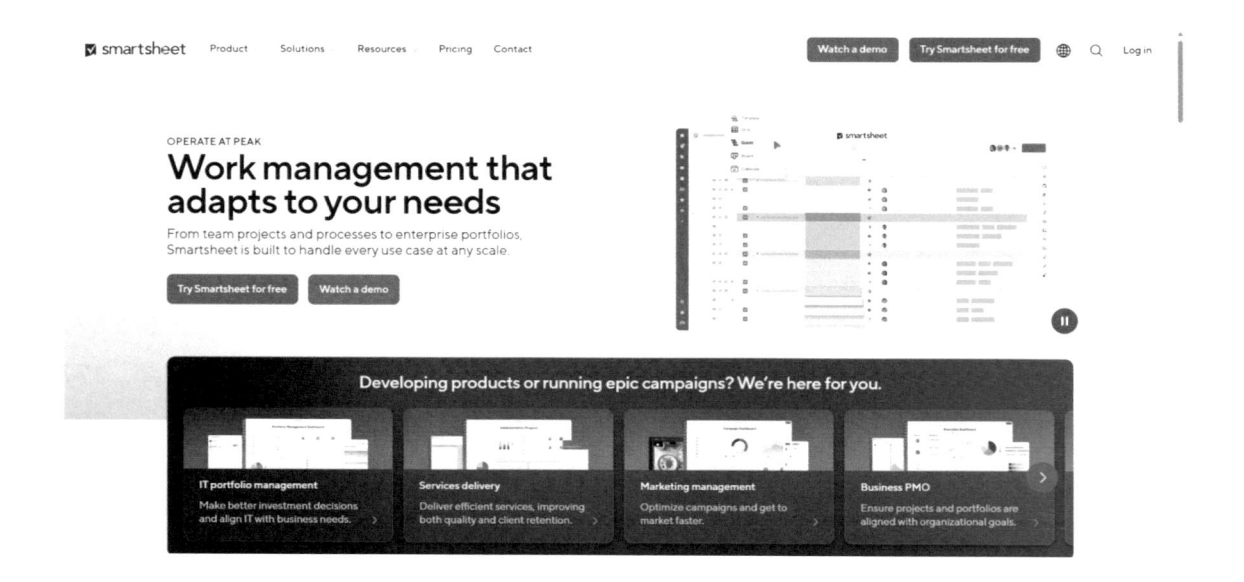

Smartsheet is a powerful cloud-based platform designed to simplify and streamline work management, project tracking, and team collaboration. It is widely used across various industries, from small startups to large enterprises, due to its intuitive interface, robust features, and ability to scale according to organizational needs.

At its core, Smartsheet combines the simplicity of spreadsheets with the power of modern project management tools. Unlike traditional spreadsheets, which are often limited to data entry and calculations, Smartsheet enables users to manage tasks, timelines, resources, and workflows in a highly visual and collaborative environment.

The Evolution of Work Management Tools

The concept behind Smartsheet emerged as a response to the limitations of traditional tools like Microsoft Excel and email for managing complex workflows. While spreadsheets were sufficient for basic data tracking, they lacked real-time collaboration, automation, and integration capabilities. Project management software, on the other hand, often proved too rigid or complex for everyday use.

Smartsheet bridges this gap by offering a flexible, user-friendly platform that adapts to a wide range of use cases. Whether you're organizing a marketing campaign, tracking construction projects, or planning personal goals, Smartsheet provides the tools you need to succeed.

Key Features of Smartsheet

1. **Flexible Sheets:** Smartsheet's foundation is the sheet, which functions like a spreadsheet but offers far more capabilities. Users can add columns for specific data types, including text, dates, dropdown menus, checkboxes, and attachments. Each sheet can be customized to fit unique project needs.

2. **Collaboration Tools**: Collaboration is seamless in Smartsheet, as multiple team members can work on the same sheet in real time. The platform supports comments, discussions, and file attachments directly within rows, reducing the need for lengthy email threads.

3. **Automation**: Smartsheet offers powerful automation tools to eliminate repetitive tasks. Users can create workflows to send notifications, request approvals, or update data automatically based on predefined triggers.

4. **Dashboards and Reports**: To help visualize progress and performance, Smartsheet includes customizable dashboards and reports. These tools provide a bird's-eye view of key metrics, helping teams and stakeholders stay informed.

5. **Integration with Other Tools**: Smartsheet integrates with numerous third-party applications, including Microsoft Office, Google Workspace, Salesforce, and Slack. These integrations enhance its functionality and enable teams to connect Smartsheet with existing systems seamlessly.

6. **Mobile Access**: With mobile apps for iOS and Android, Smartsheet ensures that users can access their work on the go. This feature is particularly valuable for teams that need to update or review project details in the field.

Use Cases for Smartsheet

One of Smartsheet's greatest strengths is its versatility. It can be tailored to suit a variety of industries and functions, including:

- **Project Management**: Plan timelines, assign tasks, and monitor progress in real time.
- **Marketing Campaigns**: Track deliverables, deadlines, and budgets for advertising initiatives.
- **Human Resources**: Manage employee onboarding, training schedules, and performance reviews.
- **Construction Projects**: Organize tasks, resources, and materials to ensure timely completion.
- **Event Planning**: Coordinate vendors, venues, and schedules for seamless events.

Smartsheet vs. Traditional Tools

While traditional tools like Excel and project management software have their place, Smartsheet offers a unique combination of features that make it stand out:

- **Real-Time Collaboration**: Unlike spreadsheets, which require manual updates and sharing, Smartsheet allows users to collaborate in real time, ensuring everyone has access to the latest information.
- **Automation**: Tasks that would require manual effort in traditional tools can be automated in Smartsheet, saving time and reducing errors.
- **User-Friendly Interface**: The learning curve for Smartsheet is much smaller compared to other project management software, making it accessible to beginners.

The Benefits of Using Smartsheet

1. **Improved Productivity**: By streamlining workflows and reducing manual tasks, Smartsheet enables teams to focus on high-value activities.
2. **Enhanced Collaboration**: With centralized data and communication tools, Smartsheet eliminates the need for scattered information across emails and documents.
3. **Better Decision-Making**: Smartsheet's reporting and dashboard capabilities provide actionable insights, helping managers and team leaders make informed decisions.

4. **Scalability**
   Whether you're managing a single project or overseeing an enterprise-wide initiative, Smartsheet scales to meet your needs.

Smartsheet in Numbers

Smartsheet's widespread adoption speaks to its effectiveness. As of recent years:

- Over 90% of Fortune 100 companies use Smartsheet.
- Millions of users worldwide rely on Smartsheet for work management.
- Smartsheet has been consistently recognized as a leader in collaborative work management tools by industry analysts.

Getting Started with Smartsheet

For beginners, Smartsheet offers a welcoming environment with ample resources to help you get started. The platform includes:

- **Templates**: Pre-built templates for common use cases, such as project planning, task tracking, and event management.
- **Help Center**: A comprehensive library of tutorials, FAQs, and guides.
- **Community Forums**: A vibrant user community that shares tips, best practices, and solutions.
- **Training and Certification**: Courses to help users deepen their Smartsheet knowledge and skills.

Conclusion

Smartsheet is more than just a tool—it's a transformative platform that empowers teams to work smarter, collaborate effectively, and achieve their goals. By understanding what Smartsheet is and its key features, you're taking the first step toward mastering this innovative solution. In the following chapters, we'll dive deeper into how you can set up your account, create sheets, and start managing projects like a pro.

INTRODUCTION

1.2 Why Use Smartsheet?

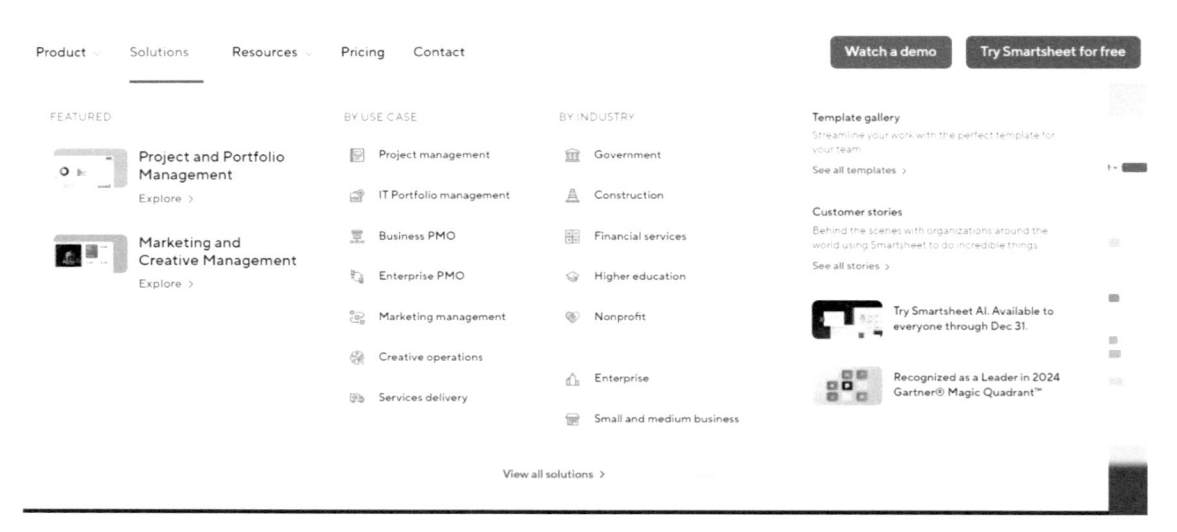

Smartsheet has emerged as one of the most popular tools for project management and team collaboration, offering a powerful, user-friendly platform that simplifies work processes. Whether you're managing a team, organizing projects, or automating workflows, Smartsheet provides tools to help you achieve your goals efficiently. In this section, we'll explore the key reasons why Smartsheet is a go-to solution for millions of users worldwide.

A Versatile Platform for Various Use Cases

One of the standout features of Smartsheet is its versatility. Unlike specialized tools that cater to narrow use cases, Smartsheet adapts to various industries and scenarios. Whether you are in marketing, IT, construction, or healthcare, the platform can be tailored to meet your needs.

- **Project Management:** Smartsheet offers robust tools for planning, tracking, and completing projects. From Gantt charts to task tracking, it covers everything you need to stay on top of deadlines and deliverables.

- **Team Collaboration:** Collaboration is seamless with Smartsheet. Teams can share files, communicate within tasks, and update project statuses in real time.

- **Resource Management:** Allocate and track resources effectively. Smartsheet makes it easy to assign roles, monitor workloads, and ensure optimal resource utilization.

- **Event Planning:** Whether you're organizing a corporate event or a personal gathering, Smartsheet templates simplify planning, tracking RSVPs, and managing budgets.

- **Process Automation:** Smartsheet excels in automating repetitive tasks, saving time and reducing human error. From sending notifications to updating task statuses, automation rules simplify workflow management.

Intuitive and User-Friendly Interface

Smartsheet's user-friendly design is a major reason for its widespread adoption. The interface is clean and intuitive, making it accessible for both beginners and experienced users.

- **Spreadsheet-Like Layout:** Smartsheet resembles a traditional spreadsheet, so users familiar with tools like Excel or Google Sheets find it easy to get started.

- **Customizable Workspaces:** Each user or team can customize their workspace to suit their specific workflow. Drag-and-drop functionality allows users to rearrange tasks, add columns, and adjust views effortlessly.

- **Multiple View Options:** Smartsheet supports different views, including Grid, Gantt, Calendar, and Card views, allowing users to work in the format that best suits their preferences.

Enhanced Collaboration and Communication

Collaboration lies at the heart of Smartsheet. The platform is designed to bring teams together, ensuring that everyone stays aligned and informed.

- **Real-Time Updates:** Team members can update tasks and statuses in real time, ensuring that everyone is working with the most up-to-date information.

- **Centralized Communication:** Smartsheet eliminates the need for endless email chains by centralizing communication within tasks and projects. Comments, attachments, and notes can be added directly to specific items.

- **Permission Settings:** The platform allows users to control who can view or edit specific sheets, ensuring data security while enabling collaboration.
- **Mobile Access:** Smartsheet's mobile app makes it easy for team members to stay connected and productive, even on the go.

Integration with Popular Tools

Smartsheet integrates seamlessly with other tools and platforms, making it a valuable addition to any tech ecosystem.

- **Microsoft Office:** Users can sync Smartsheet with Excel, Word, and Outlook for seamless data sharing and task management.
- **Google Workspace:** Smartsheet integrates with Google Sheets, Gmail, and Google Calendar, ensuring smooth collaboration for teams using Google tools.
- **Third-Party Apps:** From Salesforce to Slack, Smartsheet connects with dozens of third-party applications, enabling users to create an integrated workflow.
- **APIs and Custom Integrations:** For advanced users, Smartsheet's API allows for custom integrations, ensuring the platform fits perfectly within your organization's systems.

Powerful Automation Features

Smartsheet's automation capabilities are a game-changer for teams looking to streamline workflows and reduce manual tasks.

- **Automated Alerts and Notifications:** Users can set up rules to notify team members of task updates, upcoming deadlines, or status changes.
- **Approval Processes:** Automate approval workflows to ensure that tasks and projects move forward efficiently without manual bottlenecks.
- **Recurring Tasks:** Schedule recurring tasks and updates, so nothing falls through the cracks.
- **Data Collection with Forms:** Smartsheet's form feature allows teams to collect information directly into a sheet, automating data entry and saving time.

Robust Reporting and Visualization Tools

Managing data is only part of the equation—visualizing it effectively is just as important. Smartsheet excels in transforming raw data into actionable insights.

- **Custom Reports:** Generate detailed reports tailored to your needs. Reports can pull data from multiple sheets, making it easy to track progress across projects.
- **Dashboards:** Smartsheet dashboards provide at-a-glance updates, displaying metrics, charts, and key performance indicators (KPIs) in a visually appealing format.
- **Export and Sharing Options:** Share reports and dashboards with stakeholders or export them as PDFs, Excel files, or slides for presentations.

Scalability for Teams and Organizations

Smartsheet is designed to grow with your needs. Whether you're a solopreneur or part of a large enterprise, the platform scales effortlessly.

- **Small Teams:** Smartsheet offers affordable plans for small teams, with features that allow for effective collaboration and task management.
- **Mid-Sized Businesses:** For growing organizations, Smartsheet provides tools to manage complex projects, automate processes, and track resources.
- **Enterprises:** With advanced security, custom integrations, and premium features, Smartsheet supports enterprise-level needs.

Cost-Effective Solution

Smartsheet offers excellent value for its wide range of features. Compared to other project management tools, it provides a cost-effective solution that caters to a variety of needs.

- **Flexible Pricing Plans:** From free trials to premium plans, Smartsheet accommodates different budgets.

- **ROI Through Efficiency:** By reducing manual tasks, improving collaboration, and streamlining workflows, Smartsheet often pays for itself through increased productivity.

Continuous Improvement and Support

Smartsheet is continuously evolving, with regular updates and new features based on user feedback.

- **Active Development:** The platform frequently rolls out enhancements and new tools to meet the changing needs of users.
- **Customer Support:** Smartsheet provides excellent support through live chat, email, and an extensive knowledge base.
- **Learning Resources:** From webinars to tutorials, Smartsheet offers resources to help users make the most of the platform.

Conclusion

Smartsheet is more than just a project management tool—it's a comprehensive platform for organizing, automating, and visualizing work. Its versatility, ease of use, and powerful features make it an indispensable tool for teams and individuals looking to work smarter. By leveraging Smartsheet, you can improve collaboration, streamline processes, and achieve your goals with greater efficiency.

1.3 Who This Guide is For

Smartsheet has become a popular platform for managing tasks, projects, and workflows due to its flexibility, user-friendly interface, and ability to integrate with various tools. Whether you're a project manager, a small business owner, a student, or just someone looking to improve personal productivity, Smartsheet offers a suite of tools to help you stay organized and efficient. This guide is specifically tailored to those who are just beginning their Smartsheet journey and want to build a solid foundation. In this section, we will explore who can benefit most from this guide and how it can cater to your unique needs.

Professionals Looking to Manage Projects Efficiently

One of the primary audiences for this guide is professionals who manage projects, tasks, or teams. Whether you're a project manager, a team leader, or an executive overseeing multiple departments, Smartsheet provides a platform to streamline your workflows.

Many professionals struggle with juggling multiple spreadsheets, emails, and disconnected tools. Smartsheet consolidates these disparate processes into one cohesive system. This guide will teach you how to:

- Set up project timelines using Gantt charts.
- Assign tasks and track progress effectively.
- Automate reminders and notifications to keep everyone on the same page.

By mastering the basics of Smartsheet, you'll be able to transform your chaotic project management into a smooth, efficient process.

Small Business Owners and Entrepreneurs

Small business owners and entrepreneurs often wear multiple hats, managing everything from marketing campaigns to financial planning. For this group, time is a precious resource, and organization is critical to success.

If you're running a small business, this guide will help you:

- Organize your tasks and priorities.
- Track budgets and expenses with customizable sheets.
- Manage client relationships and communication.
- Collaborate with freelancers or remote team members.

Smartsheet's intuitive interface allows you to get up and running quickly, even if you're not tech-savvy. With the help of this guide, you'll learn how to use Smartsheet to keep your business operations running smoothly without spending hours on administrative tasks.

Students and Educators

Education is another area where Smartsheet can shine. Whether you're a student managing coursework or an educator planning lessons, Smartsheet offers tools to enhance organization and productivity.

Students can use Smartsheet to:

- Plan study schedules and assignment deadlines.
- Track group project progress and collaboration.
- Organize research data and notes.

Educators can benefit from Smartsheet by:

- Scheduling classes, exams, and office hours.
- Monitoring student performance and feedback.

- Coordinating with colleagues on curriculum planning.

This guide will introduce students and educators to Smartsheet's basic features and provide tips on how to use it to succeed academically and professionally.

Personal Productivity Enthusiasts

Not all Smartsheet users come from corporate or educational backgrounds. Many individuals use Smartsheet as a personal productivity tool to organize their lives. From managing household budgets to planning events, Smartsheet can simplify your personal workflows.

For example, you can use Smartsheet to:
- Create a weekly meal plan and grocery list.
- Track personal goals and habits.
- Organize travel itineraries and packing lists.

This guide will show you how to use Smartsheet to take control of your personal life and achieve your goals with less stress.

Teams Transitioning from Spreadsheets

Teams that rely heavily on traditional spreadsheet tools like Microsoft Excel or Google Sheets often find themselves constrained by the lack of collaboration features. Smartsheet bridges this gap by offering the familiarity of a spreadsheet interface combined with robust collaboration and automation tools.

This guide is perfect for teams who are:
- Exploring alternatives to static spreadsheets.
- Looking for ways to collaborate in real time.
- Seeking to automate repetitive tasks and workflows.

We'll walk you through the process of transitioning your team to Smartsheet, ensuring a smooth adoption that maximizes productivity and minimizes disruptions.

Nonprofits and Community Organizations

Nonprofits and community organizations often have unique challenges, such as managing volunteers, planning events, and tracking donations. Smartsheet can be a game-changer for these groups, offering a centralized platform to coordinate efforts.

In this guide, nonprofit leaders will learn how to:

- Track and manage fundraising campaigns.
- Schedule volunteer shifts and assignments.
- Create event plans and monitor their progress.

By following this guide, nonprofits can maximize their impact while minimizing the time spent on administrative tasks.

Remote and Hybrid Teams

The rise of remote and hybrid work environments has created a need for tools that facilitate seamless communication and collaboration. Smartsheet is an ideal solution for distributed teams, providing a shared platform for task management, reporting, and real-time updates.

This guide is especially helpful for:

- Team leaders managing remote employees.
- Employees collaborating across different time zones.
- Organizations looking to centralize their workflows.

You'll learn how to use Smartsheet to keep your team aligned, no matter where they are working from.

Beginners with No Technical Background

If you're completely new to project management tools or feel intimidated by technology, this guide is designed with you in mind. We'll break down each feature of Smartsheet into simple, actionable steps, ensuring that you can follow along regardless of your experience level.

You'll learn:

- How to navigate the Smartsheet interface.
- How to create and manage your first sheet.
- How to use basic automation tools without technical knowledge.

By the end of this guide, you'll feel confident using Smartsheet to organize your work and life.

Why This Guide Works for You

No matter your background or goals, this guide is structured to provide value. Each chapter builds on the previous one, allowing you to progress from understanding the basics to applying more advanced features. With plenty of examples, tips, and best practices, you'll find actionable insights tailored to your needs.

Smartsheet is a versatile tool, and this guide aims to ensure that you unlock its full potential, whether you're using it for personal projects, academic pursuits, or professional endeavors.

1.4 How to Use This Book

This book is designed as a practical, step-by-step guide for anyone new to Smartsheet. Whether you're completely unfamiliar with the tool or have some basic experience and want to build on it, this book provides everything you need to know to start using Smartsheet efficiently and effectively.

In this section, we'll walk you through how to navigate this guide, explaining the structure, the purpose of each chapter, and how you can apply the content to your learning journey. We've also included some tips to help you get the most out of this book and your Smartsheet experience.

Chapter Overview

The book is divided into several chapters, each focused on a specific aspect of using Smartsheet. Here's a brief overview of what each chapter covers:

1. **Introduction**: This chapter lays the groundwork, helping you understand what Smartsheet is, why it's valuable, and who can benefit from using it. It also explains the structure of the book and how to use it.

2. **Chapter 1: Getting Started with Smartsheet**: This chapter guides you through setting up your Smartsheet account, navigating the interface, and creating your first sheet. If you're just starting out, this chapter is your essential first step.

3. **Chapter 2: Working with Data in Smartsheet**: Once you're familiar with the basics, this chapter dives into data management. You'll learn how to input, organize, and manipulate data effectively, along with some essential tips for maintaining clean and useful sheets.

4. **Chapter 3: Collaborating in Smartsheet**: Smartsheet's collaboration features are one of its greatest strengths. This chapter explores how to share sheets, communicate with team members, and work together seamlessly in real time.

5. **Chapter 4: Automating Your Workflows**: Learn how to save time and reduce manual effort by setting up automation rules, alerts, and workflows. This chapter introduces you to the automation tools Smartsheet offers and how to use them effectively.

6. **Chapter 5: Visualizing Data**: This chapter focuses on reports, dashboards, and other visualization tools that help you present your data clearly and effectively.

7. **Chapter 6: Tips and Tricks for Beginners**: This chapter includes helpful shortcuts, troubleshooting advice, and best practices to make your Smartsheet experience smoother.

8. **Chapter 7: Expanding Your Smartsheet Skills**: For those who want to explore advanced features, integrations, and additional learning resources, this chapter points you in the right direction.

9. **Conclusion**: A recap of what you've learned and recommendations for continuing your Smartsheet journey.

How to Read This Book

This guide is designed to be flexible, so you can approach it in a way that suits your learning style:

- **For Beginners**: If you're completely new to Smartsheet, we recommend reading the chapters sequentially. Each chapter builds on the knowledge from the previous one, so following the order will ensure you develop a solid foundation.

- **For Intermediate Users**: If you're already familiar with the basics, feel free to skip the introductory chapters and focus on the areas where you want to improve. The table of contents and index can help you quickly locate specific topics.

- **As a Reference Guide**: You don't have to read this book cover to cover. Instead, treat it as a reference manual that you can consult whenever you need help with a particular feature or concept. Each chapter is self-contained and provides clear explanations and step-by-step instructions.

Features to Enhance Your Learning

This book includes several features to help you learn Smartsheet effectively:

- **Step-by-Step Tutorials**: Each chapter includes detailed instructions for completing tasks in Smartsheet, accompanied by screenshots and diagrams to guide you.

- **Examples and Case Studies**: Wherever possible, we've included practical examples and case studies to illustrate how Smartsheet can be used in real-world scenarios.

- **Tips and Best Practices**: Throughout the book, you'll find tips and best practices to help you avoid common mistakes and work more efficiently.

- **Troubleshooting Advice**: If you encounter issues, check the troubleshooting sections for solutions to common problems.

- **Checklists and Summaries**: At the end of many chapters, you'll find checklists and summaries to help you review what you've learned and ensure you're ready to move on to the next topic.

- **Additional Resources**: We've included links to Smartsheet's official documentation, online tutorials, and community forums so you can explore further if needed.

Applying What You Learn

Learning Smartsheet isn't just about reading; it's about doing. To get the most out of this book, we recommend the following approach:

1. **Follow Along in Smartsheet**: As you read each chapter, open Smartsheet and try the tasks and exercises described. This hands-on practice will help you retain what you learn and gain confidence in using the tool.

2. **Start with a Personal Project**: Create a sheet for a simple personal project, such as planning a trip or organizing a to-do list. This low-pressure environment is perfect for experimenting with features and building your skills.

3. **Apply Skills to Work Projects**: Once you're comfortable with the basics, start using Smartsheet for work-related tasks. Whether it's managing a project, tracking tasks, or collaborating with colleagues, applying your skills in a real-world context will deepen your understanding.

4. **Review and Revisit**: Don't hesitate to revisit chapters as needed. If you're unsure about a feature or concept, reviewing the relevant section can reinforce your knowledge.

Tips for Effective Learning

Here are some additional tips to help you learn Smartsheet effectively:

- **Set Goals**: Before you begin, think about what you want to achieve with Smartsheet. Are you looking to manage personal tasks, collaborate with a team, or improve your workflow? Having clear goals will keep you motivated and focused.

- **Pace Yourself**: Don't try to learn everything at once. Focus on one chapter or topic at a time, and give yourself time to practice and absorb the material.

- **Ask Questions**: If you're part of a team, ask colleagues who use Smartsheet for advice or tips. You can also join online forums and communities to connect with other users and learn from their experiences.

- **Experiment**: Don't be afraid to experiment with different features and settings. Smartsheet is a versatile tool, and exploring its capabilities will help you discover new ways to work more effectively.

- **Track Your Progress**: Keep a record of what you've learned and any challenges you've overcome. This will help you see how far you've come and identify areas where you need more practice.

Moving Forward

As you work through this book, remember that learning Smartsheet is a journey. Start with the basics, build your skills step by step, and don't hesitate to revisit topics as needed. By the end of this guide, you'll have the knowledge and confidence to use Smartsheet effectively, whether for personal projects, team collaboration, or professional workflows.

We hope this book will serve as a valuable resource on your Smartsheet journey. Let's get started!

CHAPTER I
Getting Started with Smartsheet

1.1 Setting Up Your Smartsheet Account

1.1.1 Creating an Account

Creating a Smartsheet account is the first step in leveraging the platform's powerful capabilities to streamline your workflows, organize projects, and collaborate effectively. This section will guide you through every detail of setting up your Smartsheet account, ensuring a seamless start for beginners.

Step 1: Visit the Smartsheet Website

To begin, navigate to the official Smartsheet website by typing www.smartsheet.com into your web browser. Once the website loads, you will notice a user-friendly homepage showcasing Smartsheet's key features, including project management, collaboration, and automation tools.

At the top-right corner of the homepage, click the **"Sign Up"** or **"Try Smartsheet for Free"** button. Smartsheet offers a free trial for new users, allowing you to explore its features without committing to a subscription right away.

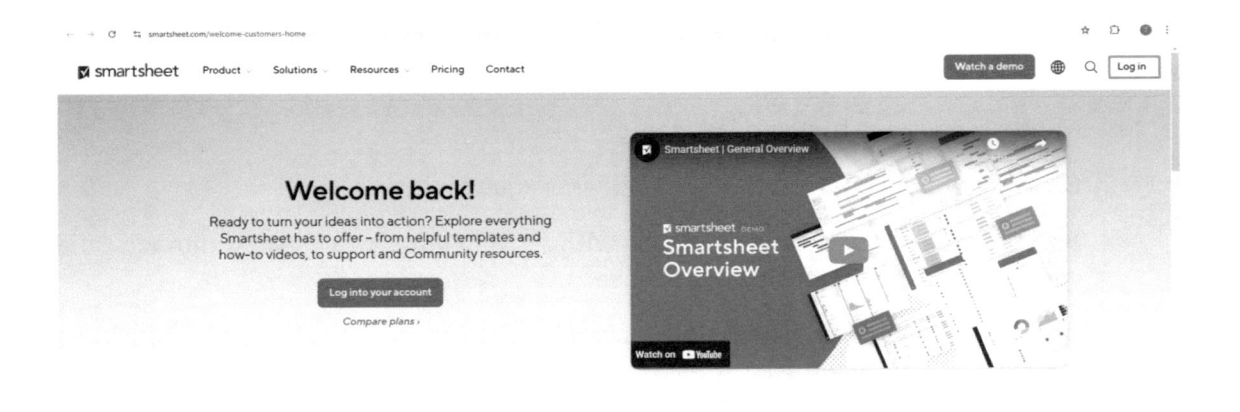

Step 2: Choose How You Want to Sign Up

Smartsheet provides multiple options for signing up, allowing flexibility for users. You can create an account using:

- **Your Email Address**: This is the most common method, where you register with a work or personal email.

- **Google Account**: If you use Google Workspace, signing up with your Google account can simplify login management.

- **Microsoft Account**: For users within a Microsoft ecosystem, this method offers seamless integration with Office 365.

Click on your preferred method and follow the prompts. If you're using an email address, you'll need to create a password and verify your email before proceeding.

Step 3: Fill in Your Details

Once you've selected your sign-up method, Smartsheet will ask for some basic information to set up your profile. This typically includes:

- **Name**: Enter your first and last name.
- **Email Address**: Confirm the email address you want to use.
- **Password**: Create a strong password with a mix of uppercase letters, numbers, and special characters to ensure account security.
- **Organization Name (Optional)**: If you're setting up Smartsheet for business purposes, you can add your organization's name to customize the workspace.

After entering these details, click **"Create Account"** or **"Continue"** to proceed.

Step 4: Email Verification

If you signed up using an email address, Smartsheet will send a verification email to the address you provided. Open your email inbox and look for a message from Smartsheet.

Click on the verification link within the email to activate your account. If you don't see the email in your inbox, check your spam or junk folder. Once verified, you can return to the Smartsheet website and log in to your new account.

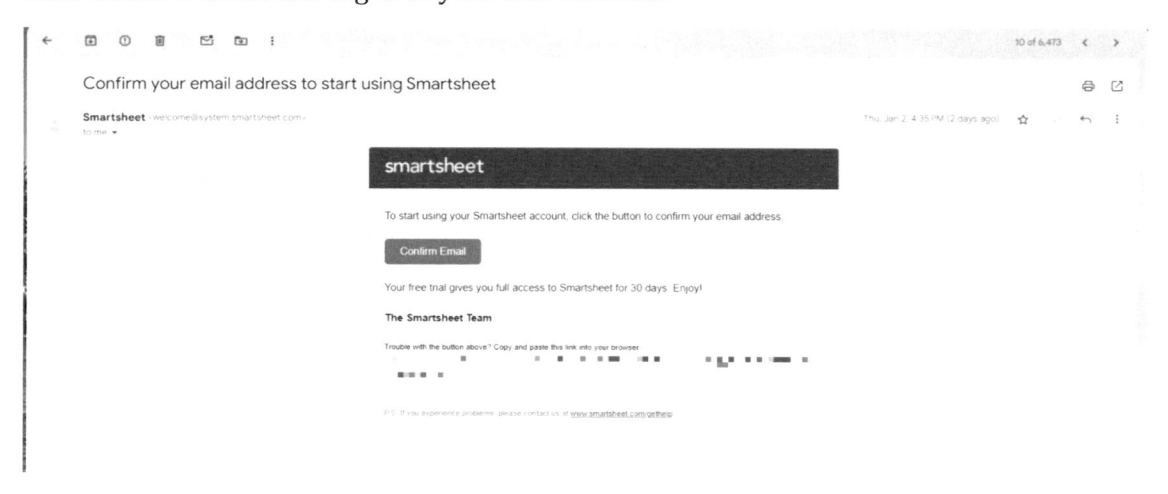

Step 5: Explore the Free Trial

After verifying your email, Smartsheet will guide you to a welcome page, where you can start exploring the platform. Smartsheet typically offers a **30-day free trial**, which grants access to most of its features, including:

- Unlimited sheets and reports.
- Collaboration tools for team projects.
- Automation and workflows.
- Dashboards and data visualization.

Take advantage of the trial period to explore how Smartsheet can meet your needs before committing to a paid plan.

Step 6: Set Up Two-Factor Authentication (Optional but Recommended)

For enhanced security, enable two-factor authentication (2FA) for your account. This adds an additional layer of protection by requiring a second form of verification, such as a code sent to your mobile device.

To enable 2FA:

1. Go to your account settings by clicking on your profile icon in the top-right corner.

2. Select **"Security"** or **"Account Settings"**.

3. Follow the prompts to set up 2FA using an authentication app or SMS.

Step 7: Log In and Familiarize Yourself with the Dashboard

Once your account is set up, log in to Smartsheet by entering your email and password on the login page. Upon logging in, you'll be greeted with the main dashboard. This is your control center, where you can access all your sheets, reports, and dashboards.

Take a few minutes to explore the interface:

- Locate the **"Home"** tab for quick access to your workspaces.

- Find the **"Solution Center"** to create new sheets or templates.

- Familiarize yourself with the **Toolbar**, where most tools and features are located.

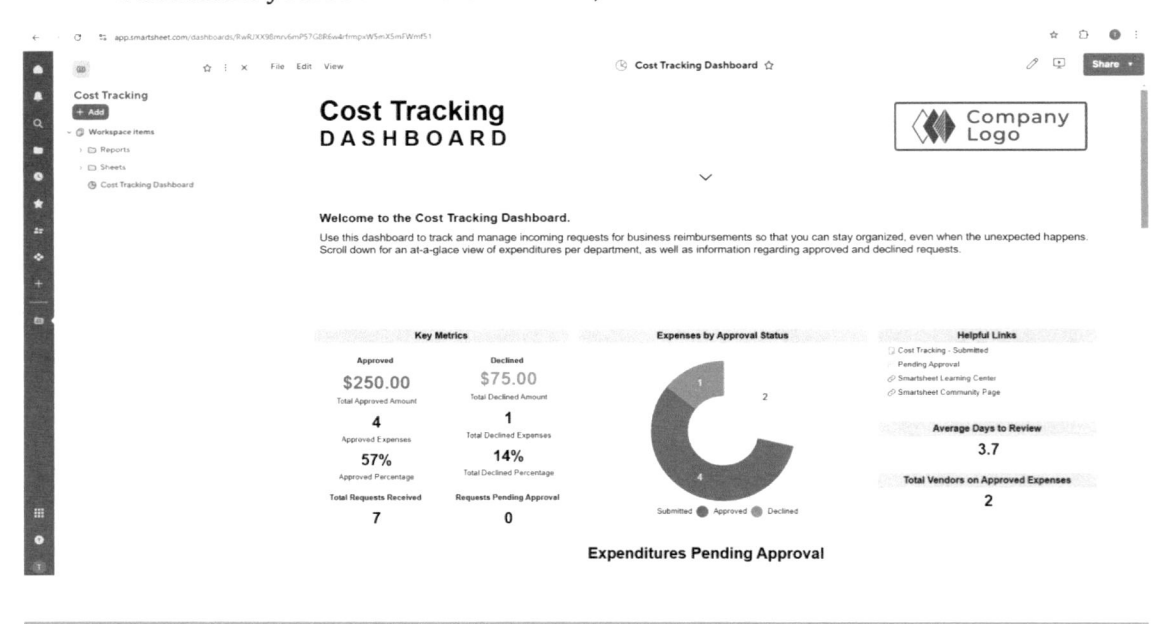

Tips for First-Time Users

1. **Bookmark the Smartsheet Login Page**

   Save the Smartsheet login page in your browser for easy access. This will save time whenever you want to access your account.

2. **Choose a Professional Email Address**

If you're using Smartsheet for work purposes, it's best to register with your work email. This ensures a more professional setup and smoother integration with your team.

3. **Use the Mobile App**

   Download the Smartsheet mobile app (available on iOS and Android) to access your account on the go. Logging in on your mobile device is quick and mirrors the desktop experience.

4. **Leverage the Free Trial Period**

   Spend time experimenting with different features during the free trial to fully understand Smartsheet's capabilities. Create sample sheets, try out automation, and collaborate with team members to get a feel for the platform.

Troubleshooting Common Sign-Up Issues

1. **Didn't Receive a Verification Email?**

- Double-check your email address for typos during registration.
- Look in your spam or junk folder.
- Resend the verification email by logging in and clicking **"Resend Email"**.

2. **Invalid Password Error**

- Ensure your password meets Smartsheet's security requirements (e.g., at least eight characters, a mix of letters and numbers).

3. **Issues with Google or Microsoft Sign-Up**

- Confirm that your Google or Microsoft account is active and linked to the correct email.
- Try clearing your browser cache and reloading the sign-up page.

4. **Free Trial Expired Before Setup**

- Contact Smartsheet support to request an extension or clarification.

Conclusion

Setting up your Smartsheet account is straightforward, but taking time to explore the features during this initial phase is crucial. By following the steps above, you can confidently create an account and start organizing your projects and workflows.

In the next section, we'll dive into **"Choosing a Pricing Plan"**, where we'll help you understand the different subscription options available and how to select the one that best fits your needs.

1.1.2 Choosing a Pricing Plan

Choosing the right Smartsheet pricing plan is a crucial step for maximizing your investment in this powerful tool. Smartsheet offers various plans tailored to different user needs, from individuals to large enterprises. In this section, we'll explore each plan in detail, helping you identify which one aligns best with your goals and budget.

Understanding Smartsheet's Pricing Model

Smartsheet operates on a subscription-based pricing model, offering monthly or annual billing options. The plans are typically divided into four categories: Free, Pro, Business, and Enterprise. Each plan includes specific features and usage limits, designed to cater to different user groups, such as freelancers, small businesses, or large organizations with complex needs.

Overview of Available Plans

1. Free Plan

The Free Plan is ideal for beginners or individuals looking to explore Smartsheet before committing to a paid plan. While it has limitations, it provides enough functionality to help users understand the basics of the platform.

Key Features of the Free Plan:

- Access for 1 user.
- Ability to create up to 2 sheets.
- Limited collaboration features, such as view-only sharing.
- Basic data entry and management.

Who Should Choose the Free Plan? The Free Plan is suitable for students, hobbyists, or individuals managing small projects without the need for advanced collaboration or automation features.

2. Pro Plan

The Pro Plan is designed for individuals or small teams who need more functionality and collaboration tools. It's a great choice for users who want to manage simple workflows while benefiting from additional features beyond the Free Plan.

Key Features of the Pro Plan:

- Access for up to 10 users.
- Unlimited sheets and up to 20 GB of storage.
- Advanced collaboration tools, including editing and commenting.
- Basic automation capabilities, such as reminders and alerts.
- Ability to generate reports.

Pricing and Billing Options: The Pro Plan typically costs around $7 per user per month when billed annually. Monthly billing is available but at a slightly higher rate.

Who Should Choose the Pro Plan? Freelancers, small teams, or project managers who require moderate collaboration and reporting features will find this plan beneficial.

3. Business Plan

The Business Plan is the most popular choice among organizations. It offers robust features suitable for managing larger teams and more complex workflows.

Key Features of the Business Plan:

- Access for an unlimited number of users.
- Unlimited sheets with up to 1 TB of storage.
- Advanced automation, including approval workflows.
- Reporting tools with cross-sheet functionality.
- Dashboards for visualizing project data.
- Integration with third-party tools like Microsoft Office, Google Workspace, and Slack.

Pricing and Billing Options: The Business Plan costs approximately $25 per user per month when billed annually.

Who Should Choose the Business Plan? This plan is ideal for mid-sized businesses or teams managing multiple projects that require advanced reporting, automation, and integrations.

---

4. Enterprise Plan

The Enterprise Plan is tailored for large organizations with complex requirements. It offers all the features of the Business Plan, plus additional tools and enterprise-grade security.

Key Features of the Enterprise Plan:

- Customizable security features, including single sign-on (SSO) and domain control.
- Unlimited storage.
- Access to Smartsheet premium add-ons like Dynamic View and Control Center.
- Enhanced support options, including a dedicated account manager.
- Compliance with industry standards, such as GDPR and HIPAA.

Pricing and Billing Options: The Enterprise Plan does not have a fixed price and is quoted based on the organization's specific needs.

Who Should Choose the Enterprise Plan? Large corporations, government agencies, or any organization requiring advanced features, scalability, and enterprise-level security should consider this plan.

Factors to Consider When Choosing a Plan

1. Team Size

The number of users who will need access to Smartsheet can significantly impact your choice. Smaller teams may find the Pro Plan sufficient, while larger organizations may require the Business or Enterprise Plan.

2. Feature Requirements

Consider the features you need to manage your workflows effectively. If automation, dashboards, or integrations are critical, the Business or Enterprise Plans are better options.

3. Budget Constraints

While advanced plans offer more features, they also come with higher costs. Evaluate your budget and weigh it against the benefits of the plan to ensure you're making the most cost-effective decision.

4. Storage Needs

If your projects involve handling large volumes of data or files, pay close attention to the storage limits of each plan. Free and Pro Plans may not suffice for data-heavy workflows.

5. Future Scalability

If you anticipate growing your team or managing more complex projects in the future, it's worth investing in a plan that allows for easy scalability, such as the Business or Enterprise Plan.

Step-by-Step Guide to Choosing a Plan

1. **Assess Your Needs:** Create a list of the features you need to manage your work effectively. Consider factors such as collaboration, automation, and reporting.
2. **Evaluate the Plans:** Review the features of each plan and compare them against your list. Pay attention to limitations such as user count, storage, and integrations.
3. **Start with a Trial:** Smartsheet offers free trials for its paid plans. Take advantage of this to test the features and ensure they meet your requirements before committing.

4. **Choose a Billing Option:** Decide between monthly or annual billing. Annual billing often comes with discounts, making it a cost-effective choice for long-term use.

5. **Upgrade or Downgrade as Needed:** Smartsheet allows you to upgrade or downgrade your plan at any time. If your needs change, you can easily adjust your subscription.

Tips for Making the Most of Your Plan

- **Leverage Free Resources:** Use Smartsheet's help center, tutorials, and community forums to maximize your plan's potential.

- **Train Your Team:** If you're managing a team, invest time in training them to use Smartsheet effectively.

- **Monitor Usage:** Regularly review how your team uses Smartsheet to ensure you're utilizing all available features.

By carefully evaluating your needs and understanding the features of each plan, you can confidently choose the Smartsheet pricing plan that aligns with your goals. Whether you're an individual looking to streamline your tasks or an organization managing complex projects, Smartsheet has a solution for you.

Choose your Smartsheet plan

US Dollar - USD

♀ Learn about Member, Guest, and Viewer user types

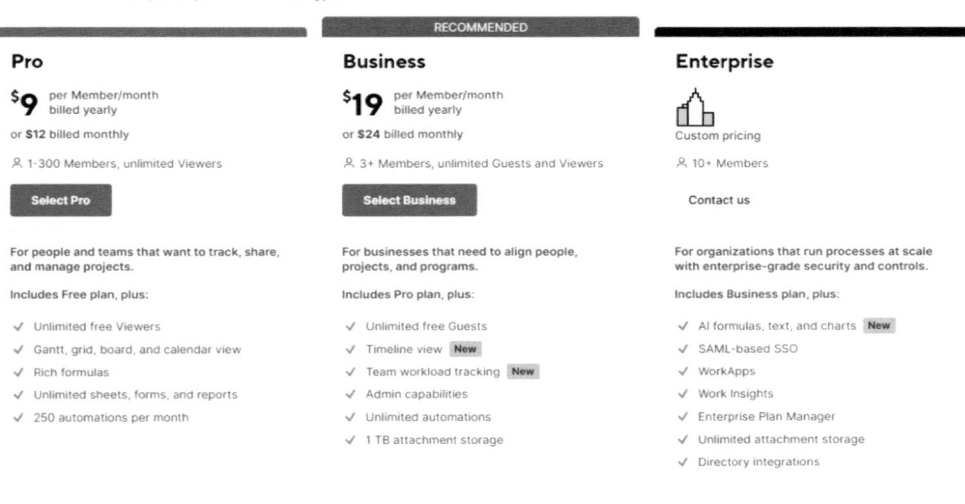

RECOMMENDED

Pro
$9 per Member/month
billed yearly
or **$12** billed monthly

♀ 1-300 Members, unlimited Viewers

Select Pro

For people and teams that want to track, share, and manage projects.

Includes Free plan, plus:
- ✓ Unlimited free Viewers
- ✓ Gantt, grid, board, and calendar view
- ✓ Rich formulas
- ✓ Unlimited sheets, forms, and reports
- ✓ 250 automations per month

Business
$19 per Member/month
billed yearly
or **$24** billed monthly

♀ 3+ Members, unlimited Guests and Viewers

Select Business

For businesses that need to align people, projects, and programs.

Includes Pro plan, plus:
- ✓ Unlimited free Guests
- ✓ Timeline view New
- ✓ Team workload tracking New
- ✓ Admin capabilities
- ✓ Unlimited automations
- ✓ 1 TB attachment storage

Enterprise

Custom pricing

♀ 10+ Members

Contact us

For organizations that run processes at scale with enterprise-grade security and controls.

Includes Business plan, plus:
- ✓ AI formulas, text, and charts New
- ✓ SAML-based SSO
- ✓ WorkApps
- ✓ Work Insights
- ✓ Enterprise Plan Manager
- ✓ Unlimited attachment storage
- ✓ Directory integrations

For more information, visit www.smartsheet.com/pricing

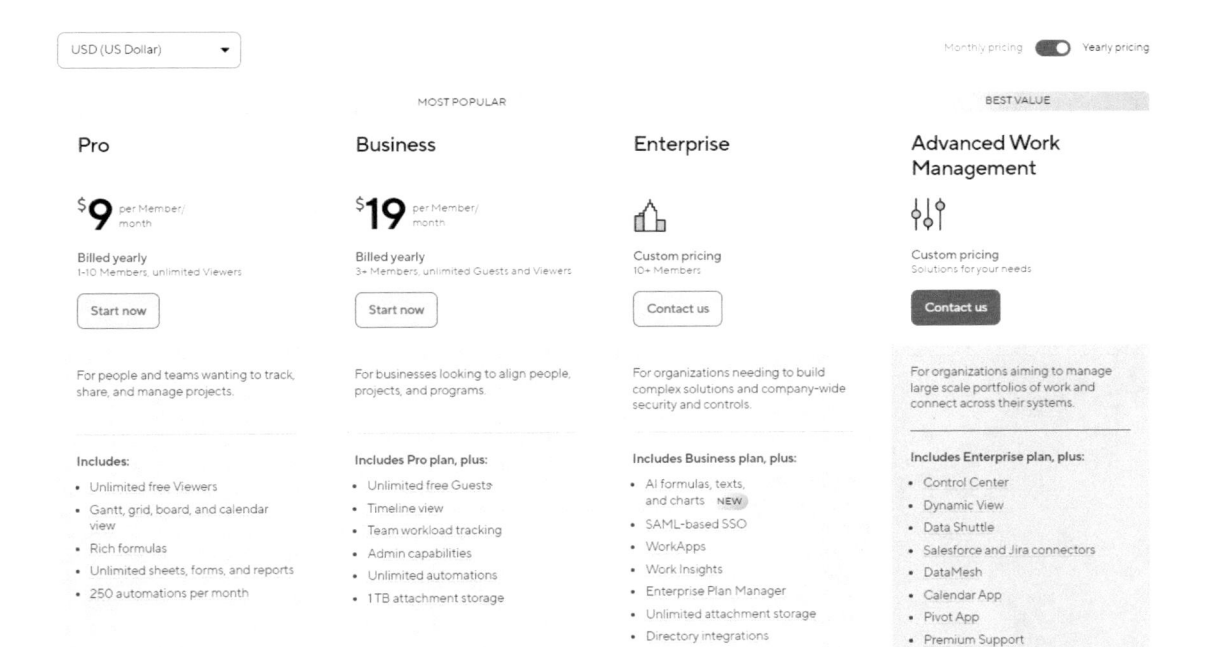

USD (US Dollar)

Monthly pricing ● Yearly pricing

MOST POPULAR   BEST VALUE

Pro
$9 per Member/month

Billed yearly
1-10 Members, unlimited Viewers

Start now

For people and teams wanting to track, share, and manage projects.

Includes:
- Unlimited free Viewers
- Gantt, grid, board, and calendar view
- Rich formulas
- Unlimited sheets, forms, and reports
- 250 automations per month

Business
$19 per Member/month

Billed yearly
3+ Members, unlimited Guests and Viewers

Start now

For businesses looking to align people, projects, and programs.

Includes Pro plan, plus:
- Unlimited free Guests
- Timeline view
- Team workload tracking
- Admin capabilities
- Unlimited automations
- 1 TB attachment storage

Enterprise

Custom pricing
10+ Members

Contact us

For organizations needing to build complex solutions and company-wide security and controls.

Includes Business plan, plus:
- AI formulas, texts, and charts NEW
- SAML-based SSO
- WorkApps
- Work Insights
- Enterprise Plan Manager
- Unlimited attachment storage
- Directory integrations

Advanced Work Management

Custom pricing
Solutions for your needs

Contact us

For organizations aiming to manage large scale portfolios of work and connect across their systems.

Includes Enterprise plan, plus:
- Control Center
- Dynamic View
- Data Shuttle
- Salesforce and Jira connectors
- DataMesh
- Calendar App
- Pivot App
- Premium Support

	Pro	Business	Enterprise	Advanced Work Management
	Start now	Start now	Contact us	Contact us
Essential features				
Sheets	Unlimited	Unlimited	Unlimited	Unlimited
Grid view	✓	✓	✓	✓
Gantt view	✓	✓	✓	✓
Calendar view	✓	✓	✓	✓
Board view	✓	✓	✓	✓
Timeline view		✓	✓	✓
Dashboards	Unlimited	Unlimited	Unlimited	Unlimited
Reports	Unlimited	Unlimited	Unlimited	Unlimited
Forms	Unlimited	Unlimited	Unlimited	Unlimited
Conditional form logic		✓	✓	✓
Templates	✓	✓	✓	✓
Widgets per dashboard	10	Unlimited	Unlimited	Unlimited
Sheets per report	1	Unlimited	Unlimited	Unlimited
Mobile app (Android & iOS)	✓	✓	✓	✓
Private sheets and reports	✓	✓	✓	✓
Export sheet	✓	✓	✓	✓
File library NEW	✓	✓	✓	✓
Team workload tracking		✓	✓	✓

CHAPTER I: GETTING STARTED WITH SMARTSHEET

	Pro	Business	Enterprise	Advanced Work Management
	Start now	Start now	Contact us	Contact us
Formulas and functions				^
Column types	✓	✓	✓	✓
Cell formulas	✓	✓	✓	✓
Column formulas	✓	✓	✓	✓
Cross-sheet formulas	✓	✓	✓	✓
Dependencies	✓	✓	✓	✓
Filters	✓	✓	✓	✓
Conditional formatting	✓	✓	✓	✓
Cell history	✓	✓	✓	✓
Cell linking	✓	✓	✓	✓
Lock or unlock rows and columns	✓	✓	✓	✓
Baselines		✓	✓	✓
Report grouping and summary		✓	✓	✓
Activity log		✓	✓	✓
Document builder		✓	✓	✓
API calls		✓	✓	✓
Custom colors & logos		✓	✓	✓
Work Insights: Instantly analyze your data			✓	✓
Custom welcome and help screens			✓	✓

CHAPTER 1: GETTING STARTED WITH SMARTSHEET

	Pro	Business	Enterprise	Advanced Work Management
	Start now	Start now	Contact us	Contact us
Sharing				
Members	Max 10	Min 3	Custom	Custom
Provisional Members NEW	✓	✓	✓	✓
Viewers	✓	✓	✓	✓
Guests		✓	✓	✓
File/Attachment storage	20 GB	1 TB	Unlimited	Unlimited
Maximum attachment size	30 MB	250 MB	250 MB	250 MB
Assign people	✓	✓	✓	✓
Conversations	✓	✓	✓	✓
Comments	✓	✓	✓	✓
Proofing (image and video)		✓	✓	✓
Publish sheets, reports, and dashboards		✓	✓	✓
Collections NEW			✓	✓
AI tools				
Generate formulas			✓	✓
Text and summaries			✓	✓
Analyze data NEW			✓	✓

	Pro	Business	Enterprise	Advanced Work Management
	Start now	Start now	Contact us	Contact us
Automated workflows				
Automated triggers	250/month	Unlimited	Unlimited	Unlimited
Alerts and notifications	✓	✓	✓	✓
Reminders	✓	✓	✓	✓
Assign people action	✓	✓	✓	✓
Update requests	✓	✓	✓	✓
Approval requests	✓	✓	✓	✓
Record a date	✓	✓	✓	✓
Move or copy row	✓	✓	✓	✓
Clear cell	✓	✓	✓	✓
Send alert to Slack	✓	✓	✓	✓
Send alert to Microsoft Teams	✓	✓	✓	✓
Integrations				
Microsoft Office 365 (Teams, Outlook, OneDrive, etc.)	✓	✓	✓	✓
Google Workspace (Gmail, Hangouts, Drive, etc.)	✓	✓	✓	✓
Slack	✓	✓	✓	✓
Adobe Creative Cloud Extension		✓	✓	✓
Power BI		✓	✓	✓
Tableau		✓	✓	✓
E-signature with DocuSign			✓	✓
Nearly 100 more	✓	✓	✓	✓

	Pro (Start now)	Business (Start now)	Enterprise (Contact us)	Advanced Work Management (Contact us)
Security				
Single sign-on (SSO)	✓	✓	✓	✓
Admin Center	✓	✓	✓	✓
User Management	✓	✓	✓	✓
Plan Insights		✓	✓	✓
Group management	—	✓	✓	✓
Account discovery		✓	✓	✓
Schedule backups		✓	✓	✓
SAML-based SSO			✓	✓
Directory integrations			✓	✓
User merge			✓	✓
Enterprise Plan Manager			✓	✓
Enterprise access controls			✓	✓
Custom email domains			✓	✓
Domain validation			✓	✓
User account provisioning			✓	✓
Safe Sharing			✓	✓
Chargeback reports			✓	✓
System admin fallback			✓	✓
Data retention policies			Add-on	Add-on
Data egress			Add-on	Add-on
Event reporting			Add-on	Add-on
Customer Managed Encryption Key (CMEK)			Add-on	Add-on

	Pro	Business	Enterprise	Advanced Work Management
	Start now	Start now	Contact us	Contact us
Premium features				
WorkApps: No-code workapps			✓	✓
Brandfolder by Smartsheet	Add-on	Add-on	Add-on	Add-on
Resource Management by Smartsheet		Add-on	Add-on	Add-on
Control Center: Portfolio management		Add-on	Add-on	✓
Dynamic View: Secure request management		Starting at $50 USD/month	Starting at $50 USD/month	✓
Data Shuttle		Starting at $20 USD/month	Starting at $20 USD/month	✓
Calendar App		Add-on	Add-on	✓
DataMesh		Add-on	Add-on	✓
Pivot App		Add-on	Add-on	✓
Connectors		Add-on	Add-on	✓
DataTable			Add-on	✓
Bridge			Add-on	✓
Support and services				
Help & Learning content	✓	✓	✓	✓
Smartsheet Community	✓	✓	✓	✓
Web-based ticketing	✓	✓	✓	✓
Standard Support Package		Add-on	✓	✓
Premium Support Package		Add-on	Add-on	✓
Smartsheet University	Add-on	Add-on	Add-on	✓
Smartsheet Professional Services		Add-on	Add-on	Add-on
Technical Account Managers		Add-on	Add-on	Add-on

1.1.3 Navigating the Dashboard

Navigating the Smartsheet dashboard effectively is crucial for any beginner as it serves as the control center for all your projects, tasks, and teams. This section will guide you through the essential components of the dashboard, explain how to access various features, and provide tips for streamlining your workflow.

Understanding the Dashboard Layout

Upon logging into Smartsheet, you are greeted by the dashboard, which offers a visual overview of your workspace, sheets, and activities. The layout is designed to help users manage their tasks efficiently by centralizing relevant information in one place.

The dashboard is made up of several key areas:

1. **Left Navigation Bar**: The top navigation bar provides access to essential features such as:

    - **Logo and Account Settings**: Click on your profile icon to access account settings, sign out, or switch between multiple accounts if needed.

    - **Search Bar**: Located at the center, this allows you to search for sheets, reports, or anything within Smartsheet quickly. The search bar is a powerful tool, especially as you accumulate more sheets and data over time.

    - **Notifications**: Smartsheet has built-in notification systems for various updates. Notifications alert you about changes made to your sheets, comments, and more. By clicking the bell icon, you can view, dismiss, or manage your notifications.

    - **Help & Resources**: The question mark icon on the right gives you quick access to Smartsheet's help center, user guides, and live chat support.

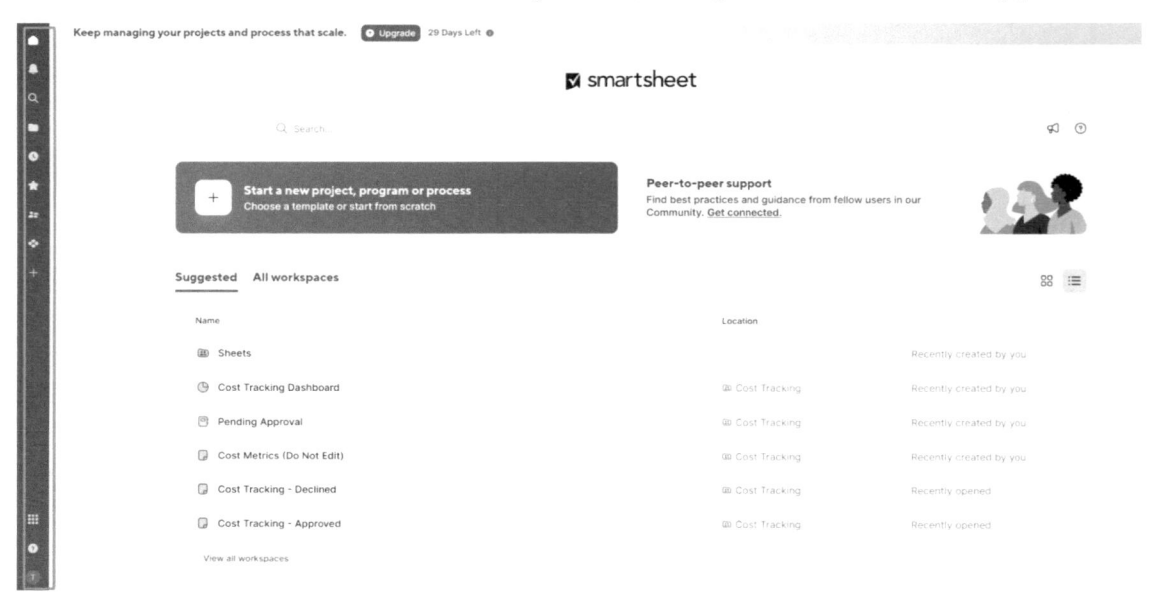

2. **Left Navigation Panel**
   The left panel is where you can access all your sheets, reports, dashboards, and other important sections within Smartsheet. Key features in this area include:
   - **Home**: The Home icon will bring you back to the main dashboard, giving you a global view of your workspace and recent activities.
   - **Sheets**: This section lists all the sheets in your workspace, where you can filter by different categories such as "Recently Opened," "Favorites," or by creating a new sheet.
   - **Reports**: Reports help you generate customized views of your data. You can create reports that filter and display specific information across various sheets, which helps in tracking and managing projects.
   - **Dashboards**: A Smartsheet dashboard acts as a data visualization tool that aggregates data from multiple sheets or reports into a single view, displaying key metrics and progress in various widgets.
   - **Workspaces**: Workspaces are where your sheets, reports, and dashboards live. You can create workspaces for different teams or projects to keep everything organized.

3. **Main Content Area**
   The main content area is the largest section of your Smartsheet dashboard. Here, you'll see a preview of your sheets, reports, or dashboards. The contents of this area change depending on what you select in the left navigation panel.

Customizing Your Dashboard

One of the most powerful aspects of Smartsheet is the ability to customize your dashboard to match your workflow. This customization ensures that the information you need is always readily available. Let's explore how you can personalize your dashboard:

1. **Widgets and Layout**
   You can add different types of widgets to your dashboard, each serving a specific purpose. Some common widgets include:
   - **Chart Widget**: Display your data in a graphical format, such as a bar chart, pie chart, or line graph.
   - **Metric Widget**: Show key statistics like totals, averages, or custom calculations.
   - **Report Widget**: Embed a live report that filters and displays data according to your specific criteria.
   - **Web Content Widget**: You can also embed links to external websites or other online resources directly into your dashboard.

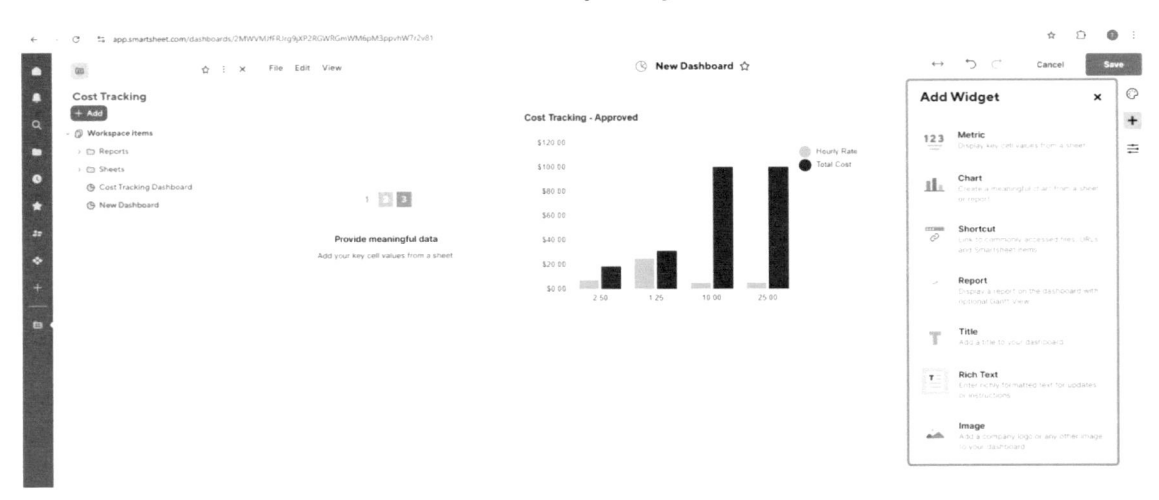

Once you've added widgets, you can adjust the layout by dragging them around, resizing them, or even removing them. This customization ensures that your dashboard contains only the most relevant information at a glance.

2. **Setting Up Alerts and Reminders**: To stay on top of tasks, Smartsheet allows you to set alerts and reminders for your projects. Alerts can be set to notify you when a specific action takes place, such as when a task is updated or when a deadline is approaching. These alerts are shown in your notifications center or sent via email,

depending on your preferences. Setting up these reminders is crucial for staying organized and making sure that deadlines are met.

3. **Adding Data from Other Sheets**: Smartsheet is highly integrated, and the dashboard allows you to pull data from other sheets into your widgets. This means you don't have to navigate between multiple sheets or constantly update the dashboard manually. Data is pulled in real-time, ensuring you're always viewing the latest updates. You can create relationships between sheets and display key information across your projects using widgets like reports and charts.

Smartsheet Views on the Dashboard

Your Smartsheet dashboard is not just a static page; it's a dynamic workspace that can be displayed in several different views, depending on your needs. These views allow you to analyze data in ways that are most useful for your projects.

1. **Grid View**: This is the default view for sheets in Smartsheet. The grid view displays your data in a traditional spreadsheet format, where rows represent tasks or data entries, and columns represent fields or attributes like task names, deadlines, and owners. From the dashboard, you can quickly open any sheet in grid view and get to work editing or reviewing data.

2. **Card View**: Card view is especially useful for tracking tasks. It displays data as individual cards or tiles, with each card representing a row from your sheet. You can move cards between different categories or stages, which is particularly useful for project management and task tracking.

3. **Gantt View**: Smartsheet's Gantt View is a powerful tool for project management. It allows you to visualize your projects on a timeline, making it easier to understand dependencies, deadlines, and progress. On the dashboard, you can add Gantt charts as widgets, giving you a quick overview of how your project is progressing over time.

4. **Calendar View**: The calendar view integrates tasks with deadlines into a calendar format. This makes it easy to see when specific tasks are due and ensures that no deadlines are overlooked. You can add this view to your dashboard to track important milestones.

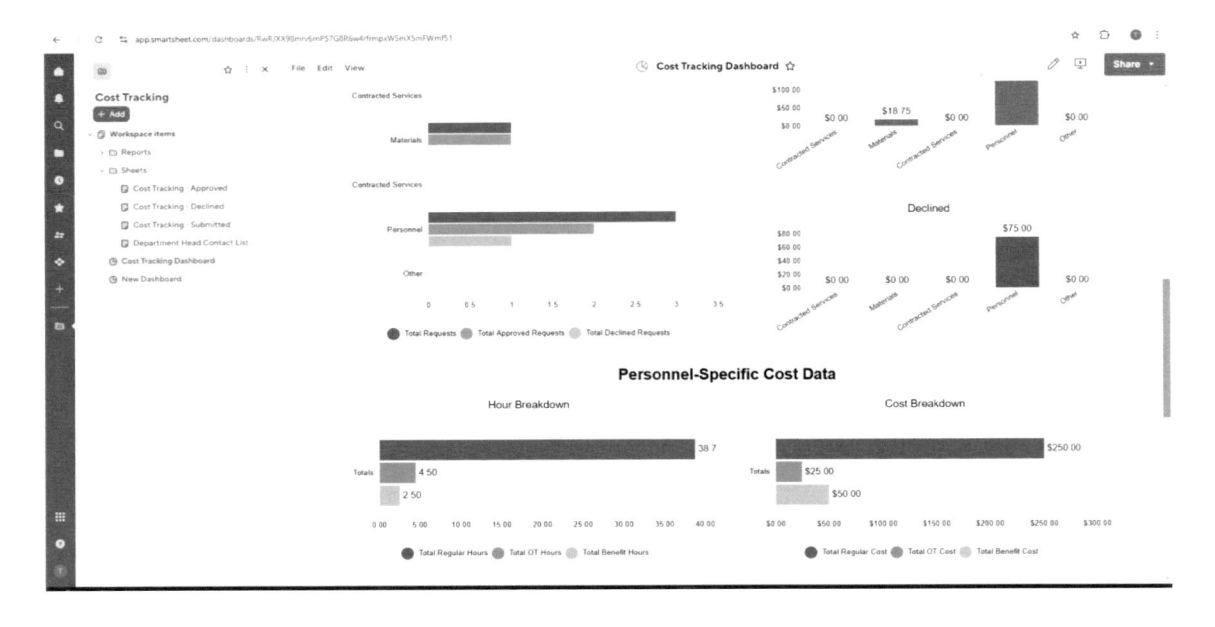

Using Shortcuts and Quick Access Tools

Smartsheet also allows you to navigate your workspace quickly using shortcuts. These tools and shortcuts are designed to save you time and streamline your navigation.

- **Favorites**: You can mark certain sheets, reports, or dashboards as "favorites" so you can access them more quickly from the left panel.

- **Recent Items**: Smartsheet tracks your recent activities, so you can quickly jump back to a sheet you were recently working on.

- **Keyboard Shortcuts**: Smartsheet supports a variety of keyboard shortcuts that allow you to perform common actions, such as opening a sheet, editing a row, or switching between views, without using the mouse. Mastering these shortcuts can significantly boost your efficiency.

Collaborating and Communicating from the Dashboard

Your Smartsheet dashboard is not just a tool for managing data; it also serves as a hub for collaboration. You can interact with team members directly from the dashboard, making communication easier and more efficient.

1. **Sharing and Permissions**

    You can share your dashboard with other team members by clicking on the "Share" button at the top of the page. From here, you can manage permissions, deciding who can view or edit the dashboard. Smartsheet gives you fine control over permissions, so you can ensure that sensitive information remains secure.

2. **Commenting and Notifications**

    Collaboration is key in Smartsheet, and the dashboard includes commenting features that allow you to communicate with team members directly on tasks, projects, or reports. By adding comments, you can ask questions, give feedback, or request updates, and team members will be notified in real time.

3. **Activity Log**

    The activity log provides a history of all changes made to the sheet, report, or dashboard. You can track who made what changes, when they were made, and what exactly was modified. This is invaluable for project managers who need to keep track of progress and resolve any potential issues.

Final Thoughts on Navigating the Dashboard

The Smartsheet dashboard is an essential feature that enables you to manage your projects and tasks efficiently. By understanding the layout, customizing your workspace, and utilizing the powerful tools Smartsheet provides, you can streamline your workflow and improve productivity. As you become more comfortable with the dashboard, you'll find that it becomes second nature to navigate, making your projects easier to manage and more successful.

1.2 Understanding the Smartsheet Interface

Smartsheet provides a highly flexible and collaborative environment for teams and individuals to manage various types of work. To truly harness the power of Smartsheet, it's essential to understand its core elements: **Sheets**, **Dashboards**, and **Workspaces**. These components allow you to organize, track, and visualize your data, ensuring that your projects run smoothly and efficiently. Let's break each one down in detail.

1.2.1 Sheets, Dashboards, and Workspaces

Smartsheet Sheets: The Foundation of Your Work

At the heart of Smartsheet is the **sheet**. A sheet is essentially a flexible workspace where you track tasks, projects, or any other kind of data you need to manage. If you're familiar with spreadsheets, you'll find that Smartsheet's sheets feel quite similar, but with added functionality and collaboration features that are unique to Smartsheet.

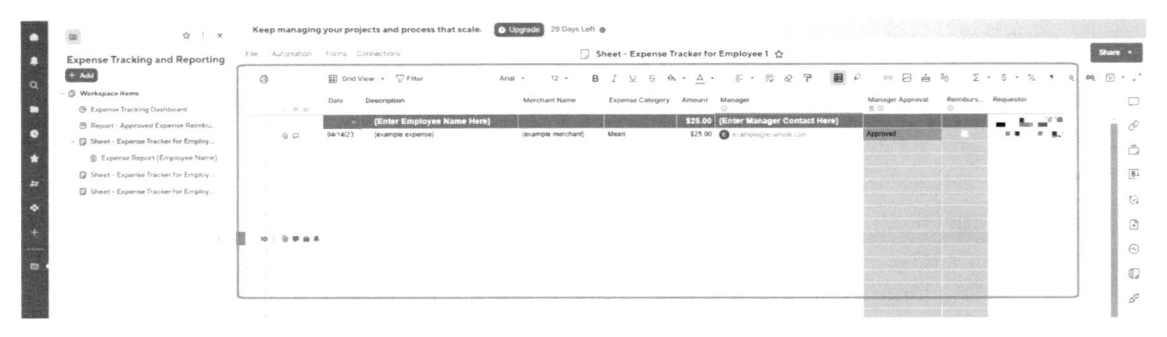

What is a Sheet?

A sheet in Smartsheet is comparable to an Excel spreadsheet, but it's designed specifically for project management, team collaboration, and work automation. It has rows and columns, and the data you input can be anything from project tasks, deadlines, and team members to resource allocations and financial details.

Sheets can be customized to meet the needs of your projects by adding various types of columns. For example, you can use columns for:

- **Text data** (e.g., task names, descriptions)

- **Date fields** (e.g., start and end dates, deadlines)
- **Checklists** (e.g., task completion status)
- **Dropdown menus** (e.g., task priority levels or responsible individuals)
- **Currency or number fields** (e.g., budget estimates, cost tracking)

You can also use formulas and functions (like in Excel) to automatically calculate values, update information, or link data between sheets. Smartsheet sheets are often the starting point for tracking and managing individual projects or tasks.

Types of Sheets in Smartsheet

There are different types of sheets depending on what you want to manage:

- **Project Sheets**: These are used to track projects, milestones, tasks, deadlines, and resources.
- **Task Sheets**: These focus on individual tasks and can be linked to larger project sheets for greater context.
- **Inventory Sheets**: You can track inventory, including quantities, suppliers, and restocking schedules.

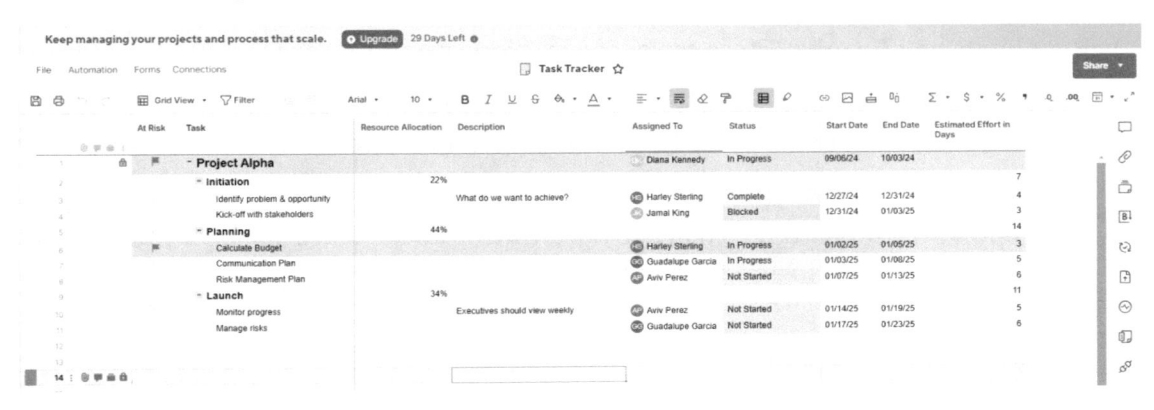

The beauty of Smartsheet is the flexibility it provides in choosing the format and structure of your sheets based on your specific needs.

Key Features of Smartsheet Sheets

- **Collaboration**: Just like Google Docs or Microsoft Word, Smartsheet allows real-time collaboration. Team members can comment, ask questions, and make changes directly on the sheet. This feature is incredibly valuable for keeping everyone on the same page, especially when working with large teams.

- **Attachments and Links**: You can attach files, documents, or links to any cell in a sheet. This is helpful for storing related documents like project reports, images, and meeting notes directly within the context of the project.

- **Cell Linking**: This allows you to link data from one sheet to another, enabling you to track dependencies or consolidate information across multiple sheets.

Dashboards: Visualizing Your Work

Smartsheet dashboards are the next step in organizing and presenting your work. While sheets are excellent for managing the granular details of your projects, **dashboards** give you a high-level overview of everything. Dashboards combine multiple data points from your sheets and display them visually through charts, graphs, and metrics.

What is a Dashboard?

A Smartsheet dashboard is a customized, visual representation of the most critical data from your sheets. It's designed to provide at-a-glance insights into your project's progress and health. Dashboards can be set up to display a variety of data from your sheets, including:

- **Charts and Graphs**: These can show progress over time, resource usage, or budget allocation.

- **Summary Fields**: These fields display key metrics like task completion percentages or upcoming deadlines.

- **Reports**: Dashboards can pull live reports from your sheets, displaying filtered and summarized data in an easy-to-read format.

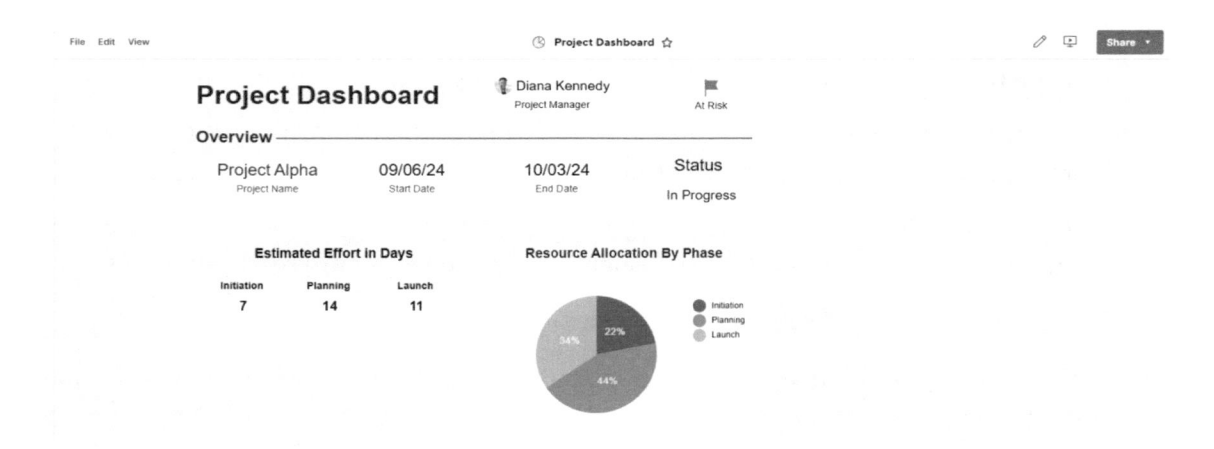

Dashboards are dynamic, meaning that any changes made to your sheets automatically update the data displayed on your dashboard. This ensures that you're always viewing the most current and relevant information.

Creating Dashboards

When creating a dashboard, you can choose from a variety of widgets and tools to build the most useful visual representation of your work. Some key widgets include:

- **Metric Widgets**: Display key numerical data (e.g., total budget spent, number of tasks completed).
- **Chart Widgets**: Display graphical representations of your data, such as bar charts, pie charts, and line graphs.
- **Web Content Widgets**: Embed external web content such as videos, instructions, or forms directly within your dashboard.
- **Report Widgets**: Show filtered lists or reports that summarize information from your sheets.

Dashboards are often used by managers and team leads to track overall project progress or monitor multiple projects simultaneously. For example, a project manager might create a dashboard that pulls in data from all the tasks in a project sheet and visualizes the status of each task, the project timeline, and any budget overruns.

Key Benefits of Dashboards

- **Real-Time Monitoring**: Dashboards pull live data from your sheets, so you always have the most up-to-date information at your fingertips.
- **Customizable Views**: Tailor your dashboard to show the most important metrics for your role, whether you're a project manager, team member, or executive.
- **Quick Insights**: Dashboards give you a high-level overview, so you can quickly identify areas that need attention, such as overdue tasks or exceeded budgets.

Workspaces: Organizing Your Sheets and Projects

Smartsheet **workspaces** are the overarching containers that hold your sheets, reports, and dashboards. They are the logical structure that helps you organize all your work by grouping related sheets, dashboards, and reports into one central location. Workspaces are particularly useful when you have multiple projects or teams that need to collaborate on the same set of data.

What is a Workspace?

A workspace in Smartsheet is a container for organizing all your Smartsheet assets. It's essentially a folder that holds multiple sheets, reports, and dashboards related to a specific project or team. You can have as many workspaces as you need, and each workspace can be tailored to a different department, project, or business unit.

For example:

- A **Marketing Team Workspace** might contain a sheet for social media campaigns, a dashboard for tracking performance, and a report on advertising spend.
- A **Product Development Workspace** might have a sheet for tracking product features, a dashboard for overall product progress, and a report showing customer feedback.

Managing Workspaces

Within each workspace, you can control the access permissions for each sheet, dashboard, or report. Workspaces can be shared with teams or individuals, and you can set different permission levels, such as:

- **Admin**: Full access to all items within the workspace, including the ability to delete sheets and change permissions.
- **Editor**: Can view and modify sheets and reports within the workspace, but cannot delete or change permissions.

- **Viewer**: Can view but not edit the contents of sheets or dashboards.

Workspaces also allow you to maintain organization and consistency. For example, by creating standardized templates within a workspace, teams can ensure that they are using the same structure for tasks, reports, and project tracking across all projects.

Key Benefits of Workspaces

- **Centralized Organization**: Workspaces provide a central hub where you can store all project-related assets. This makes it easy for team members to access relevant files, sheets, and reports without searching through multiple locations.

- **Collaborative Environment**: By grouping related resources in a workspace, teams can collaborate more effectively. Everyone involved can access the same data, share feedback, and track progress, fostering smoother communication and teamwork.

- **Permission Management**: Workspaces allow you to set different levels of access for different team members, ensuring that sensitive information is protected while others can contribute to or view data as needed.

How to Create and Use Workspaces

Creating a workspace in Smartsheet is simple and can be done from the Smartsheet homepage. Here's a step-by-step guide:

1. **Create a New Workspace**: On the Smartsheet homepage, click on the "+" button to create a new workspace. You'll be prompted to enter a name for the workspace.

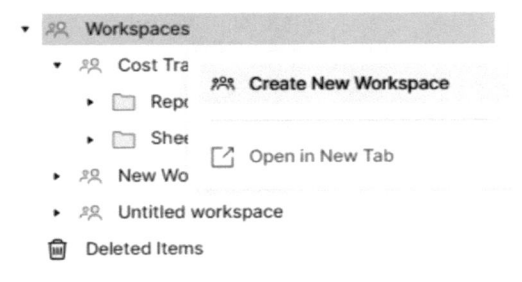

2. **Add Sheets, Reports, and Dashboards**: Once your workspace is created, you can begin adding sheets, reports, and dashboards. You can either create new ones from within the workspace or move existing ones into the workspace.

CHAPTER I: GETTING STARTED WITH SMARTSHEET

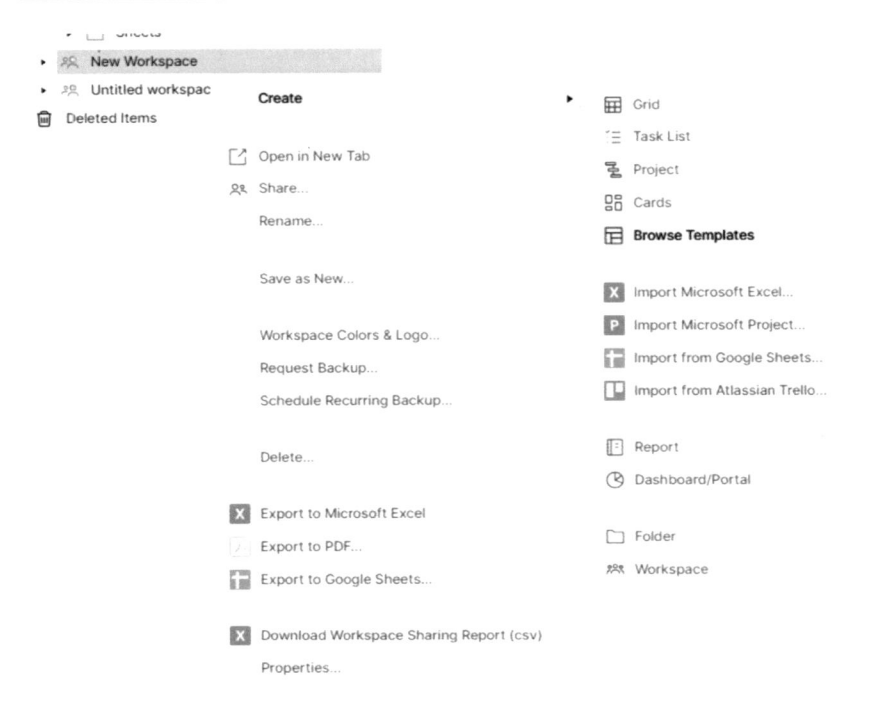

3. **Share the Workspace**: After adding your sheets and dashboards, you can share the workspace with your team members. Depending on their role, they may be able to view or edit the content in the workspace. You can do this by clicking on the workspace settings and adjusting the sharing permissions.

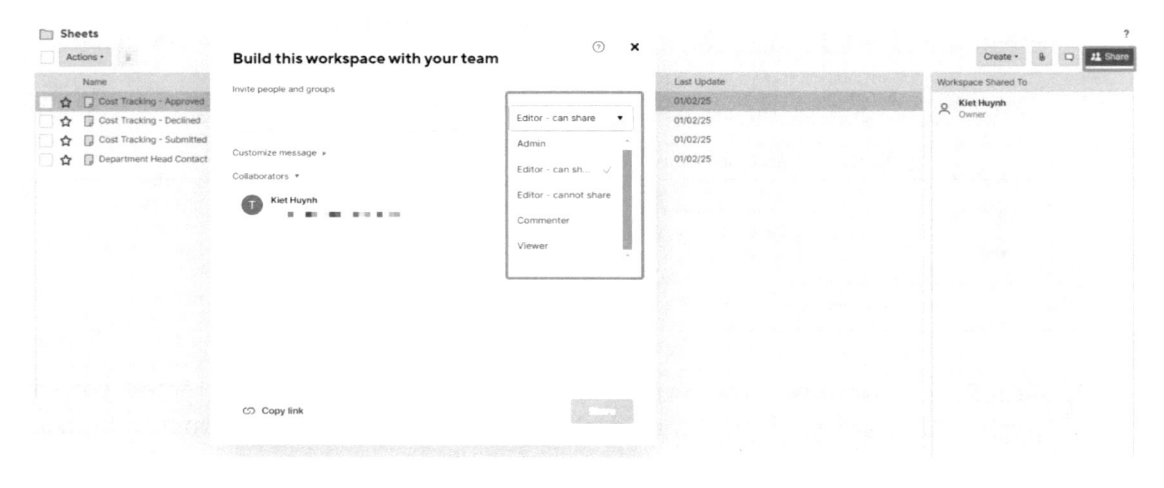

Workspaces can also be used to standardize project management processes. For example, if your team regularly works on similar types of projects, you can create a workspace with pre-built templates for task tracking, status reporting, and project timelines. This ensures consistency across all projects and saves time by using templates that are already set up.

Integrating Sheets, Dashboards, and Workspaces Together

The power of Smartsheet comes when you use **sheets**, **dashboards**, and **workspaces** together. These elements work seamlessly to create a highly effective system for tracking, managing, and reporting on projects.

- **Sheets** provide the data and granular detail needed for task management and project tracking.
- **Dashboards** give you a visual summary of that data, so you can quickly understand project status, timelines, and key metrics.
- **Workspaces** serve as the organizational framework that brings everything together, ensuring that all relevant resources are easily accessible and shareable among the team.

Together, these components allow you to move from raw data (in sheets) to actionable insights (via dashboards), all within a cohesive and organized environment (workspaces).

Best Practices for Organizing Smartsheet Resources

Here are some best practices to consider when organizing your sheets, dashboards, and workspaces in Smartsheet:

1. **Use Workspaces to Group Related Projects**: If your organization is working on multiple projects simultaneously, create separate workspaces for each project or department. For example, you can have a workspace for **Marketing**, one for **Product Development**, and another for **Customer Support**. This will keep everything organized and easily accessible.

2. **Use Sheets to Track Individual Tasks and Projects**: Each sheet should represent a specific project, task list, or data set. Don't overcomplicate your sheets by cramming too much information into one. Keep them focused on a specific purpose, and use multiple sheets as needed.

3. **Leverage Dashboards for Real-Time Insights**: Dashboards are designed to give you a quick snapshot of your work. Don't be afraid to use multiple dashboards for different teams or stakeholders. For instance, your team may have one dashboard

for daily project tracking, while the executives may have a separate dashboard for high-level project performance metrics.

4. **Standardize Sheet and Dashboard Templates**: To save time and maintain consistency, create templates for frequently used sheets and dashboards. For example, create a template for project timelines, task tracking, or performance reports that can be easily duplicated and customized for different projects.

The Role of Collaboration in Sheets, Dashboards, and Workspaces

One of the key features of Smartsheet is its ability to facilitate collaboration across teams. Collaboration in Smartsheet is not only about sharing sheets, but also about creating a system where everyone has access to the data they need, can contribute in real-time, and can stay updated on the progress of projects.

Collaboration in Sheets

In Smartsheet, you can share sheets with team members and give them different levels of access:

- **Editor**: Team members with editor access can update rows, add comments, and make changes directly to the sheet.
- **Viewer**: If you only want team members to see the data, you can give them viewer access, which allows them to view but not edit the sheet.

In addition to sharing sheets, you can also use **comments** to provide context or ask questions on specific cells. Comments in Smartsheet are threaded, which means that multiple team members can participate in a conversation without cluttering up the sheet.

Collaborating through Dashboards

Dashboards enable team members to keep track of a variety of data points. However, collaboration goes beyond just displaying data; you can also share dashboards with your team members, who can view and interact with the data. This allows everyone to stay updated on key metrics and project status without having to dive into detailed sheets.

For example, if you're working on a product launch, a shared dashboard could show real-time sales data, campaign performance, and inventory levels. Everyone involved can view this data and make informed decisions based on the dashboard's insights.

Collaboration within Workspaces

Workspaces offer the ultimate collaboration environment in Smartsheet. Since workspaces contain all the sheets, reports, and dashboards for a project, they allow everyone involved in that project to have access to everything they need in one place. Furthermore, workspaces are easy to share with teams or clients, which means you can grant access to the entire team or only to specific stakeholders.

Conclusion

Understanding the Smartsheet interface—specifically the relationship between **Sheets**, **Dashboards**, and **Workspaces**—is essential for leveraging the full power of the tool. Each element has its own distinct role:

- **Sheets** track the data and details of your work.
- **Dashboards** provide visual summaries and insights.
- **Workspaces** organize everything into cohesive, shareable projects.

By utilizing all three in tandem, you can create a streamlined, collaborative project management system that enables teams to stay on top of tasks, track progress, and make data-driven decisions.

1.2.2 The Toolbar Overview

The toolbar in Smartsheet is an essential element of the interface, providing easy access to a variety of tools and features that allow users to interact with their sheets, automate workflows, and efficiently manage data. This section will give you an overview of the toolbar, covering its primary components and how to use them effectively.

What is the Toolbar?

The toolbar is located at the top of the Smartsheet interface, just below the header, and it acts as the central hub for performing most of the sheet-related tasks. It includes buttons for file management, formatting options, data manipulation, and collaboration tools. As you work on your sheets, the toolbar will be your go-to place for executing common commands.

It is divided into several sections, each catering to a different aspect of your work in Smartsheet. Let's take a closer look at the various elements within the toolbar and explore what each one does.

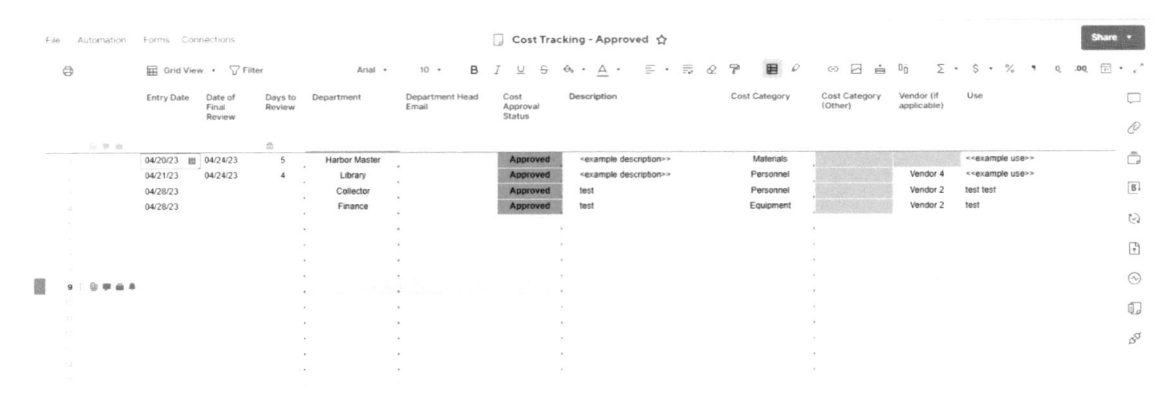

File Options: Managing Your Sheets

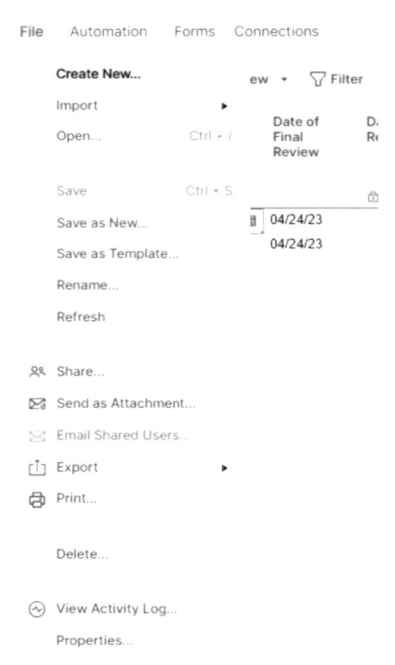

At the far left of the toolbar, you will find a set of file-related options. These options allow you to manage your sheet, collaborate with others, and customize settings to fit your needs.

• **Save**: The save button is automatically enabled in Smartsheet. While other applications may require you to click "Save," Smartsheet saves your progress in real-time. However, if you are working with a template or importing data, you may occasionally need to click the save icon to store your changes.

• **New Sheet**: The "New Sheet" button allows you to create a fresh sheet from scratch. When you click this button, you are prompted to choose whether you want to create a blank sheet or use one of the available templates. Templates are especially helpful for beginners because they provide pre-built structures for specific use cases like project tracking, inventory management, and event planning.

- **Open**: Clicking the "Open" button brings up a window where you can select and open any sheet or report you have recently worked on. This is a great feature for quick access to your frequently used sheets.

- **Share**: Sharing your work with others is a fundamental part of Smartsheet, and the "Share" button lets you send your sheet to others or generate a public link. You can customize permissions to control who can view, edit, or comment on your sheet.

- **Publish**: If you want to make your sheet available to the public or embed it on a website, you can use the "Publish" button. This allows you to share a read-only view of your sheet, which is perfect for keeping stakeholders or clients updated without allowing them to make changes.

- **History**: The "History" button opens a version history menu, which shows all changes made to your sheet over time. This feature is particularly useful if you need to restore a previous version or track changes made by collaborators. You can review who made the changes, what changes were made, and when they occurred.

Data and Formatting Tools: Modifying Your Sheet

The middle section of the toolbar is dedicated to data management and formatting tools. These tools allow you to manipulate your sheet's content, adjust its appearance, and ensure your data is presented in a professional and readable way.

- **Undo/Redo**: At the far left of the data toolbar, you will see the Undo and Redo buttons. These buttons give you the ability to quickly reverse any changes you've made to your sheet. The "Undo" button lets you go back to the previous state, while "Redo" restores the last undone change. These buttons are invaluable if you make a mistake or want to experiment with different options without fear of losing your work.

- **Font and Text Formatting**: The toolbar provides a range of options for customizing the appearance of text in your sheet. You can change the font type, size, and style (bold, italics, underline) to make your text stand out or adhere to your company's branding guidelines. You can also adjust the text alignment (left, center, or right) to ensure it appears exactly as you want.

- **Cell Color and Bordering**: Color-coding cells and adding borders is an excellent way to enhance the visual organization of your sheet. The toolbar allows you to change the background color of individual cells, rows, or columns. You can also add borders to highlight specific data or create a clean layout for your information. These features are especially helpful when presenting data to stakeholders or organizing large amounts of information.

- **Number Formatting**: Smartsheet provides several number formatting options to ensure that numerical data is displayed correctly. You can format cells as currency, percentages, dates, or plain numbers. You can also customize the decimal places and apply rounding as necessary. This feature is crucial for financial tracking, project management, and data analysis.

- **Conditional Formatting**: This tool enables you to apply formatting based on specific conditions, such as highlighting tasks that are overdue or marking high-priority items in red. You can create rules that automatically adjust the appearance of cells based on the data they contain, making it easy to identify trends and outliers. Conditional formatting improves readability and helps draw attention to key pieces of information.

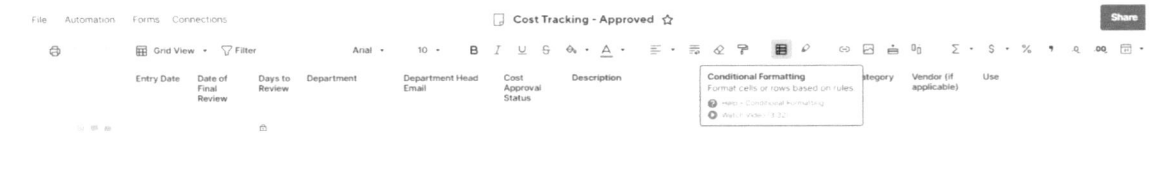

Collaboration and Communication Tools: Working with Your Team

The right side of the toolbar is focused on collaboration tools, enabling you to interact with your team members, assign tasks, and track progress.

- **Comments**: The "Comments" button opens a pane where you can add comments to specific rows or cells within your sheet. Comments allow you to communicate directly with your collaborators and leave feedback or questions about the data. This feature eliminates the need for external communication channels and keeps all discussions within the context of the sheet.

- **Attachments**: Smartsheet makes it easy to attach files, such as documents, images, or links, directly to your sheet. By clicking the "Attachments" button, you can upload files that your team may need to reference while working on the sheet.

Attachments can be linked to individual rows or added to the sheet as a whole, making it easier for everyone to find the resources they need.

- **Cell History**: If you want to view the change history for a specific cell or track who modified a particular piece of data, the "Cell History" button allows you to access this information. This feature is helpful for auditing purposes and ensuring data integrity within your sheet.

- **Alerts and Actions**: Alerts and actions help you automate communication and keep everyone informed. You can set up triggers that send automatic notifications when certain events occur, such as when a task is completed or when a deadline is approaching. The toolbar allows you to configure and manage these alerts, keeping your team on track and minimizing the risk of missed deadlines.

- **Task Assignments**: The toolbar includes buttons that allow you to assign tasks to specific team members directly within your sheet. You can select a row or task and assign it to a collaborator, specifying their responsibilities and deadlines. This feature is vital for project management, ensuring that everyone knows what they need to do and by when.

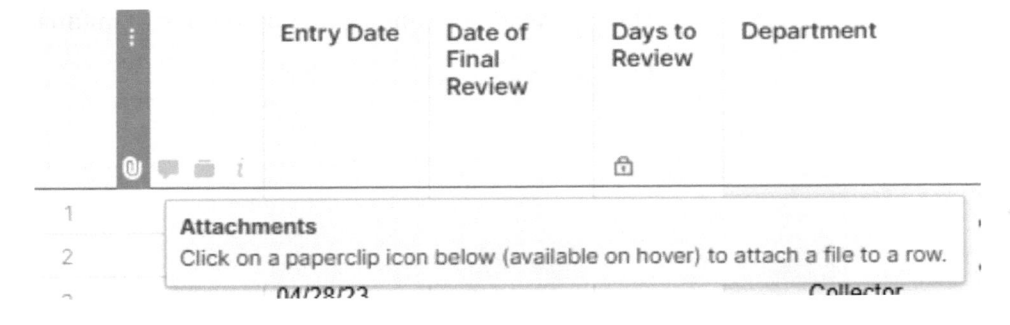

Advanced Tools: Streamlining Your Workflows

In addition to the basic data and collaboration tools, the Smartsheet toolbar also includes several advanced features for power users looking to optimize their workflows.

- **Reports**: The "Reports" button allows you to create customized reports that pull data from multiple sheets. Reports can be filtered and grouped to provide a clear overview of key metrics, such as project status or task progress. This feature is ideal for managers and team leads who need to consolidate data from various sources into one cohesive view.

- **Automation**: Smartsheet includes an automation feature that allows you to create rules and workflows that automate repetitive tasks. The "Automation" button enables you to set up triggers, actions, and alerts, streamlining your processes and reducing the need for manual updates. You can automate everything from task reminders to project approvals, improving efficiency and reducing human error.

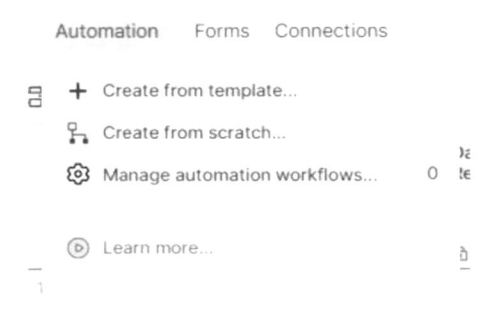

- **Forms**: Smartsheet also provides a form feature that enables you to collect data from external sources. The "Forms" button allows you to create custom forms that can be sent to stakeholders, clients, or team members to gather information, such as feedback, survey responses, or progress updates. The collected data is automatically entered into your sheet, saving time and reducing the risk of manual entry errors.

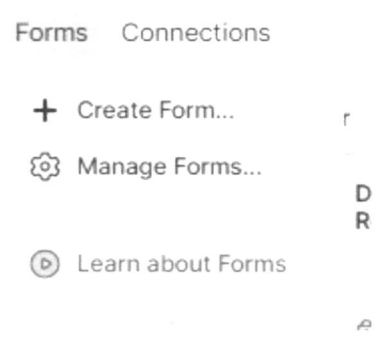

Conclusion: Mastering the Toolbar for Efficient Smartsheet Use

The Smartsheet toolbar is designed to simplify your workflow, improve collaboration, and streamline project management. By familiarizing yourself with the features and tools available in the toolbar, you can work more efficiently, automate repetitive tasks, and maintain better control over your projects.

As you continue to use Smartsheet, you will find that these tools become second nature, helping you manage and execute projects with ease. Whether you're creating reports, collaborating with team members, or automating workflows, the toolbar is your primary tool for making the most of Smartsheet's powerful capabilities.

1.2.3 Key Features and Their Uses

Smartsheet is a robust platform designed to help users organize, manage, and automate tasks and projects efficiently. In this section, we will explore the key features of Smartsheet and their practical applications, making it easier for you to harness the full potential of the platform.

1. Task Management and Collaboration

At its core, Smartsheet is all about managing tasks, tracking progress, and collaborating with your team members. Let's take a look at some of the key task management features:

a. Task Lists: Task lists are the fundamental building blocks of a Smartsheet. They allow users to create and organize tasks, set due dates, assign owners, and track progress. Each row in a sheet represents a task, and you can add multiple columns to capture additional information like priority, status, start date, and more.

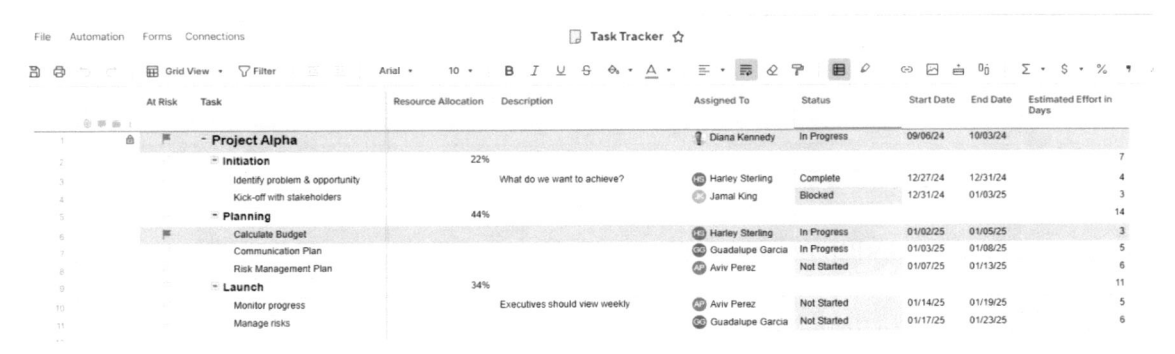

#	At Risk	Task	Resource Allocation	Description	Assigned To	Status	Start Date	End Date	Estimated Effort in Days
1		− **Project Alpha**			Diana Kennedy	In Progress	09/06/24	10/03/24	
2		− Initiation	22%						7
3		Identify problem & opportunity		What do we want to achieve?	Harley Sterling	Complete	12/27/24	12/31/24	4
4		Kick-off with stakeholders			Jamal King	Blocked	12/31/24	01/03/25	3
5		− Planning	44%						14
6		Calculate Budget			Harley Sterling	In Progress	01/02/25	01/05/25	3
7		Communication Plan			Guadalupe Garcia	In Progress	01/03/25	01/08/25	5
8		Risk Management Plan			Aviv Perez	Not Started	01/07/25	01/13/25	6
9		− Launch	34%						11
10		Monitor progress		Executives should view weekly	Aviv Perez	Not Started	01/14/25	01/19/25	5
11		Manage risks			Guadalupe Garcia	Not Started	01/17/25	01/23/25	6

How to Use:

- **Add Rows:** To create a task, simply click on the row and start typing the task name in the left-most column.

- **Assign Owners:** You can assign tasks to team members by selecting their names from a drop-down list.
- **Set Due Dates:** You can specify start and end dates for tasks using the calendar view or date picker tool.

Use Case Example: Imagine you are managing a product launch. Each task can be entered as a row in the sheet, such as "Design product logo," "Develop marketing materials," and "Set up online store." By assigning each task to different team members and setting deadlines, you can easily track progress and ensure that no task falls behind.

b. Dependencies and Predecessors: Dependencies allow you to link tasks based on their relationships. You can set up task dependencies by establishing predecessors. This means that some tasks will only start after others are completed. Dependencies help you maintain proper project timelines, ensuring that tasks happen in a logical order.

How to Use:

- **Predecessor Column:** You can add a "Predecessor" column to your sheet, where you specify which task must be completed before the current task starts.
- **Gantt Chart View:** Smartsheet provides a Gantt chart that visually represents the dependencies between tasks, helping you see how delays in one task might impact others.

Use Case Example: In a construction project, the task "Order materials" would be a predecessor to "Build foundation." The foundation can't be built until the materials have arrived. By linking these tasks, Smartsheet will automatically adjust timelines if a delay occurs.

2. Reports and Views

Smartsheet offers multiple ways to view and report on your data, allowing you to customize how information is displayed. This feature is particularly useful for keeping track of large projects or portfolios.

Grid View: The Grid View is Smartsheet's default view and offers a spreadsheet-like interface where you can see all of your rows (tasks) and columns (attributes). This view allows for easy data entry and editing.

CHAPTER I: GETTING STARTED WITH SMARTSHEET

How to Use:

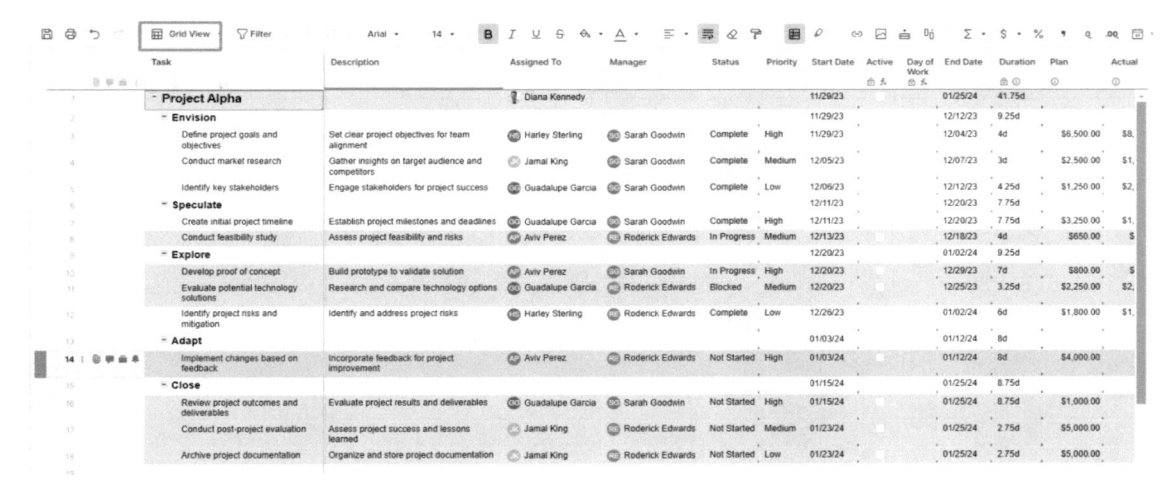

- **Edit Directly in Cells:** You can click into any cell to enter or edit data.
- **Sorting and Filtering:** You can sort data based on specific columns or filter out unnecessary information.

Use Case Example: In the Grid View, you can easily filter tasks to show only those that are overdue, enabling you to prioritize and address critical tasks first.

Gantt View: Gantt View is a visual representation of your project timeline, ideal for showing the start and end dates of tasks. It displays tasks as horizontal bars on a timeline, allowing you to see project progress at a glance. Task dependencies are also displayed here, making it easy to spot any potential bottlenecks.

How to Use:

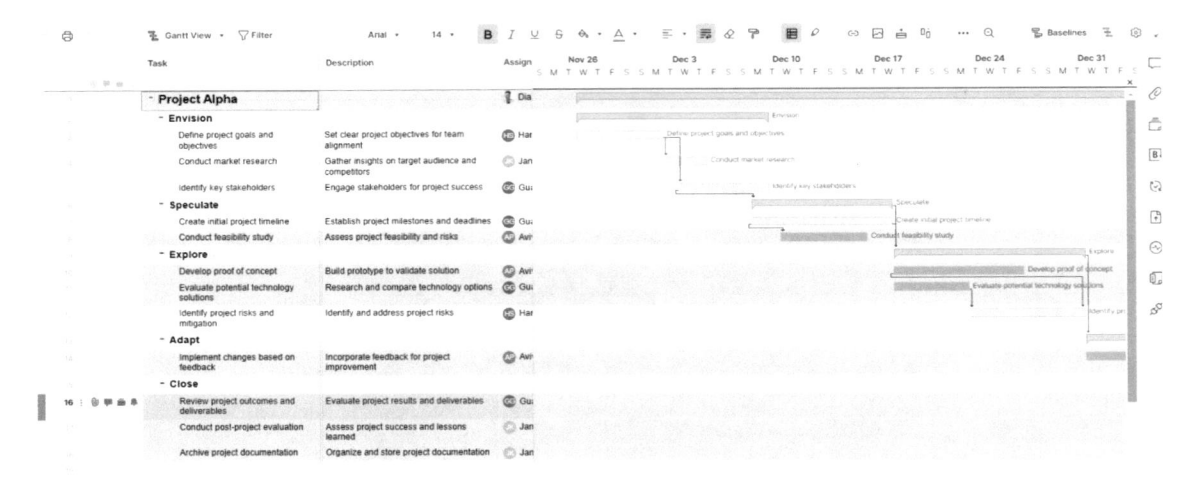

- **Adjust Dates:** You can drag and adjust the Gantt bars to update start and end dates.
- **Color Code Tasks:** You can apply color coding to tasks to visually represent status or priority.

Use Case Example: In a project with many overlapping tasks, the Gantt View gives you a clear view of task durations and how they relate to each other. If any task is delayed, you can quickly see which subsequent tasks might be impacted.

Card View: Card View transforms your tasks into visually distinct cards, often used for agile project management, such as Kanban-style boards. It provides a clear and intuitive way to track progress, especially when working with multiple tasks across different stages.

How to Use:

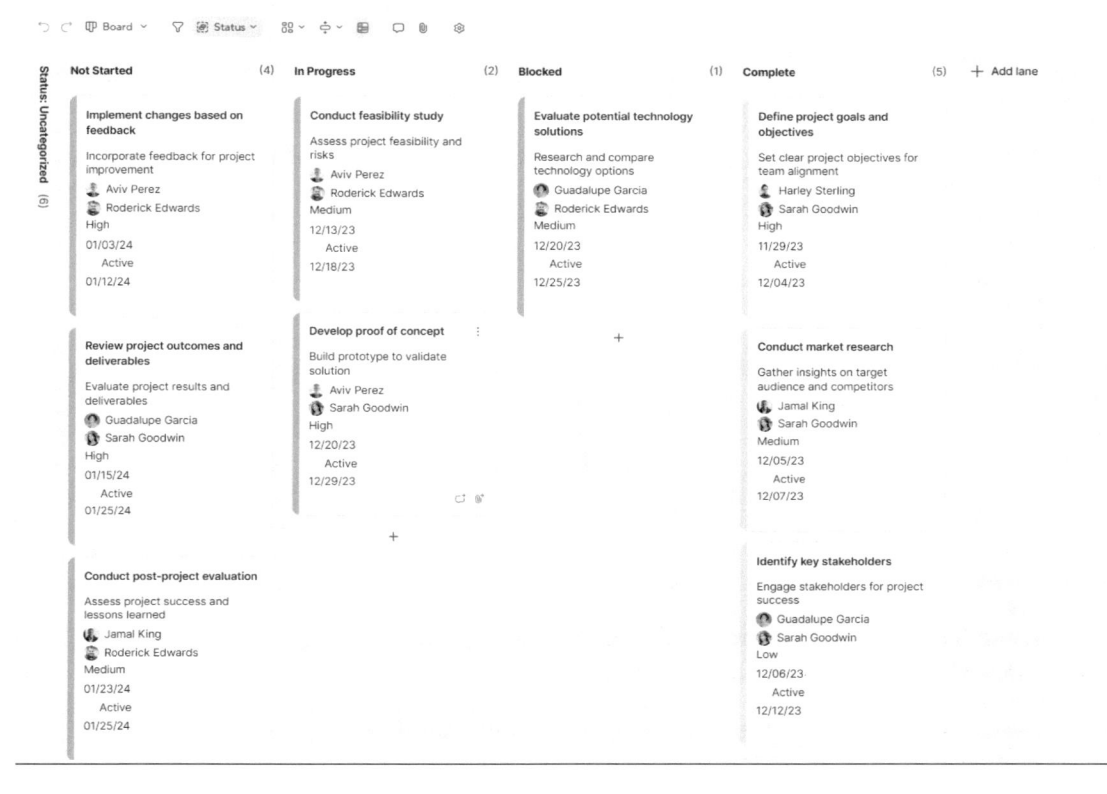

- **Drag and Drop:** You can move cards across columns (e.g., from "To Do" to "In Progress") to visually track task status.

- **Customization:** Customize the columns to represent different stages in your workflow (e.g., "Backlog," "In Progress," "Completed").

Use Case Example: A marketing team may use the Card View to manage content creation. Each card represents an article, and it can be moved across columns like "Idea," "In Progress," and "Published." This allows everyone to visualize the work pipeline at a glance.

Calendar View: The Calendar View allows you to see your tasks and deadlines on a calendar format. This is particularly useful for managing deadlines and ensuring that tasks are completed on time.

How to Use:

- **Drag Tasks into Calendar:** You can drag tasks from the grid or Gantt view and place them directly on the calendar.
- **Sync with Google Calendar:** Smartsheet allows integration with Google Calendar so that you can see tasks alongside other calendar events.

Use Case Example: A project manager may use the Calendar View to track milestone deadlines, ensuring that the project stays on schedule.

3. Automation and Alerts

One of Smartsheet's most powerful features is its ability to automate workflows and set up alerts. Automation helps streamline repetitive tasks, saving time and reducing human error. You can set up triggers to notify team members when a task is due, or automatically move tasks between different stages.

a. Alerts and Reminders: You can set up automated email alerts to notify specific team members when a task is due, delayed, or completed.

How to Use:

- **Create a Rule:** Go to the Automation menu and select "Create Rule." You can set conditions such as "When a task's status changes to 'Complete,' notify the project manager."
- **Schedule Alerts:** You can set up reminders that alert team members a certain number of days before a task's due date.

Use Case Example: In a product launch, you could set up an automated reminder to notify the responsible team members one week before the product testing phase begins, helping to ensure that preparations are on track.

b. Workflow Automation: Workflow automation allows you to automate multi-step processes. For instance, when a task is marked as completed, Smartsheet can automatically notify stakeholders, update project status, and even generate a report.

How to Use:

- **Create Triggers:** Set triggers based on specific actions, like when a task reaches a certain status or when a date is approaching.
- **Create Actions:** Actions can include sending an email, changing a row's status, or moving data between sheets.

Use Case Example: A marketing team might set up a workflow automation to notify team members whenever a task's status changes, keeping everyone informed in real-time.

4. Sharing and Collaboration Tools

Collaboration is a core feature of Smartsheet, and there are various tools within the platform to facilitate smooth teamwork.

a. Comments and Discussions: Smartsheet allows you to add comments to any row or cell, making it easy to discuss specific details with team members.

How to Use:

- **Add Comments:** Click on any row or cell and use the comment feature to add feedback, ask questions, or provide updates.
- **Threaded Discussions:** Comments can be threaded, allowing for organized discussions related to each task.

Use Case Example: A task in the sheet might involve "Designing marketing materials." Team members can leave comments on that row, discussing design feedback or asking for approval, keeping the conversation centered around the task itself.

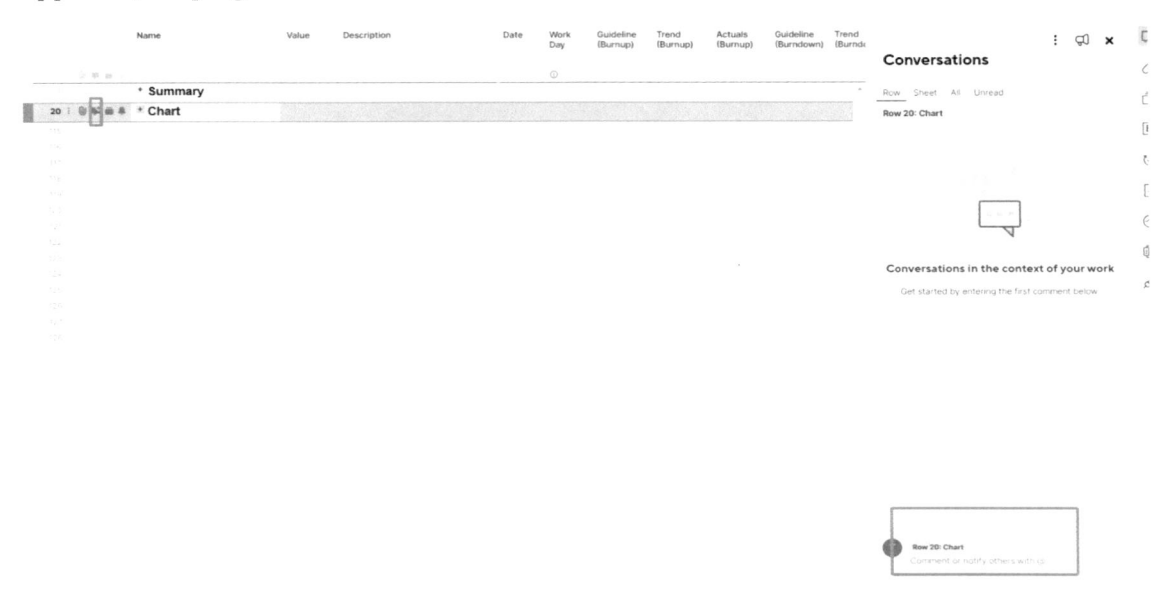

b. Sharing Sheets and Reports: Smartsheet makes it easy to share your data with collaborators. You can share individual sheets, reports, or even entire workspaces with team members.

How to Use:

- **Set Permissions:** When sharing, you can assign different permission levels (Viewer, Editor, Admin) to control who can view, edit, or manage your sheets.

- **Public Sharing:** You can make certain sheets publicly accessible by creating a shareable link.

Use Case Example: If you're working with external contractors, you can share specific sheets with them, giving them read-only access to the progress of certain tasks without compromising the rest of the project.

5. Reporting and Dashboards

One of the most powerful aspects of Smartsheet is its ability to collect, organize, and present data in a way that supports decision-making and strategic planning. Through **Reports** and **Dashboards**, users can easily gain insights into their projects, monitor performance, and track KPIs (Key Performance Indicators).

Reports: Reports allow users to filter and compile data from various sheets and display it in a consolidated view. This feature is invaluable when working across multiple projects or departments, allowing you to create custom reports based on specific criteria.

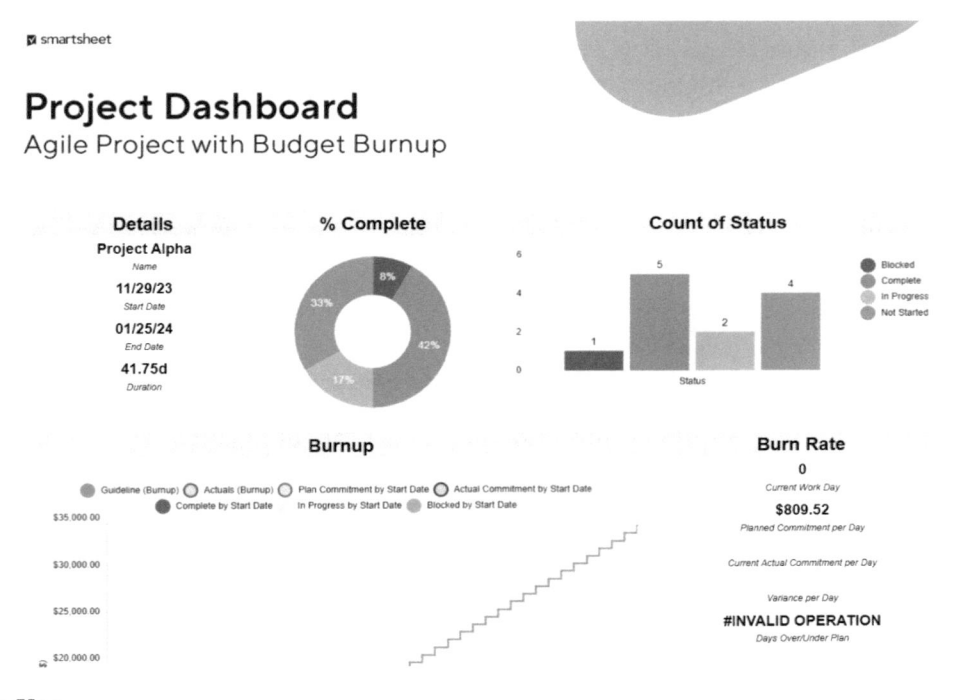

How to Use:

- **Create a Report:** From the Home tab, click on the "Create" button and choose "Report." You can select multiple sheets to pull data from, and apply filters based on specific conditions (e.g., tasks assigned to a particular person, or tasks due within the next week).

- **Customize Columns:** Select the columns you want to display in the report and arrange them in the desired order. You can also modify the layout and appearance to suit your needs.

- **Save and Share Reports:** Once your report is created, save it and share it with team members. Reports can be scheduled for automatic updates, so stakeholders always have access to the latest information.

Use Case Example: A project manager working on multiple client projects can create a report that pulls data from each project sheet, showing tasks that are due in the next week, who they are assigned to, and the status of each task. This can be shared weekly with the client for progress updates.

Dashboards: Dashboards provide a visual, real-time overview of project performance. They aggregate data from multiple sheets and present it using charts, graphs, and widgets, allowing stakeholders to track key metrics at a glance. Dashboards are highly customizable and can be configured to highlight the most important information.

How to Use:

- **Create a Dashboard:** Navigate to the Home tab, select "Create," and choose "Dashboard." You can then add widgets like charts, graphs, and data summaries to display key metrics.

- **Widgets and Data Sources:** Smartsheet allows you to add widgets such as:
    - **Chart Widgets** for visualizing data trends (e.g., pie charts, bar charts).
    - **Metric Widgets** for showing real-time data such as the number of completed tasks or project budget status.
    - **Report Widgets** to display data from a specific report.

- **Customizing the Layout:** Dashboards can be organized into rows and columns, and the layout can be adjusted based on what information is most crucial for your audience.

Use Case Example: A senior executive may use a dashboard to track the overall health of a company's projects. The dashboard could display key performance indicators (KPIs) such as budget utilization, overdue tasks, and project completion percentage across multiple projects.

---

6. Integration with Other Tools

Smartsheet offers several integration options with popular business tools to enhance collaboration and streamline workflows. By connecting Smartsheet with other platforms, you can reduce manual effort and ensure smooth data flow between systems.

a. Integrations with Google Workspace: Smartsheet integrates with Google Workspace, allowing you to seamlessly link documents, calendar events, and emails with your Smartsheet tasks.

How to Use:

- **Google Drive Integration:** Attach Google Docs, Sheets, and Slides directly to your Smartsheet tasks for easy access.
- **Google Calendar Sync:** Sync Smartsheet tasks with Google Calendar to track deadlines and milestones. Changes made in Smartsheet automatically reflect in Google Calendar, helping you stay aligned.

Use Case Example: If you're managing a marketing campaign, you can link Google Docs for drafts or final versions of marketing materials to each task in Smartsheet. This makes it easy for everyone to access and collaborate on the documents without leaving the Smartsheet platform.

b. Integration with Microsoft Office 365: Smartsheet also integrates with Microsoft Office 365, including Outlook, Excel, and OneDrive, enhancing your ability to share, track, and collaborate on files.

How to Use:

- **Microsoft Excel Integration:** Import and export data between Excel and Smartsheet. You can use Smartsheet's advanced features like dependency management and Gantt charts with the data you bring over from Excel.
- **Outlook Integration:** Sync Smartsheet tasks with Outlook calendar events. Additionally, you can send task-related email reminders and notifications directly from Smartsheet to Outlook.

Use Case Example: A project manager might use Excel to prepare a detailed project schedule, then import the data into Smartsheet for better task tracking, dependencies, and team collaboration.

c. Integration with Slack and Other Communication Tools: Smartsheet integrates with Slack, allowing teams to communicate more effectively by bringing Smartsheet updates directly into Slack channels.

How to Use:

- **Set up Notifications:** You can configure Smartsheet to send alerts or updates to Slack when specific actions happen, such as when a task is completed, or when a project milestone is reached.

- **Slack Commands:** Users can update tasks or check statuses directly within Slack using Smartsheet commands.

Use Case Example: A development team may use Slack to communicate project updates. By integrating Smartsheet with Slack, the team can receive automatic notifications about task changes or upcoming deadlines, ensuring everyone is on the same page without needing to check Smartsheet constantly.

7. Security and Permissions

Smartsheet offers a variety of tools to ensure that your data remains secure and only accessible to authorized individuals. The platform provides multiple levels of security and permissions, allowing you to control who can view, edit, or manage your sheets.

a. Role-Based Permissions: With Smartsheet, you can assign different roles to users based on their involvement with the project. Permissions control access at both the sheet level and the workspace level, ensuring that sensitive information is only available to the right individuals.

How to Use:

- **Admin Permissions:** Administrators can manage sheet settings, user permissions, and access to all functionalities within the sheet.

- **Editor and Viewer Roles:** Editors can make changes to the sheet, while Viewers can only see data without making edits.

Use Case Example: A project manager can assign a team member as a Viewer for a particular sheet, ensuring they can access the data but not modify it, while other members are given Editor access to make updates.

b. Data Protection and Audit Logs: Smartsheet provides features like data encryption, audit logs, and user activity tracking to maintain the integrity of your data.

How to Use:

- **Audit Logs:** You can track changes made to your sheets, including who made the change and when it occurred. This is especially helpful for troubleshooting and ensuring compliance.

- **Data Encryption:** Smartsheet uses encryption to protect sensitive data both in transit and at rest, ensuring that your project information is secure.

Use Case Example: In a highly regulated industry such as healthcare or finance, it's crucial to keep a record of every update and modification made to project sheets. Smartsheet's audit logs provide that transparency, allowing teams to remain compliant with industry standards.

8. Mobile App for On-the-Go Management

Smartsheet's mobile app extends its capabilities, allowing you to manage tasks and projects from anywhere. Whether you're in the office or on-site at a construction project, you can stay updated and ensure your work stays on track.

How to Use:

- **Download the App:** Smartsheet's mobile app is available for both iOS and Android devices. You can download it from the respective app stores.

- **Access Sheets and Tasks:** You can access your Smartsheet projects, view task details, update progress, and even share information with your team while on the go.

Use Case Example: A field manager on a construction site can use the Smartsheet mobile app to check off completed tasks, upload photos or documents related to the project, and update task statuses directly from their mobile device.

By mastering these key features, you will be able to use Smartsheet efficiently, whether you are managing a simple task list or a complex project portfolio. Smartsheet's flexibility and wide range of features ensure that you can tailor it to meet your unique needs, improving collaboration, enhancing productivity, and optimizing workflows across your team or organization.

1.3 Creating Your First Sheet

1.3.1 Selecting a Template

When you first start using Smartsheet, one of the most important decisions you'll make is selecting a template. A template is a pre-designed sheet with predefined structure and fields, designed to help you quickly start tracking and managing your projects, tasks, or data. Smartsheet offers a wide range of templates suited to various industries and use cases, including project management, marketing campaigns, event planning, and more. In this section, we'll explore how to choose the right template, how to customize it to fit your needs, and how to use the built-in features to get the most out of your chosen template.

Why Use a Template?

Before diving into the selection process, it's important to understand why templates are so helpful. Templates serve as a shortcut to setting up a new sheet, saving you time and effort by providing you with a structure already in place. You don't need to start from scratch every time you need to create a new sheet. Templates are especially useful for beginners who may not yet be familiar with all the functionalities of Smartsheet or for those looking to quickly replicate an existing workflow.

Some key advantages of using templates include:

- **Time Savings**: Templates help you get started quickly. You don't need to worry about creating columns, setting up formulas, or figuring out what data you need to track. Templates give you a ready-made foundation to build upon.

- **Consistency**: If you're managing multiple projects or collaborating with teams, templates ensure that everyone is working from the same layout and structure. This leads to better consistency across all your work.

- **Best Practices**: Templates are often designed with industry best practices in mind, meaning they come with optimized structures and configurations based on real-world use cases.

- **Customization**: While templates are designed to provide a starting point, they are fully customizable, allowing you to adjust the columns, data fields, and even add advanced features as your needs evolve.

Navigating the Template Gallery

When creating a new sheet in Smartsheet, you'll be presented with the option to choose from a variety of templates. To access the template gallery, follow these steps:

1. **Open Smartsheet**: Once logged into your Smartsheet account, navigate to the Home tab.

2. **Create New Sheet**: Click the "**+ Create New**" button in the top left corner of your screen. This will open a menu where you can choose from different sheet creation options.

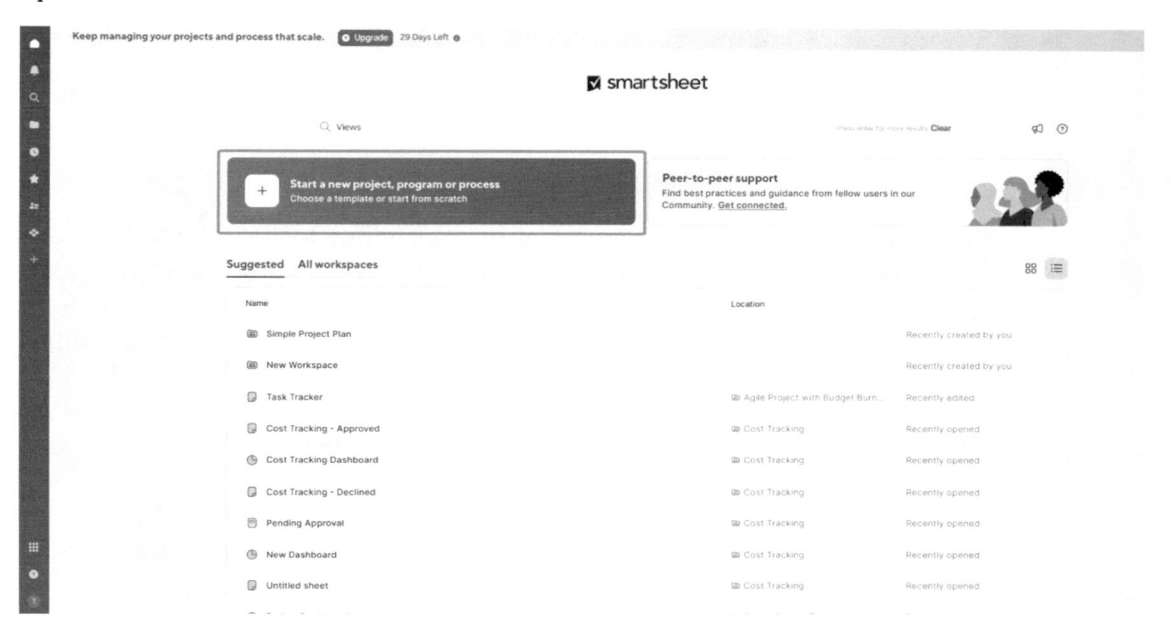

3. **Select Template**: In the creation menu, you'll see an option for **"Browse Templates"**. Click this to access the Template Gallery, where you can explore the available templates.

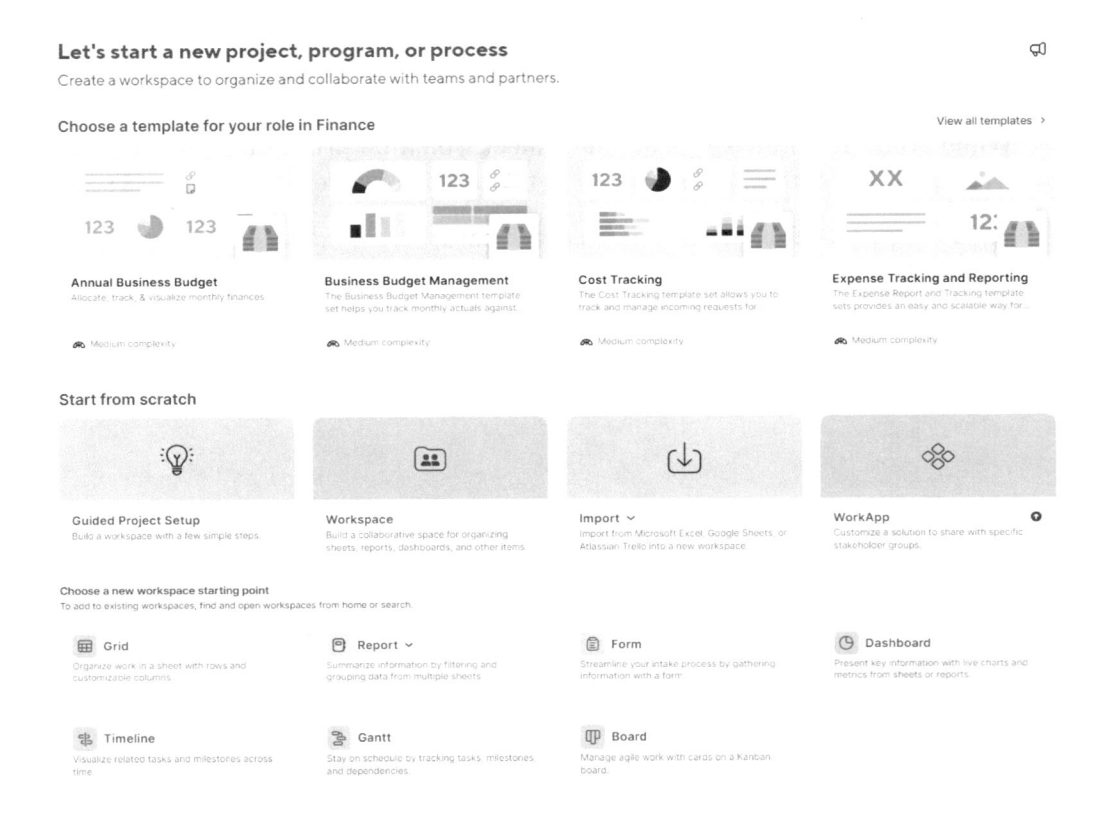

4. **Browse or Search**: You can either browse templates by category (such as Project Management, Marketing, IT, etc.) or use the search bar to find a template that fits your specific needs. Smartsheet offers dozens of categories and hundreds of templates, so you're likely to find one that fits your project type or industry.

Choosing the Right Template

Selecting the right template can make all the difference in how efficiently you work within Smartsheet. Here are some factors to consider when choosing a template:

1. Determine Your Purpose

Before you choose a template, take a moment to consider the primary purpose of your sheet. Are you managing a project timeline? Tracking employee performance? Planning a marketing campaign? Knowing your primary objective will help narrow down your choices.

- **Project Management**: Smartsheet offers a wide range of project management templates, such as Gantt charts, task lists, and timelines. These templates are ideal for organizing and tracking progress on specific tasks or milestones.
- **Marketing**: If you're working on a marketing campaign, you may find templates designed specifically for tracking campaigns, content calendars, or advertising budgets.
- **HR and Employee Management**: Templates designed for HR purposes may include employee information sheets, performance reviews, and onboarding trackers.
- **Sales and CRM**: If you're in sales or customer relationship management (CRM), there are templates available for managing leads, tracking sales pipelines, and forecasting revenue.

By identifying the purpose of your sheet, you can quickly filter out templates that aren't relevant to your needs.

2. Consider Your Team's Needs

If you are collaborating with a team, consider their needs as well. Does your team require a template with a built-in Gantt chart for visualizing timelines? Or will a simple task tracker suffice? In a collaborative environment, it's essential to ensure that the template you choose supports team workflows and communication needs.

- **Collaboration**: Choose a template that allows team members to easily track progress, add comments, and update statuses. Templates with built-in notifications and automated workflows can enhance team collaboration.
- **Permissions**: If multiple people are contributing to the sheet, consider a template that allows you to set permissions for various team members, ensuring that they can only access and edit the sections relevant to them.

3. Flexibility and Customization

While templates provide a structure, they should also be flexible enough to accommodate your unique requirements. Look for templates that are easily customizable—whether it's adding new columns, changing formulas, or adjusting the layout to match your preferred workflow.

For instance, if you're using a project management template but need additional fields for budget tracking, you should be able to add custom columns for cost, expenses, or budget status.

Types of Templates in Smartsheet

Smartsheet's template gallery is divided into various categories, each designed for different use cases. Here's a breakdown of some of the most popular types of templates available:

1. Project Management Templates

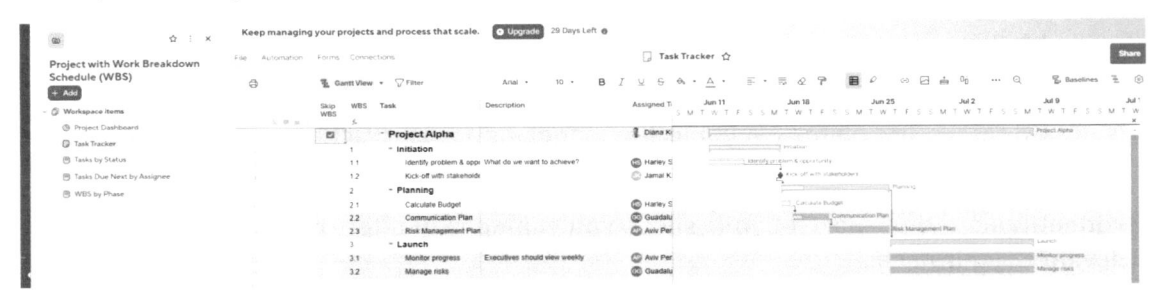

Project management templates are among the most widely used. These templates help you plan, organize, and track the progress of your projects. Some popular project management templates include:

- **Gantt Chart Template**: Ideal for visualizing project timelines and task dependencies. It's a great tool for tracking milestones, deadlines, and task assignments.
- **Task List Template**: A simple checklist format that allows you to track tasks, assign owners, and set due dates.
- **Agile Project Management Template**: If you follow Agile methodologies, this template allows you to plan sprints, track user stories, and monitor progress.

2. Marketing Templates

For marketing professionals, Smartsheet offers templates for content planning, campaign tracking, and social media management. Examples include:

CHAPTER I: GETTING STARTED WITH SMARTSHEET

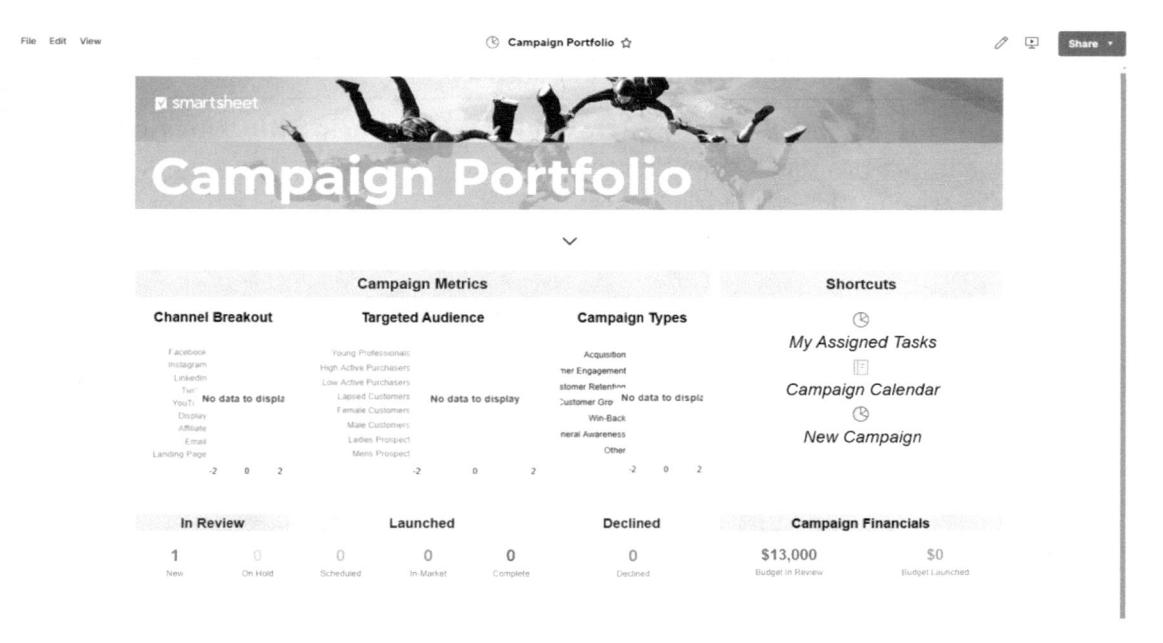

- **Content Calendar Template**: Track content creation, deadlines, and publishing schedules for blogs, social media, and other marketing efforts.
- **Campaign Tracker Template**: This template helps you plan, execute, and monitor marketing campaigns, including tasks, deadlines, and budgets.

3. HR and Employee Management Templates

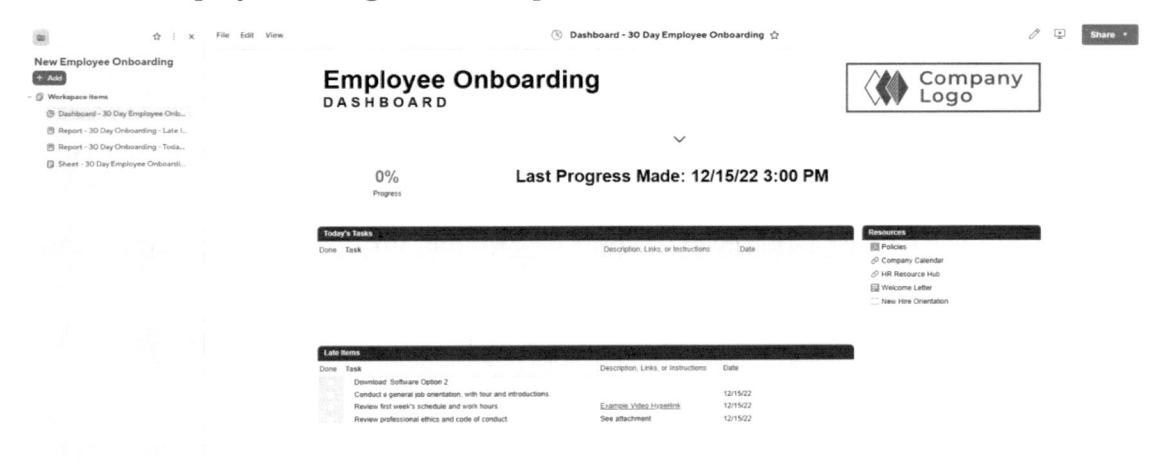

Page 81 | 383

If you work in human resources or need to manage employee-related data, there are several HR-focused templates to choose from, such as:

- **Employee Onboarding Template**: This template helps HR teams manage the onboarding process for new hires, track progress, and ensure that all necessary tasks are completed.

- **Performance Review Template**: Track employee performance reviews, feedback, and goals.

4. Finance Templates

Finance-related templates help you manage budgets, expenses, and financial reporting:

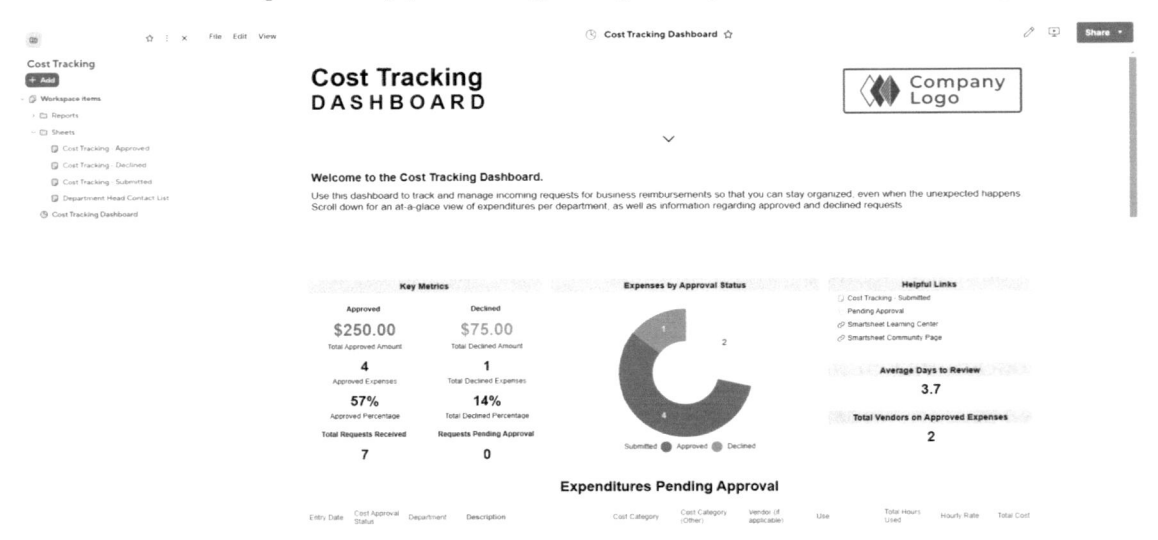

- **Budget Tracking Template**: Use this template to track income, expenses, and financial goals.

- **Expense Report Template**: A simple way to track business expenses and generate reports.

Customizing Your Template

After selecting a template, it's time to customize it to your specific needs. While templates come pre-configured with many useful fields, they are fully customizable, and you can make changes to better fit your project or workflow.

1. Adding and Editing Columns

One of the first things you may want to do is add or remove columns to match the data you need to track. To add a column:

1. Right-click on the column header where you want to insert a new column.
2. Select **"Insert Column"** from the drop-down menu.
3. Choose the type of column (text, date, dropdown, etc.) and give it a name.

To edit a column, simply click on the column header and update its settings, including changing the column name, data type, or format.

2. Updating Data Types and Formats

Templates may come with predefined data types for each column (e.g., date, dropdown list, text). You can modify the data type to better suit your needs. For example, if a date column is too rigid, you can switch it to a text column to allow for more flexibility.

3. Adding Rows and Additional Sheets

Depending on your template, you may need to add additional rows for new tasks, data points, or people. To add a row, click the **"+ Row"** button at the bottom of the sheet. Similarly, if your project grows and you need more sheets, you can create additional sheets within the same workspace for better organization.

Conclusion

Choosing the right template in Smartsheet is the first step in getting your projects off the ground efficiently. Smartsheet provides a wide range of templates designed for various industries, and understanding how to select and customize the template best suited for your needs can save you a significant amount of time and effort. By considering your project's purpose, your team's needs, and your flexibility requirements, you can quickly set up a Smartsheet that's ready to track, manage, and optimize your work.

In the next section, we'll explore how to add and edit columns to customize your sheet further, and how to start entering data to make your project come to life.

1.3.2 Adding and Editing Columns

When you first begin using Smartsheet, one of the most essential steps in organizing your data is understanding how to add and edit columns. Columns act as the structural framework of your sheets, allowing you to categorize, organize, and manage your information effectively. In this section, we'll explore how to add, edit, and manage columns in Smartsheet to help you create the perfect sheet for your projects.

Why Columns Matter in Smartsheet

Columns in Smartsheet represent the categories of data you want to track, whether you are managing projects, tasks, resources, or deadlines. Each column in Smartsheet can hold specific types of information, and understanding how to manage them efficiently can make the difference between a cluttered, hard-to-read sheet and an organized, easy-to-manage one.

Smartsheet offers a range of column types, from simple text fields to more complex data types like drop-down lists, checkboxes, and dates. Knowing how to add and edit these columns allows you to customize your sheet to meet the unique needs of your project.

Step 1: Adding New Columns

Adding new columns to a Smartsheet is a straightforward process that you'll likely perform frequently as you continue to work within the tool. Follow these steps to add a column to your sheet:

1.1 Navigating the Column Toolbar

First, open your sheet and navigate to the column toolbar located at the top of your sheet. You'll see the existing columns and an empty space to the right of the last column. Here is where you'll add new columns.

1.2 Clicking the "+" Button

Next, locate the "+" button at the far right of the column list. This button allows you to insert a new column into your sheet. When you click on it, Smartsheet will provide options for creating a new column.

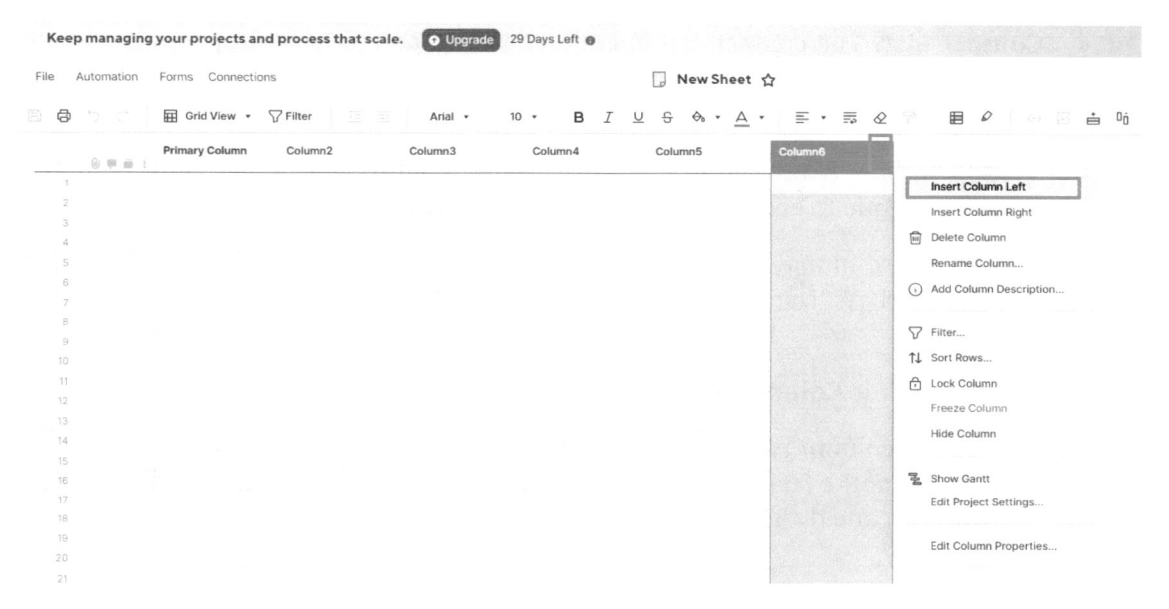

1.3 Selecting Column Type

Smartsheet provides multiple column types, and it's essential to choose the correct one for the data you're going to track. Here are the most common column types available:

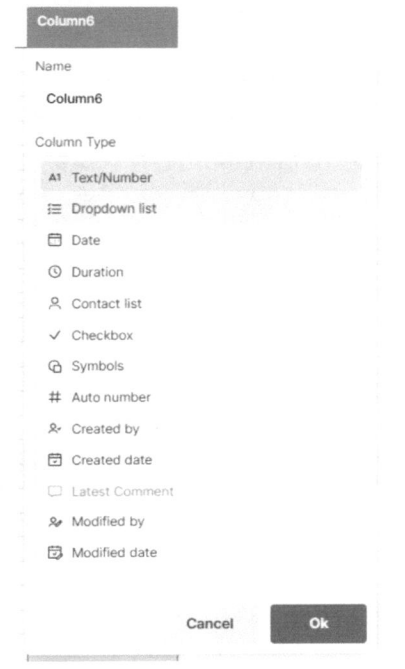

- **Text/Number**: This is a standard column used for general text or numerical data. It's versatile and can be used for almost anything, such as task names, descriptions, or numeric values like project costs.

- **Date**: If you want to track dates (such as deadlines or milestones), you'll need to add a "Date" column. This type ensures your data is formatted consistently, and you can easily sort tasks by date.

- **Dropdown List**: Dropdown columns are used for predefined options. For example, you might have a column titled "Status" with dropdown options like "Not Started," "In Progress," and "Completed." This type helps standardize responses across your sheet.

- **Checkbox**: A checkbox column allows you to mark items as either completed or incomplete. It's ideal for simple binary data, such as "Task Completed" or "Verified."

- **Contact List**: The contact column allows you to assign tasks to people, allowing team members to be notified when their tasks are approaching deadlines or need action.

- **Text/Number (Auto-Number)**: This column automatically assigns a unique number or code to each row, useful for project IDs or task numbers.

Once you select the column type, give it a name. You can name it something descriptive like "Task Name," "Priority," "Due Date," or whatever best fits the information the column will hold.

1.4 Inserting the New Column

After selecting the column type and naming the column, click "OK" to insert it. The new column will appear at the far-right side of your sheet. If you want to reposition the column, you can simply click and drag it into the desired location.

Step 2: Editing Existing Columns

In addition to adding columns, Smartsheet also allows you to edit columns. Whether you need to rename a column, change the column type, or adjust other settings, here's how to edit your existing columns:

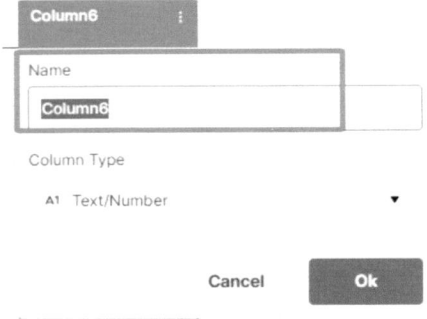

2.1 Renaming a Column

If you've added a column but realize that the name doesn't quite reflect the data it holds, it's easy to rename it.

- **Hover over the Column Name**: Navigate your mouse to the column header, where the column name is displayed.

- **Click the Drop-down Arrow**: A drop-down menu will appear when you click the small arrow next to the column name.

- **Select "Rename Column"**: From the drop-down menu, click "Rename Column." You can then type the new name for the column and press Enter to confirm.

2.2 Changing Column Type

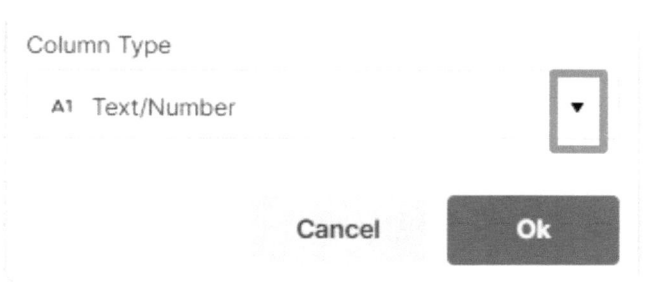

At any point, you may realize that you need to change the column type (for example, changing a text column to a date column). To do this:

- **Click the Drop-down Arrow**: Hover over the column name and click the small drop-down arrow next to it.

- **Select "Edit Column Properties"**: From the menu, select "Edit Column Properties."

- **Change Column Type**: In the settings window, you can choose a different column type (such as changing a "Text/Number" column to a "Dropdown List" column). Be aware that changing the column type may affect your data, so review it carefully.

- **Save Changes**: After making your adjustments, click "OK" to save the changes.

2.3 Adjusting Column Width

Another essential aspect of managing columns in Smartsheet is ensuring your data is visible and well-organized. You can adjust the width of a column to ensure that all of your data fits neatly within the sheet. Here's how:

- **Hover Over the Column Border**: Move your mouse cursor to the line between two column headers.

- **Drag to Adjust Width**: Click and hold the border, then drag it to the left or right to adjust the column width. Release the mouse to set the new width.

- **Double-Click to Auto-Adjust**: If you want Smartsheet to automatically adjust the column width to fit the longest piece of data in that column, double-click on the border between two columns.

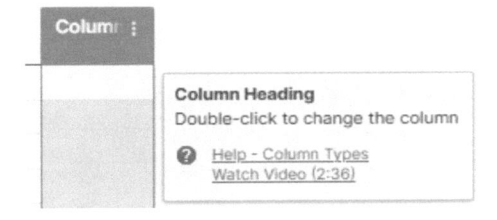

2.4 Adding and Editing Dropdown Options

If you've added a dropdown list column and want to modify the options, follow these steps:

- **Click the Drop-down Arrow**: Hover over the column name and click the small drop-down arrow next to it.

- **Select "Edit Column Properties"**: Click this option to open the column settings.

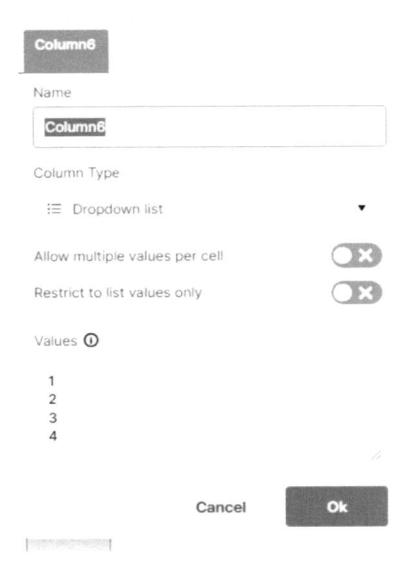

- **Modify the Dropdown List**: In the column properties window, you can add, remove, or modify the options available in the dropdown list. You can also set default values for the column.

- **Save Changes**: Once you've made your adjustments, click "OK" to save the changes.

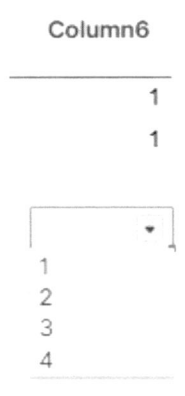

2.5 Adding or Removing Default Values

For columns that require specific data entries (such as dates or checkboxes), you may want to set default values. For example, you might want to set today's date as the default value in a "Due Date" column.

- **Select Column Properties**: Follow the same steps to open the column properties as before.
- **Set Default Value**: In the settings, look for an option to set a default value and configure it as needed.
- **Save**: Confirm the default value and save your changes.

Step 3: Managing Column Data

Once your columns are set up and customized, managing data within them becomes a crucial part of working effectively in Smartsheet. Here are a few tips for managing column data:

3.1 Filtering Data

Smartsheet allows you to filter data by column values. This is useful if you want to quickly view only specific rows based on column criteria. For example, you could filter all tasks with a "High" priority.

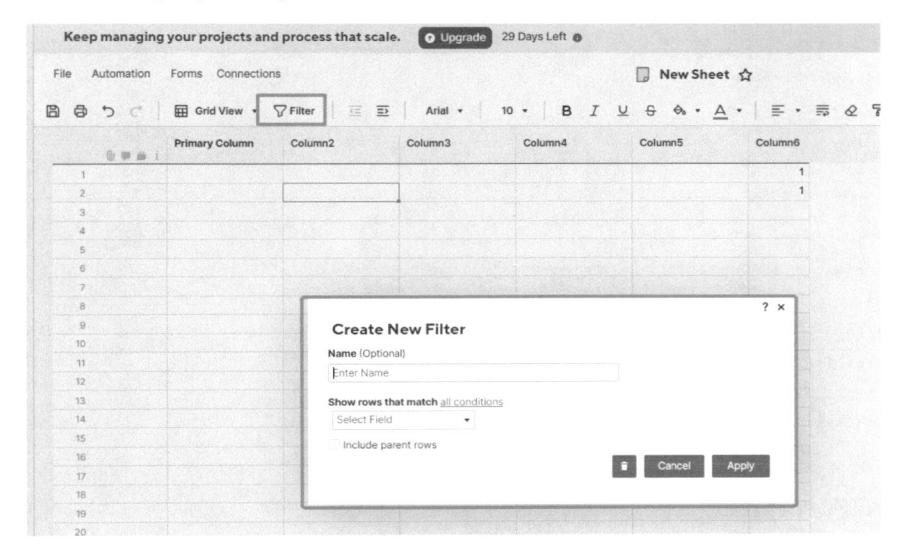

- **Click on the Filter Icon**: In the column header, click the filter icon (a funnel shape).
- **Set Filter Criteria**: Choose your filter options (for example, choose "High" in the "Priority" column).
- **Apply the Filter**: Once the filter criteria are set, only rows matching those criteria will appear on the sheet.

3.2 Sorting Data

Sorting columns help to organize data logically. For example, you may want to sort tasks by their due dates.

- **Click the Drop-down Arrow**: In the column header, click the small drop-down arrow.
- **Choose Sort Option**: Select either "Sort Ascending" or "Sort Descending" based on your preference.
- **Apply Sorting**: Once sorted, your data will be arranged according to the selected column's values.

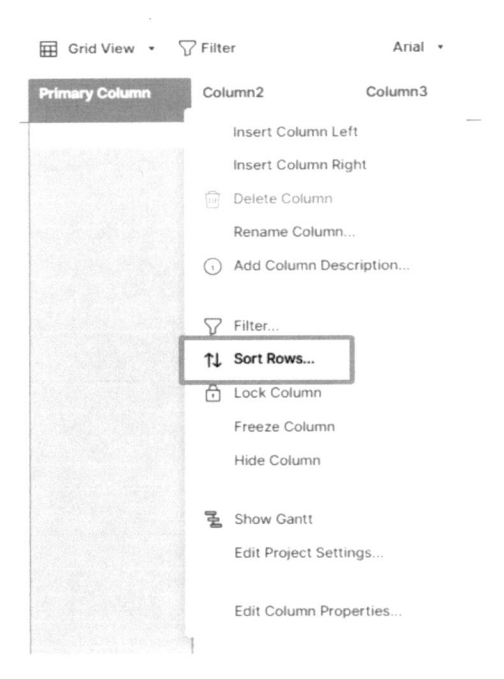

3.3 Using Conditional Formatting

Conditional formatting allows you to automatically apply different styles (like color changes) to cells based on their content. This can be helpful for quickly spotting key information, such as overdue tasks or completed items.

- **Select Column**: Click the column header to select the entire column.
- **Go to Conditional Formatting**: Open the toolbar and choose "Conditional Formatting."

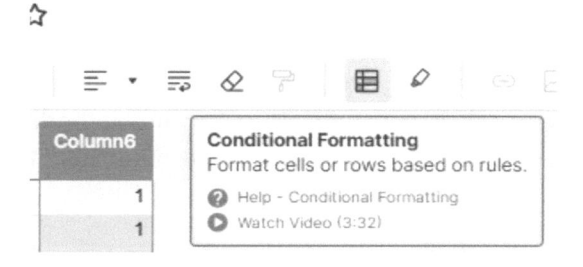

- **Set Formatting Rules**: Define the conditions (such as values greater than a certain number or dates in the past), and select the formatting style.
- **Apply Changes**: Once you've configured the rules, the formatting will automatically apply to matching cells.

Conclusion

Adding and editing columns in Smartsheet is a fundamental skill that will help you manage your data effectively. By learning how to structure your sheet with the right columns, you can ensure that your projects are organized, easily tracked, and aligned with your team's needs. From simple text columns to more advanced dropdowns and checkboxes, Smartsheet gives you the flexibility to adapt your sheets to your specific requirements.

As you continue to explore Smartsheet, keep these techniques in mind as you customize your sheets for even greater functionality and efficiency.

1.3.3 Saving and Sharing Your Sheet

Once you have created your sheet and added all the necessary data, the next step is to save and share it with collaborators. This ensures that your work is accessible and editable by others, fostering collaboration and effective project management. In Smartsheet, saving and sharing are simple, but there are several important features and settings you should be familiar with to make the most out of this process.

Saving Your Sheet

Smartsheet automatically saves your work as you make changes, so there is no need to manually save every time you add or update data. This auto-save feature ensures that you don't lose any progress if you accidentally close the application or encounter an internet issue.

1. Auto-Save in Smartsheet

Smartsheet operates in the cloud, which means that your data is constantly saved as you work on it. Every change you make is synced across all devices where your Smartsheet account is logged in. Whether you are on your desktop, laptop, or mobile device, all your changes are automatically updated in real-time, reducing the chances of losing information.

This cloud-based system allows you to access your work from anywhere and anytime, ensuring that your data is always up-to-date. In contrast to traditional desktop-based software, you do not need to worry about manually saving your work or losing unsaved changes.

2. Manual Save (Optional)

Although Smartsheet auto-saves your work, there are still times when you may want to manually save a version of your sheet before making significant changes. You can do this by clicking the "File" menu at the top left corner of the screen and selecting "Save". This creates a backup of your current version, and you can refer to this version if needed.

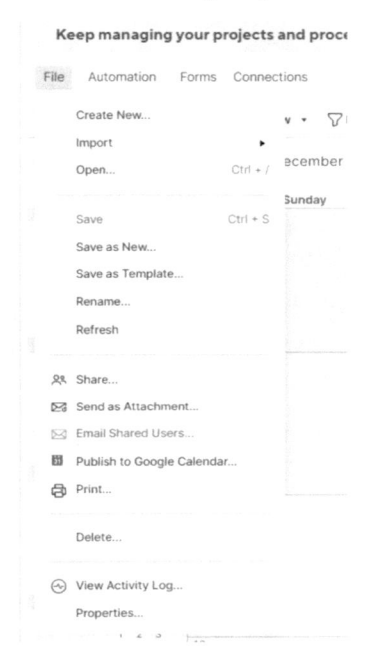

Sharing Your Sheet

Sharing your sheet in Smartsheet is essential for collaboration, whether you're working with a team on a project or need to provide stakeholders with access to a report. Smartsheet provides various sharing options, allowing you to control who has access to your sheet and what level of permissions they have.

1. Sharing a Sheet with Specific Users

To share a sheet with others, click on the "Share" button located at the top-right corner of the screen. This opens a sharing dialog box where you can enter the email addresses of the people you want to share the sheet with.

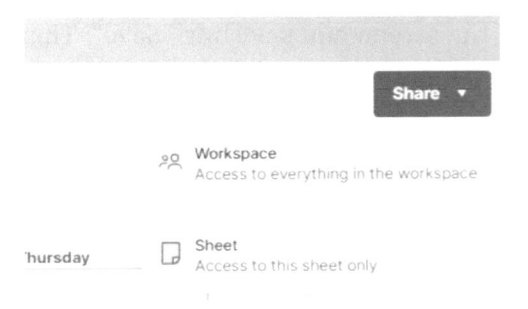

Once you enter the email addresses, you can choose the permission level for each person:

- **Viewer:** This permission level allows users to view the sheet but not make any changes. This is ideal for stakeholders who need to track progress but do not need to edit the sheet.

- **Editor:** Editors can make changes to the sheet, including adding or modifying data, adding new rows or columns, and reformatting the sheet. This permission level is useful for team members actively collaborating on the sheet.

- **Admin:** Admins have full access to the sheet. They can edit the sheet, change the structure of the sheet, and manage sheet settings, including sharing settings and permissions. Admins also have the ability to delete the sheet if necessary. This permission level should be reserved for project managers or team leaders.

You can assign different permission levels to each user depending on the role they will play in your project.

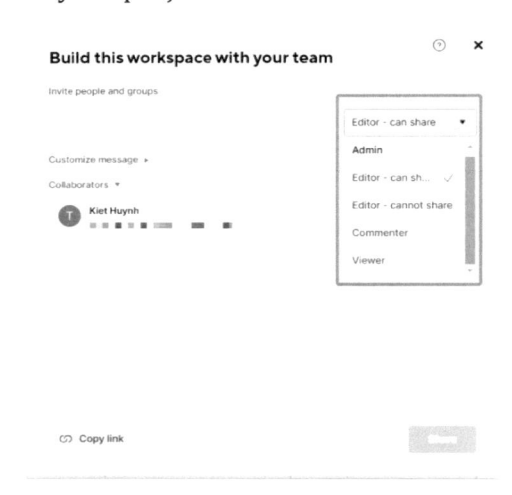

2. Sharing a Sheet with a Group

Instead of sharing your sheet with individual users, you can also share it with an entire group. This feature is particularly useful for teams and organizations that have multiple members. To share with a group, you need to set up groups within Smartsheet beforehand.

Once the group is created, you can simply enter the group name into the sharing dialog, and all members of that group will receive access to the sheet. This is an efficient way to share sheets with large teams or departments.

3. Generating Shareable Links

Smartsheet allows you to generate a shareable link to your sheet, making it easy to provide access to others without manually entering their email addresses. This is particularly useful if you need to share the sheet with a larger audience, such as external partners, clients, or stakeholders.

To generate a shareable link, click the "Share" button and choose the "Get Link" option. You will then be presented with a URL that you can copy and send to others. You can control the level of access for the link:

- **View-Only Link:** Users who access the sheet via this link will only be able to view the sheet. They will not be able to make any changes or edits.
- **Editor Link:** If you want users to be able to make changes, select this option. This grants users full editing rights to the sheet.

4. Enabling Comments and Attachments

As part of the sharing process, Smartsheet allows collaborators to leave comments and attach files directly to the sheet. This feature is useful for team discussions, clarifications, or file sharing without leaving the sheet.

To enable comments and attachments, simply check the relevant boxes when setting permissions for users. You can also restrict comment and attachment permissions if you want to limit access to those features.

5. Sharing a Sheet with External Parties

If you need to share a sheet with someone outside your organization, Smartsheet makes this easy while maintaining control over data security. You can share a sheet with external collaborators by entering their email addresses in the sharing dialog.

For additional security, you can set a password for the sheet or limit access based on a specific time frame. These options are useful for sensitive projects where you want to ensure that only authorized individuals can view or edit your sheet.

Managing Sheet Permissions

After sharing your sheet, you may need to manage the permissions of users to ensure that only authorized people can make changes. To manage permissions, go to the "Share" button again and review the list of users who have access.

- You can modify a user's permission level at any time. For example, if someone no longer needs editing access, you can downgrade them to a viewer.

- You can also remove a user from the sheet by clicking the "Remove" button next to their name. This is useful if someone no longer needs access or if they have finished their part of the project.

Best Practices for Sharing and Collaboration

When sharing your Smartsheet with others, there are several best practices to keep in mind to ensure smooth collaboration:

- **Set clear permissions:** Only grant editing rights to those who actively need to make changes. Others should be given view-only access to avoid confusion or accidental changes.

- **Organize sheet access:** If you are sharing your sheet with multiple people, keep track of who has access and their role. This helps prevent any conflicts or unauthorized edits.

- **Communicate within the sheet:** Use comments to leave notes and feedback, especially when collaborating with remote team members. Smartsheet allows you to tag users in comments using the "@" symbol, which sends them a notification and helps keep conversations organized.

- **Use version history:** Smartsheet automatically tracks all changes made to a sheet, so you can always revert to an earlier version if needed. This is particularly useful if multiple users are making changes simultaneously, and you need to roll back to a previous state.

Conclusion

Saving and sharing your sheet in Smartsheet is a key part of the collaboration process. By understanding how to set permissions, share sheets with specific users or groups, and manage access, you can ensure that your team works efficiently and effectively. As you continue to use Smartsheet, these sharing and saving features will help you maintain control over your data while empowering your team to contribute and collaborate in real time.

CHAPTER II
Working with Data in Smartsheet

2.1 Adding and Managing Data

2.1.1 Inputting Data Manually

When you first begin using Smartsheet, one of the most straightforward tasks is manually inputting data. This process serves as the foundation for creating your sheets and organizing information effectively. Whether you're tracking a project, managing a list, or creating a schedule, understanding how to input data manually is an essential first step. In this section, we'll walk you through the fundamentals of entering data into Smartsheet, exploring best practices and tips to make the process efficient and error-free.

Understanding the Layout of a Smartsheet

Before inputting data, it's important to familiarize yourself with Smartsheet's layout. A Smartsheet is essentially a grid-based platform that resembles a spreadsheet, but with added features tailored for project and data management. Here are the key components:

- **Columns and Rows**: Each column represents a category or data type (e.g., Task Name, Due Date, Status), while rows hold individual entries or records.
- **Cells**: A cell is the intersection of a column and a row, where you input specific pieces of data.
- **Column Types**: Columns can be formatted for different data types such as text, dropdown lists, checkboxes, dates, or numbers.

Take a moment to plan your sheet's structure before you start inputting data. Clearly define the purpose of each column and ensure it aligns with the type of data you'll be working with.

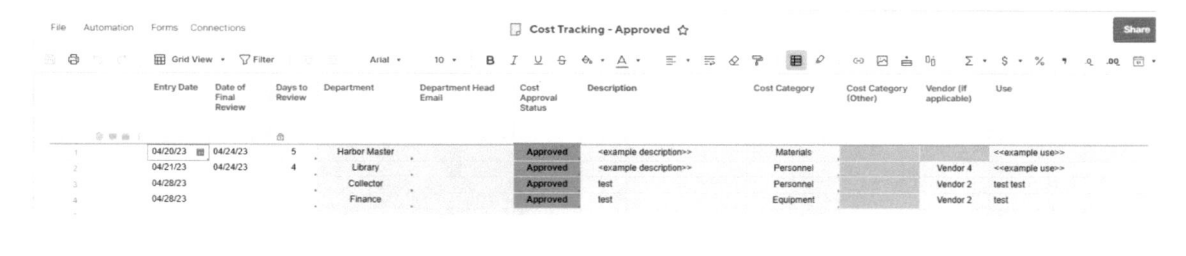

Step-by-Step Guide to Inputting Data

1. Creating or Opening a Sheet

Start by opening an existing sheet or creating a new one. If you're creating a new sheet:

- Click the **"+" icon** in the Smartsheet interface to create a blank sheet or choose a pre-designed template.

- Name your sheet appropriately to reflect its purpose (e.g., "Project Tracker" or "Marketing Campaign 2025").

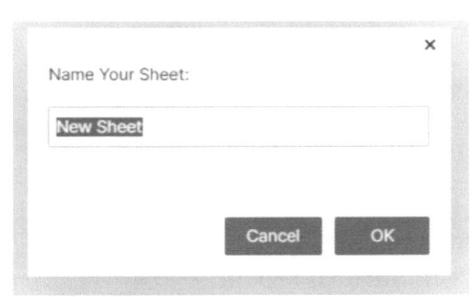

2. Adding Columns

Columns define the structure of your sheet and are essential for organizing your data. To add columns:

- Click the **"+" icon** at the top-right corner of the grid to insert a new column.

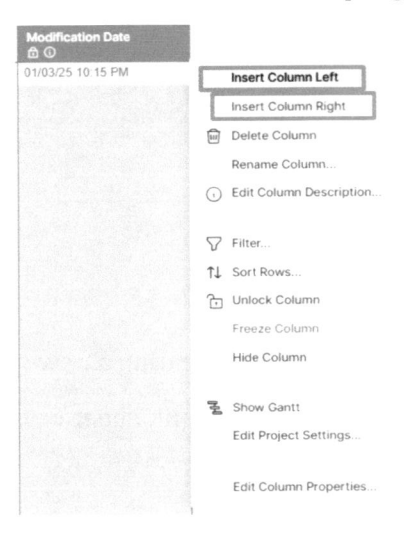

- Select a column type (e.g., text, number, date) based on the kind of data you'll input. For instance, use a **text/number column** for names or descriptions, a **date column** for deadlines, and a **checkbox column** for tasks that require completion tracking.

- Rename the column to match its purpose by double-clicking the header and typing the desired name.

3. Entering Data into Cells

To manually input data:

- Click on a cell to activate it. A cursor will appear, allowing you to type directly into the cell.

- Press **Enter** to save the data and move to the next cell in the column, or use the **Tab** key to move to the next cell in the same row.

For example, if you're creating a task list:

- In the first column, enter the task names (e.g., "Draft Proposal," "Submit Budget").

- In the second column, enter due dates (e.g., "01/15/2025").

- In the third column, use a dropdown list or checkbox to track task status.

Best Practices for Manual Data Entry

1. Start with Small Batches of Data

Avoid overwhelming yourself by entering too much information at once. Start small, focusing on a few rows or columns until you're comfortable with the interface.

2. Use Consistent Formatting

Maintaining consistency in how you enter data ensures your sheet remains organized and easy to understand. For instance:

- Use a standard date format (e.g., MM/DD/YYYY).

- Capitalize names or titles uniformly.

- Avoid unnecessary spaces or special characters that might disrupt data sorting.

3. Utilize Dropdown Lists for Repeated Values

If you need to input repeated values (e.g., "In Progress," "Completed"), consider creating a dropdown list column. This minimizes typing errors and ensures uniformity. To set up a dropdown:

- Right-click the column header, select **Column Properties**, and choose **Dropdown (Single Select)** or **Dropdown (Multi-Select)**.

- Add the options you want to appear in the dropdown menu.

4. Use Auto-Fill for Large Datasets

For repetitive data, Smartsheet allows you to auto-fill cells by dragging the small blue square at the bottom-right corner of a selected cell. This saves time and reduces manual errors.

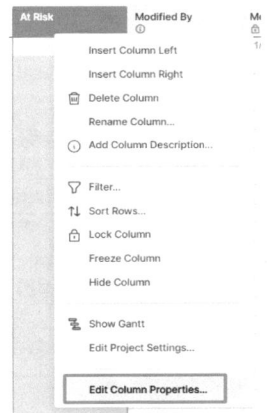

Troubleshooting Common Issues with Manual Data Entry

Even with a straightforward task like manual data entry, users may encounter challenges. Here's how to address them:

1. Incorrect Column Formatting

If you're unable to input certain data (e.g., a date in a text column), check the column type:

- Right-click the column header, choose **Edit Column Properties**, and adjust the type as needed.

2. Unintended Overwriting of Data

Accidentally overwriting data can be frustrating. Use Smartsheet's **Undo** feature (Ctrl+Z or Command+Z) to revert changes instantly.

3. Data Loss After Entry

If you find that data disappears after you've entered it, ensure that you've clicked **Enter** or moved to another cell to save the input. Smartsheet doesn't save data until you confirm your input.

Examples of Manual Data Entry Use Cases

1. Task Management

Manually enter tasks, assign them to team members, and set due dates. For instance:

Task Name	Assignee	Due Date	Status
Draft Project Plan	John Smith	01/10/2025	In Progress
Submit Final Report	Jane Doe	01/20/2025	Not Started

2. Inventory Tracking

Input product details, stock levels, and reorder dates to maintain an up-to-date inventory record:

Product Name	Stock Level	Reorder Date
Office Chairs	25	01/15/2025
Whiteboard Markers	50	02/01/2025

3. Budget Planning

Add line items, costs, and descriptions for budget tracking:

Expense Name	Amount ($)	Description
Marketing Campaign	5000	January Social Media Ads
Website Maintenance	1200	Monthly Hosting Fee

Conclusion

Manually inputting data into Smartsheet is a fundamental skill that sets the stage for creating powerful and organized sheets. While it may seem simple, following best practices can save you time and effort as your data grows. By understanding the interface, using consistent formatting, and leveraging features like dropdown lists and auto-fill, you can efficiently build sheets that meet your needs. With this foundation in place, you're ready to explore more advanced features, such as importing data and automating workflows, to take your Smartsheet experience to the next level.

2.1.2 Importing Data from Excel and Google Sheets

Importing data from other tools such as Excel and Google Sheets into Smartsheet is a fundamental skill that can save time, improve accuracy, and streamline your workflow. Smartsheet allows you to seamlessly integrate existing data into its platform, enabling you to manage, analyze, and collaborate on data more effectively. This section provides a step-by-step guide to importing data, tips for ensuring a smooth transition, and best practices to maximize efficiency.

Understanding the Import Process

Before diving into the process, it's essential to understand how Smartsheet handles imported data. When you import data from Excel or Google Sheets, Smartsheet converts the file into a Smartsheet-compatible format. This includes preserving the structure (columns, rows, and data types) while adapting it to Smartsheet's features, such as column types (e.g., dropdown, checkbox) and automation rules.

Smartsheet supports importing:

- Excel files in .xls or .xlsx formats.
- Google Sheets via direct integration.
- CSV files for simpler data structures.

Step-by-Step Guide: Importing Data from Excel

Step 1: Preparing Your Excel File

1. **Organize Your Data**: Ensure your Excel file is clean and well-organized. Use a clear header row that defines column names. Avoid merged cells, as they may disrupt the import process.

2. **Check Data Formats**: Ensure data types (e.g., text, numbers, dates) are consistent within each column. Smartsheet will attempt to match column types, so clean up any inconsistencies.

3. **Remove Unnecessary Data**: Delete any empty rows, columns, or irrelevant data that you don't want to import.

Step 2: Starting the Import

1. **Log In to Smartsheet**: Open Smartsheet and navigate to your workspace or the folder where you want to import the data.

2. **Select 'Import'**: Click the "+" button in the left-hand navigation panel to create a new sheet. From the options, select **Import**.

3. **Choose Excel File**: In the import dialog box, select the option to import an Excel file. Locate and upload the file from your computer.

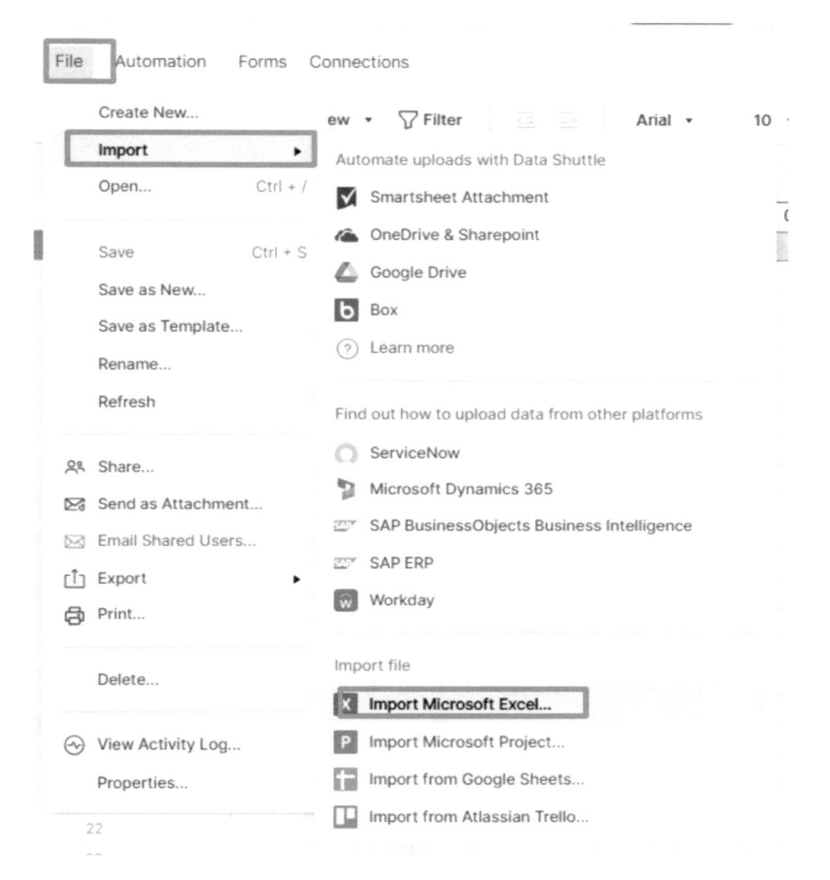

Step 3: Mapping Data to Smartsheet Columns

1. **Review Column Mapping**: Smartsheet will automatically create columns based on the header row in your Excel file. Review these columns to ensure accuracy.

2. **Adjust Column Types**: If needed, manually adjust column types (e.g., convert a text column to a dropdown list or a number column to a checkbox).

3. **Verify Data Accuracy**: Check that the data appears correctly in the preview. If any issues arise, you may need to adjust the source file and re-import.

Step 4: Finalizing the Import

1. **Save the Sheet**: Once you're satisfied with the imported data, click **Save** to create the sheet.

2. **Customize Further**: After import, you can add conditional formatting, automation rules, or additional columns to optimize the sheet for your workflow.

Step-by-Step Guide: Importing Data from Google Sheets

Step 1: Connecting Smartsheet to Google Sheets

1. **Enable Integration**: Ensure that your Smartsheet account is connected to Google Workspace. You may need to enable permissions for integration.

2. **Access Google Sheets**: Open the Google Sheet that you want to import and verify that it's properly formatted.

Step 2: Starting the Import

1. **Log In to Smartsheet**: Open Smartsheet and navigate to your workspace or folder.

2. **Select 'Import'**: Click the "+" button in the left-hand navigation panel and select **Import**.

3. **Choose Google Sheets**: Select the Google Sheets option, and you'll be prompted to log in to your Google account. Once authenticated, Smartsheet will display a list of available Google Sheets.

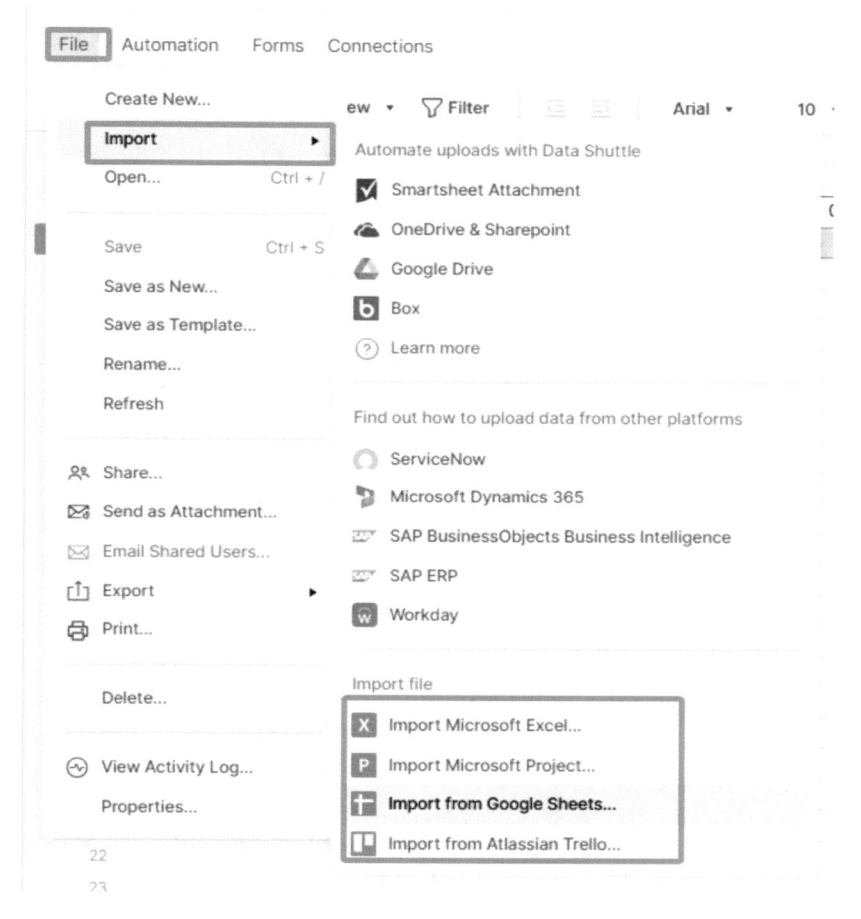

Step 3: Mapping Data to Smartsheet Columns

1. **Select the Sheet**: Choose the specific Google Sheet you want to import. If the file has multiple tabs, select the desired tab for import.

2. **Verify and Adjust**: Similar to Excel, Smartsheet will create columns based on your header row. Review and adjust the column types if necessary.

3. **Preview Data**: Check that all data appears correctly. Fix any discrepancies directly in the Google Sheet if required.

Step 4: Finalizing the Import

1. **Save and Name the Sheet**: Once you're happy with the data, save the new sheet in Smartsheet.

2. **Apply Customizations**: Enhance the imported sheet by adding Smartsheet-specific features such as automated workflows, formulas, or reports.

Best Practices for Importing Data

1. **Double-Check Data Before Importing**: Clean and organize your data to prevent errors during the import process. Ensure all relevant data is included and formatted consistently.

2. **Leverage Column Types**: Smartsheet offers various column types, such as date, text/number, dropdown, and checkbox. Assign appropriate types to maximize functionality.

3. **Use Templates for Repeated Imports**: If you frequently import data with a similar structure, create a Smartsheet template. This will save time and ensure consistency across projects.

4. **Test on a Sample File**: Before importing a large or complex dataset, test the process with a smaller file to identify potential issues.

5. **Regularly Sync with Google Sheets**: For ongoing projects, consider using Smartsheet's integration with Google Sheets to sync changes automatically, reducing the need for manual imports.

Common Issues and Troubleshooting

1. **Problem: Data Doesn't Appear Correctly**
   - **Solution**: Review your original file for merged cells, missing headers, or inconsistent data formats. Correct these and re-import.

2. **Problem: Column Types Are Incorrect**
   - **Solution**: Adjust column types during the import process or edit them in Smartsheet after import.

3. **Problem: File Is Too Large**
   - **Solution**: Break the file into smaller sections and import them individually. Alternatively, optimize the file by removing unnecessary data.

4. **Problem: Google Sheets Integration Fails**
    - **Solution**: Ensure your Google account is correctly linked to Smartsheet. Reauthorize the connection if needed.

Conclusion

Importing data from Excel and Google Sheets into Smartsheet is an essential skill for beginners. By following the steps outlined above, you can easily transition your existing data into Smartsheet and start leveraging its powerful features. With practice, importing data will become a seamless part of your workflow, saving you time and enhancing collaboration.

2.1.3 Editing and Deleting Data

Smartsheet is a dynamic tool that allows users to manage, update, and modify data efficiently. Once you've entered data into a sheet, it's inevitable that you'll need to make adjustments, whether it's correcting errors, refining information, or deleting outdated entries. This section will walk you through the process of editing and deleting data effectively in Smartsheet, ensuring that your sheets remain accurate and up-to-date.

Editing Data in Smartsheet

Editing data in Smartsheet is a straightforward process that accommodates changes with ease. Whether you need to update a cell, revise a row, or adjust a column, Smartsheet offers tools to make these tasks intuitive.

Editing Cells

1. **Direct Editing:** To edit a cell, simply double-click on it. The cell will become editable, allowing you to modify the existing content. Once you're done, press "Enter" to save the changes or "Esc" to cancel. This method is best for quick edits to single cells.

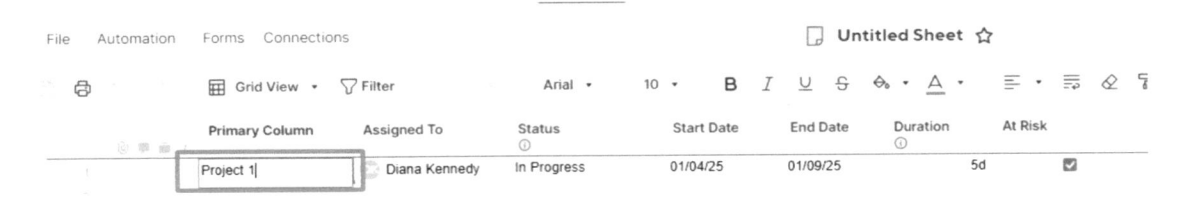

2. **Replacing Values:** If you want to completely replace the content of a cell, select the cell, start typing, and press "Enter" when you're done. The new data will overwrite the old content immediately.

3. **Adjusting Dropdown Options:** If the cell uses a dropdown menu, click on the dropdown arrow to select a new value from the predefined options. Dropdowns ensure consistency across your data and help prevent errors.

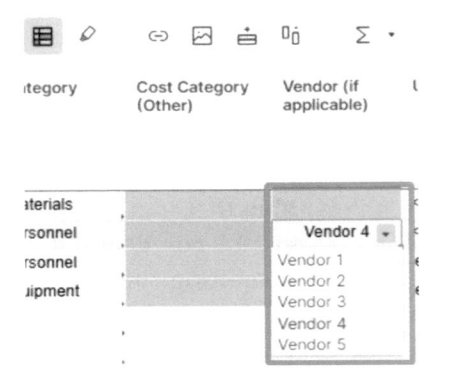

Editing Rows

1. **Inline Editing:** You can edit multiple cells within the same row by selecting each cell individually and making the necessary changes. This is especially helpful when updating related information across columns.

2. **Expanding Row Details:** For rows with complex data, such as attachments, comments, or additional notes, click the row number to open the row details panel. Here, you can edit any associated data in a more detailed view.

Editing Columns

1. **Renaming Columns:** To rename a column, right-click on the column header and select "Rename Column." Enter the new name and press "Enter" to confirm. Make sure the new column name accurately reflects the data it contains to maintain clarity.

2. **Changing Column Types:** If a column's format (e.g., text, dropdown, checkbox) no longer suits your needs, you can update it by right-clicking the column header, selecting "Edit Column Properties," and choosing a new column type. Note that changing column types may affect existing data, so proceed with caution.

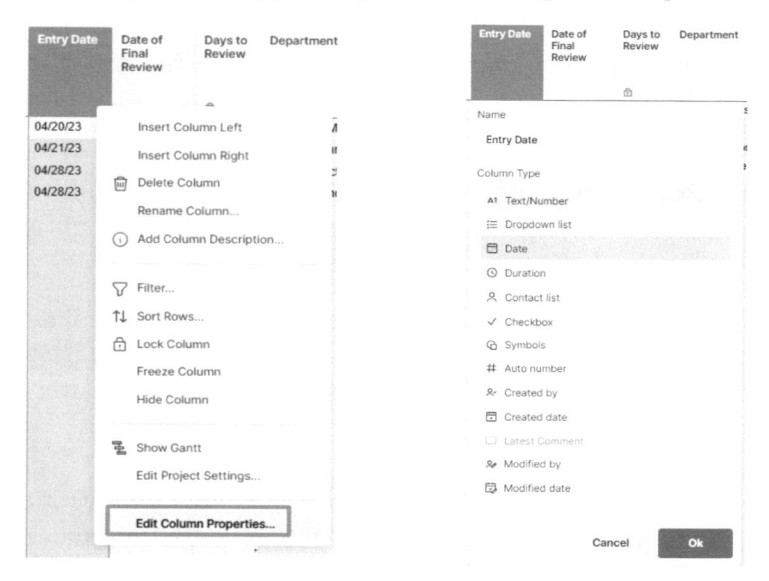

3. **Reordering Columns:** Drag and drop column headers to rearrange them. This is useful when you need to prioritize specific columns for better visibility or workflow optimization.

Deleting Data in Smartsheet

Sometimes, data becomes irrelevant or incorrect, and removing it is necessary to maintain the integrity of your sheet. Smartsheet provides flexible options for deleting data at the cell, row, or column level.

Deleting Data from Cells

1. **Clearing Content:** To clear the content of a specific cell, click on it and press the "Delete" or "Backspace" key on your keyboard. This will erase the data but retain the cell itself for future use.

2. **Mass Clearing:** Select multiple cells by clicking and dragging your mouse or holding "Shift" and clicking on individual cells. Once selected, press "Delete" to clear the content of all highlighted cells simultaneously.

Deleting Rows

1. **Single Row Deletion:** To delete a single row, right-click on the row number and select "Delete Row." The row will be removed entirely, along with all the data it contains.

2. **Deleting Multiple Rows:** Select multiple rows by holding the "Shift" or "Ctrl" (Windows) / "Command" (Mac) key while clicking on row numbers. Right-click and choose "Delete Rows" to remove them in one action.

3. **Undoing Deletions:** If you accidentally delete a row, you can immediately press "Ctrl + Z" (Windows) / "Command + Z" (Mac) to undo the action. Smartsheet also retains a revision history, which allows you to recover deleted rows if needed.

Deleting Columns

1. **Removing Entire Columns:** Right-click on the column header you want to delete and select "Delete Column." This will permanently remove the column and all its associated data from the sheet.

2. **Impact on Dependencies:** Before deleting a column, ensure that it isn't linked to formulas, conditional formatting, or automation workflows. Deleting such columns may disrupt your sheet's functionality.

Best Practices for Editing and Deleting Data

To manage your data efficiently and minimize errors, consider the following best practices when editing or deleting data in Smartsheet:

1. **Use Filters Before Making Changes:** Apply filters to isolate the data you want to edit or delete. This reduces the likelihood of accidental changes to unrelated information.

2. **Leverage Permissions:** If you're working in a shared sheet, ensure that only authorized users can edit or delete data. Adjust permissions to restrict access as needed.

3. **Track Changes with Revision History:** Use the "View Cell History" feature to track changes made to individual cells. This is especially helpful for collaborative projects where multiple users edit the same sheet.

4. **Backup Your Sheet:** Before making significant edits or deletions, create a backup of your sheet by saving it as an Excel file or duplicating it within Smartsheet. This ensures you have a reference point if issues arise.

5. **Review Automation Rules:** If your sheet uses automation workflows, double-check how edits or deletions might impact those rules. For example, deleting a row could trigger or disable alerts.

6. **Use Conditional Formatting:** Set up conditional formatting to highlight cells or rows requiring updates. This visual cue helps you prioritize edits effectively.

Common Mistakes to Avoid

While editing and deleting data is simple, it's important to avoid these common pitfalls:

1. **Overwriting Data Without Verification:** Always verify the accuracy of new data before overwriting existing information, especially if the changes affect critical calculations or reports.

2. **Deleting Dependent Data:** Be cautious when deleting data linked to formulas or automation. Smartsheet doesn't always warn you about the ripple effects of such deletions.

3. **Editing in Shared Sheets Without Notifying Others:** If you're collaborating with a team, communicate significant changes to avoid confusion or conflicts.

By mastering the tools for editing and deleting data, you can keep your Smartsheet projects clean, accurate, and organized. Whether you're working on a personal task list or managing a complex team project, these techniques will empower you to maintain control over your data.

2.2 Organizing Your Sheet

2.2.1 Sorting and Filtering Data

Organizing your data in Smartsheet is a critical skill that ensures your sheets are not just functional but also easy to navigate. Sorting and filtering are two powerful features that enable you to structure your data logically and retrieve specific information efficiently. This section will guide you through the basics of sorting and filtering in Smartsheet, provide practical examples, and share best practices for organizing your sheets effectively.

What is Sorting in Smartsheet?

Sorting is the process of arranging data in a specific order, either ascending or descending, based on one or more columns in your sheet. Sorting helps to bring order to your data and makes it easier to find trends or key entries. For example, you can sort a task sheet by due date, a contact list by last name, or a sales sheet by revenue.

Key Benefits of Sorting in Smartsheet:

- Makes large datasets easier to analyze.
- Highlights priorities (e.g., deadlines or high-value deals).
- Creates logical order for easier data review and navigation.

How to Sort Data in Smartsheet

Smartsheet provides a straightforward interface for sorting your data. Here's how you can perform sorting:

Step 1: Open Your Sheet

- Log into your Smartsheet account and navigate to the sheet you want to organize.
- Ensure the sheet contains structured data with clearly defined column types (e.g., Text/Number, Date, Dropdown, etc.).

Step 2: Select the Column to Sort By

- Hover over the column header you want to use for sorting.
- Click the down arrow that appears next to the column header.

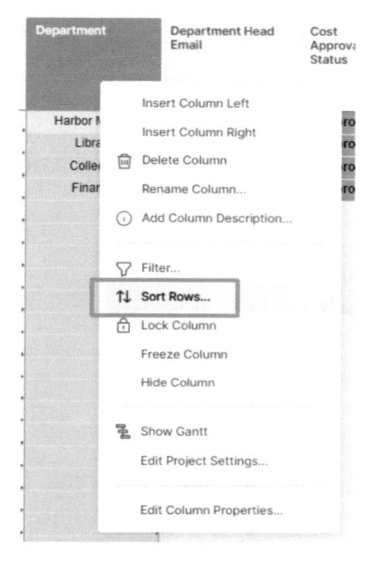

Step 3: Choose the Sort Option

- From the dropdown menu, select either:

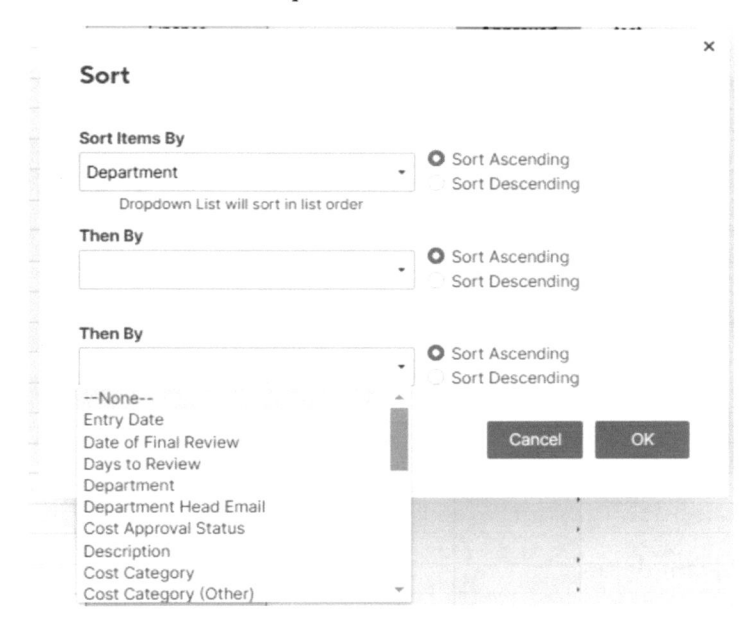

  - **Sort Ascending**: Arranges data from smallest to largest (e.g., A to Z, 1 to 100, earliest to latest).

  - **Sort Descending**: Arranges data from largest to smallest (e.g., Z to A, 100 to 1, latest to earliest).

Step 4: Apply Sorting Across Multiple Columns (Optional)

- Smartsheet allows you to sort by multiple columns

Page 115 | 383

simultaneously to create more nuanced order.

- To do this, click the dropdown menu in the toolbar and choose **Sort Rows**.
- In the dialog box, select the primary column for sorting, then add secondary and tertiary sorting criteria.

Example:
Imagine you manage a project tracker with columns for "Task Name," "Due Date," and "Priority." To prioritize tasks:

1. Sort by "Priority" in descending order (High to Low).
2. Add "Due Date" as a secondary criterion in ascending order (earliest to latest).

Best Practices for Sorting Data

1. **Keep Column Types Consistent**: Ensure the column type matches the data it holds. For example, date columns should use the "Date" column type to enable chronological sorting.
2. **Use Hierarchies Wisely**: If your sheet uses parent and child rows, be cautious when sorting, as it may disrupt the hierarchy. To maintain structure, consider using filters instead.
3. **Save Before Sorting**: Always save a copy of your sheet or create a snapshot before applying complex sorting, as sorting changes the order of rows permanently.
4. **Communicate Changes to Team Members**: If you're collaborating on a shared sheet, let your team know about significant sorting updates to avoid confusion.

What is Filtering in Smartsheet?

Filtering involves displaying only the rows that meet specific criteria while hiding the rest. This feature is invaluable when working with large datasets or when you need to focus on a subset of information.

Key Benefits of Filtering in Smartsheet:

- Allows you to focus on relevant data.

- Simplifies complex sheets for specific use cases.
- Reduces visual clutter and increases productivity.

How to Filter Data in Smartsheet

Filters in Smartsheet can be created easily using the built-in filtering tool. Follow these steps to filter your data effectively:

Step 1: Open the Filter Menu

- Click the **Filter** icon (funnel symbol) in the toolbar.
- If no filters exist, click **New Filter** to start creating one.

Step 2: Define Your Filtering Criteria

- In the filter creation window, choose the column you want to filter.
- Select the condition you want to apply. For example:
  - **Equals**: Display rows matching a specific value.
  - **Does Not Equal**: Exclude rows with a specific value.
  - **Contains**: Include rows that contain a particular word or phrase.
  - **Is Blank**: Show rows where the selected column is empty.

Step 3: Combine Multiple Conditions (Optional)

- Add additional criteria to refine your filter. For instance, you can filter tasks by "Priority = High" and "Due Date = This Week."

Step 4: Apply the Filter

- Once you've defined your criteria, click **Apply** to filter your sheet.
- Only rows that match your criteria will remain visible, while all others are hidden.

Step 5: Save or Share Your Filter

- Save the filter for future use or share it with your team. Note that shared filters are visible to everyone who has access to the sheet.

Best Practices for Filtering Data

1. **Name Filters Clearly**: Use descriptive names for saved filters (e.g., "High-Priority Tasks" or "Overdue Items") to make them easy to identify later.

2. **Use Filters for Temporary Views**: If you need a temporary view of specific data, create an unsaved filter to avoid cluttering the filter menu.

3. **Combine Filters with Conditional Formatting**: Highlight important data using conditional formatting, then apply filters to focus on specific subsets.

4. **Train Your Team**: If your sheet is shared, ensure team members understand how to apply and remove filters without disrupting the workflow.

Practical Examples: Sorting and Filtering Combined

Example 1: Managing a Sales Pipeline: Imagine you're managing a sales pipeline sheet with columns for "Client Name," "Deal Value," "Stage," and "Closing Date."

- **Sorting**: Arrange the sheet by "Deal Value" in descending order to prioritize high-value deals.
- **Filtering**: Create a filter to display only rows where "Stage" equals "Negotiation" or "Proposal."

This approach ensures you focus on critical deals that are close to closing.

Example 2: Tracking Project Deadlines: In a project tracker with columns for "Task Name," "Assigned To," "Priority," and "Due Date":

- **Sorting**: Sort by "Due Date" in ascending order to view the most urgent tasks first.
- **Filtering**: Apply a filter to display only tasks where "Priority" equals "High" and "Assigned To" is your name.

This allows you to focus on your high-priority tasks without distraction.

Common Challenges and How to Overcome Them

1. **Disrupted Hierarchies**: Sorting may reorder child rows under the wrong parent. Use filters instead when working with hierarchical data.

2. **Accidental Changes**: Collaborative sheets may be affected by unintended sorting or filtering. Regularly communicate with your team to ensure everyone is aligned.

3. **Data Inconsistencies**: Ensure consistent formatting (e.g., text, numbers, dates) to avoid unexpected sorting results.

Conclusion

Sorting and filtering are fundamental tools in Smartsheet that enable you to organize and manage your data efficiently. By mastering these techniques, you can transform even the most complex sheets into streamlined, actionable datasets. Whether you're managing a personal to-do list or leading a large project, sorting and filtering will empower you to work smarter, not harder.

In the next section, we'll explore **2.2.2 Grouping and Highlighting Key Information**, diving into how you can further enhance your sheets for maximum clarity and impact.

2.2.2 Grouping and Highlighting Key Information

Organizing data effectively is one of the essential steps in making Smartsheet work for you. Grouping and highlighting key information allows you to bring clarity and focus to your sheets, ensuring that the most important data is easily accessible and visually distinguishable. In this section, we'll explore the techniques and best practices for grouping and highlighting your data in Smartsheet to enhance visibility and usability.

Why Grouping and Highlighting Are Important

When working with large data sets, it's easy to lose sight of critical details. Grouping and highlighting serve the following purposes:

- **Improved Readability:** By logically grouping related data, you make it easier for yourself and others to navigate through the sheet.

- **Quick Decision-Making:** Highlighted data draws attention to what matters most, enabling faster and more informed decisions.
- **Error Prevention:** Clearly defined groups and color-coded information reduce the chances of misinterpreting or overlooking important details.

Grouping Key Information

Grouping involves organizing data into categories or clusters that share similar characteristics. Smartsheet doesn't have a built-in "grouping" feature like pivot tables in Excel, but you can achieve similar functionality through sorting, filtering, and layout adjustments.

```
- Summary
    Variable

    + Duraton
    + Plan commitment           $3
    + Actual commitment         $1
      Variance                 -$1
      Variance per work day
    + Trend
+ Chart
```

1. Using Hierarchies for Grouping

Smartsheet allows you to create hierarchies by indenting rows to group related items visually.

- **How to Create Hierarchies:**
    1. Identify rows that belong to the same category.

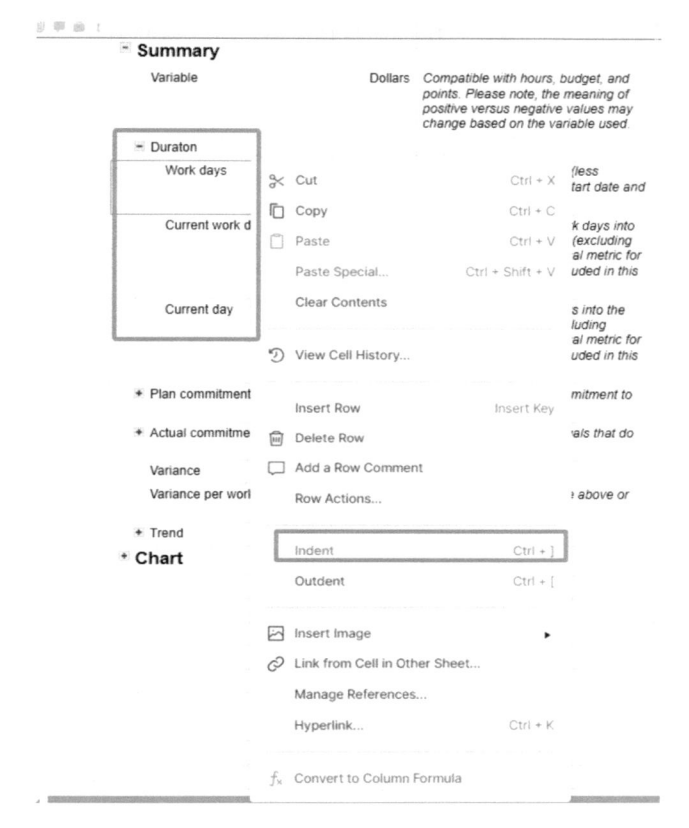

2. Use the "Indent" button on the toolbar to nest rows under a parent row.

```
- Summary
    Variable                    Dollars   Compatible with hours, budget, and
                                          points. Please note, the meaning of
                                          positive versus negative values may
                                          change based on the variable used.
    - Duraton
        Work days           ✂ Cut              Ctrl + X    (less
                                                            tart date and
                            📋 Copy             Ctrl + C
        Current work d                                      k days into
                            📄 Paste            Ctrl + V    (excluding
                                                            al metric for
                               Paste Special...  Ctrl + Shift + V  uded in this
                               Clear Contents
        Current day                                         s into the
                                                            luding
                                                            al metric for
                            🕐 View Cell History...           uded in this
    + Plan commitment                                       mitment to
                               Insert Row              Insert Key
    + Actual commitme       🗑 Delete Row                    als that do
        Variance            💬 Add a Row Comment
        Variance per worl      Row Actions...              above or
    + Trend
    + Chart                    Indent              Ctrl + ]
                               Outdent             Ctrl + [

                            🖼 Insert Image            ▶
                            🔗 Link from Cell in Other Sheet...
                               Manage References...
                               Hyperlink...             Ctrl + K

                            𝑓ₓ Convert to Column Formula
```

3. Collapse or expand the parent rows to hide or display the grouped items as needed.

- **Best Practices for Using Hierarchies:**
    o Use clear and concise parent row titles that summarize the grouped items.
    o Avoid excessive nesting to maintain readability.
    o Use hierarchy colors or formatting (discussed below) to make parent rows stand out.

2. Sorting Data by Categories

Sorting data is another effective way to group information without creating permanent structures.

- **Steps for Sorting:**
    1. Click on the column header of the data you want to sort by.
    2. Choose "Sort Ascending" or "Sort Descending" from the menu.
    3. Combine multiple sorts if needed, such as sorting by department and then by due date.
- **Best Practices for Sorting:**
    o Sort data by columns that are most relevant to your goals (e.g., status, priority, owner).
    o Save your sheet's current view before sorting to preserve the original order.

3. Using Filters for Custom Grouping

Filters enable you to create temporary views of your data based on specific criteria.

- **How to Apply Filters:**
    1. Click on the filter icon at the top-right corner of your sheet.
    2. Define filter conditions, such as showing only tasks assigned to a specific team member or due within a certain timeframe.
    3. Save the filter for reuse or share it with collaborators.
- **Best Practices for Filters:**
    o Create filters for recurring tasks, such as overdue items or high-priority projects.
    o Name filters clearly so that collaborators understand their purpose.
    o Use multiple filter criteria for more refined views.

Highlighting Key Information

Highlighting in Smartsheet is achieved through conditional formatting and manual customization. These methods ensure that critical data stands out and can be recognized instantly.

1. Using Conditional Formatting

Conditional formatting automates the process of highlighting based on predefined rules.

- **Steps for Applying Conditional Formatting:**

    1. Go to "Conditional Formatting" in the toolbar.

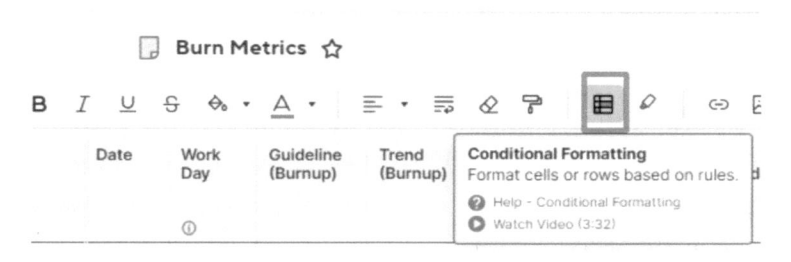

    2. Click "New Rule" and define your condition (e.g., highlight rows where status is "Overdue").

    3. Select the formatting options, such as font color, background color, or bold text.

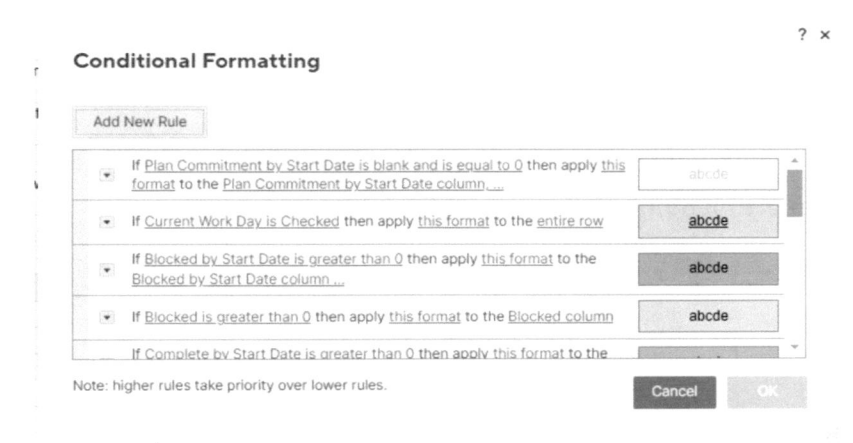

    4. Save and apply the rule.

- **Common Use Cases:**

    o Highlight overdue tasks with a red background.

    o Use green text for tasks marked as "Complete."

    o Color-code tasks by priority (e.g., high = red, medium = yellow, low = green).

- **Best Practices:**

- o Limit the number of rules to avoid overwhelming users with too many colors.
- o Test rules to ensure they don't conflict or overlap.
- o Use contrasting colors for better visibility.

2. Manually Highlighting Rows or Columns

While conditional formatting is ideal for automation, you may occasionally need to highlight data manually for unique situations.

- **How to Highlight Manually:**
    1. Select the rows, columns, or cells you want to highlight.
    2. Use the toolbar to change the background color, font style, or text color.
    3. Add comments or notes to explain the significance of the highlighted information.

- **When to Use Manual Highlighting:**
    - o For one-time events or exceptions that don't justify a conditional rule.
    - o To provide additional context for a specific audience or purpose.

3. Adding Icons and Symbols for Visual Cues

Icons and symbols can supplement color-based highlighting to provide additional visual cues.

- **Steps for Adding Symbols:**
    1. Use columns formatted as "Dropdown" or "Checkbox" to display symbols.
    2. Populate the column with emojis or predefined icons to represent statuses (e.g., ✓ for completed, ⚠☐ for issues).

- **Best Practices for Icons:**
    - o Use a consistent set of symbols across all sheets in your workspace.
    - o Avoid excessive use of icons to maintain a clean and professional look.

Combining Grouping and Highlighting

Grouping and highlighting work best when used together. For example:

- Create hierarchies to group related tasks and use conditional formatting to emphasize overdue items within each group.

- Filter data to display specific categories and manually highlight the most critical rows in the filtered view.

Common Mistakes to Avoid

1. **Overusing Highlighting:** Too many colors or icons can make the sheet look cluttered and reduce its effectiveness.

2. **Neglecting Accessibility:** Choose color schemes that are easy to read for all users, including those with color blindness.

3. **Ignoring Updates:** Regularly update grouping and highlighting rules to reflect changes in your data or priorities.

Conclusion

Grouping and highlighting are powerful tools for organizing your sheets in Smartsheet. By combining hierarchies, sorting, filters, conditional formatting, and manual customization, you can transform complex data into actionable insights. Remember to keep your designs clean and intuitive, ensuring that your sheets remain a valuable resource for your team.

2.2.3 Using Conditional Formatting

Conditional Formatting is a powerful feature in Smartsheet that allows you to visually emphasize important information within your sheet. By applying rules to specific rows, columns, or cells, you can dynamically highlight data based on its content. This tool is particularly helpful when managing large datasets, as it enables you to spot trends, identify outliers, or track deadlines at a glance.

In this section, we will explore the ins and outs of Conditional Formatting in Smartsheet, including how to set up rules, customize formatting, and use this feature effectively to enhance your workflows.

What Is Conditional Formatting in Smartsheet?

Conditional Formatting in Smartsheet allows you to apply predefined styles—such as colors, bold text, or icons—to cells that meet specific criteria. For example, you can configure a rule that highlights overdue tasks in red or marks completed items with a green background. This helps you visually organize data and prioritize tasks efficiently.

Some key features of Conditional Formatting in Smartsheet include:

- Applying rules to one or multiple columns.
- Using formulas to create complex conditions.
- Customizing formatting options such as text color, background color, and cell styles.

How to Access Conditional Formatting

To start using Conditional Formatting:

1. Open your sheet in Smartsheet.
2. Locate and click the **Conditional Formatting** icon in the toolbar. It looks like a paintbrush.

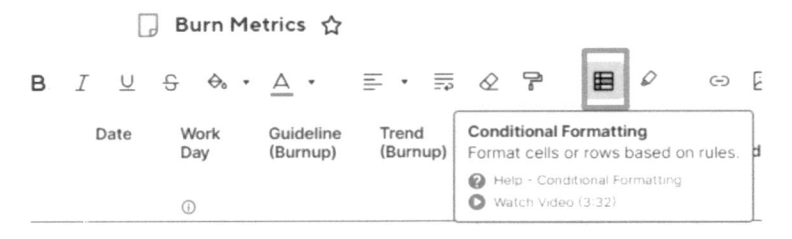

3. The **Conditional Formatting Rules** window will appear, displaying all existing rules (if any).

From here, you can create, edit, or delete rules as needed.

Creating a Conditional Formatting Rule

Here's a step-by-step guide to creating a rule:

1. **Click on "New Rule"**: In the Conditional Formatting Rules window, click the **New Rule** button.

2. **Define the Condition**:

    o   Select the range of cells, rows, or columns you want to apply the rule to.

    o   Choose the condition. For example, you can specify "if a due date is in the past" or "if the status is 'Completed.'"

3. **Choose Formatting Options**:

    o   Customize how the cells should look when the condition is met. Options include changing the text color, background color, font style, or adding icons.

4. **Save the Rule**: Click **OK** to save the rule. The formatting will automatically apply to all cells that meet the condition.

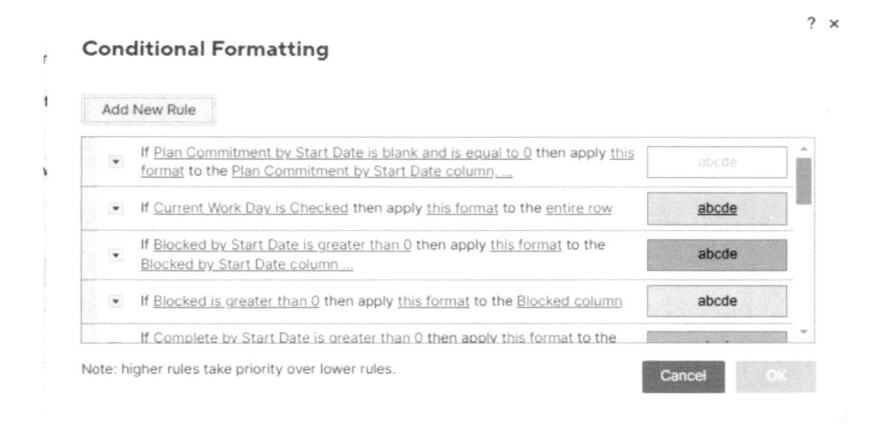

Practical Examples of Conditional Formatting

1. Highlighting Overdue Tasks

- **Condition**: If the date in the "Due Date" column is before today's date.
- **Formatting**: Apply a red background and bold text to make overdue tasks stand out.

2. Tracking High-Priority Items

- **Condition**: If the "Priority" column equals "High."
- **Formatting**: Use a bright yellow background with bold black text to emphasize high-priority tasks.

3. Identifying Completed Tasks

- **Condition**: If the "Status" column equals "Completed."
- **Formatting**: Apply a green background with strikethrough text for completed rows.

4. Flagging Empty Cells

- **Condition**: If a cell in the "Assigned To" column is blank.
- **Formatting**: Add a light gray background with italicized text to prompt users to fill in the missing information.

Advanced Features of Conditional Formatting

1. **Using Formulas in Conditional Formatting**
   - Smartsheet supports using formulas to create complex conditions. For example:
     - Highlight rows where the sum of hours exceeds a certain threshold.
     - Flag rows where two columns have mismatched values.

2. **Applying Multiple Rules**
   - You can apply more than one rule to the same range of cells. Smartsheet evaluates the rules in the order they are listed, with later rules overriding earlier ones if conflicts occur.

3. **Managing Conditional Formatting Rules**

- To rearrange rules, drag and drop them in the **Conditional Formatting Rules** window.
- To temporarily disable a rule, uncheck the box next to it.

Tips for Effective Use of Conditional Formatting

1. **Keep It Simple**: Avoid using too many formatting rules on the same sheet, as this can make your data harder to read instead of easier. Focus on highlighting only the most critical information.

2. **Use Consistent Colors**: Use consistent colors for similar conditions across different sheets or projects. For example, use red for overdue items and green for completed tasks to maintain uniformity.

3. **Combine with Filters**: Use Conditional Formatting alongside Smartsheet's filtering feature to focus on specific subsets of data. For example, filter for high-priority tasks and use Conditional Formatting to highlight those that are overdue.

4. **Test Your Rules**: After creating a rule, test it with a variety of data to ensure it works as expected. Modify the rule if necessary to refine its effectiveness.

Common Challenges and How to Overcome Them

1. **Rule Conflicts**
    - When two rules apply to the same cell, the formatting from the rule listed last will take precedence. Rearrange your rules to resolve conflicts.

2. **Performance Issues**
    - Applying too many rules to a large dataset may slow down your sheet. Simplify or consolidate your rules to improve performance.

3. **Misaligned Conditions**
    - If formatting isn't applied as expected, double-check your conditions. Ensure column names, values, and operators are correctly defined.

Real-World Applications of Conditional Formatting

1. **Project Management**
    - Highlight overdue tasks, incomplete milestones, or dependencies.
    - Track progress by using colors to represent different completion stages.

2. **Sales and Marketing**
    - Flag leads with missing contact information.
    - Identify high-value deals using specific formatting.

3. **Human Resources**
    - Highlight employees with overdue performance reviews.
    - Mark unapproved leave requests.

4. **Finance and Budgeting**
    - Flag expenses exceeding budget limits.
    - Highlight overdue invoices or payments.

Conclusion

Using Conditional Formatting in Smartsheet can dramatically improve your ability to manage and interpret data. By strategically applying formatting rules, you can make key information stand out, streamline workflows, and improve team collaboration.

Experiment with different rules and settings to find what works best for your specific needs. With practice, you'll master this feature and unlock the full potential of Smartsheet as a productivity tool.

2.3 Leveraging Formulas and Functions

Smartsheet provides a wide array of formulas and functions to enhance the utility of your sheets. Whether you're managing a project, tracking financials, or analyzing data, formulas can automate calculations, summarize data, and streamline complex processes. This section introduces the fundamental formulas in Smartsheet: **SUM**, **AVERAGE**, and **COUNT**, which are essential for handling numeric data efficiently.

2.3.1 Basic Formulas (SUM, AVERAGE, COUNT, IF ...)

Understanding the Basics of Formulas in Smartsheet

Formulas in Smartsheet are used similarly to those in Excel or Google Sheets. Each formula starts with an equal sign (=) and references cells, rows, or entire ranges of data. Smartsheet formulas are designed to be intuitive and accessible, even for beginners. The three core functions covered here—**SUM**, **AVERAGE**, and **COUNT**—form the foundation of many more advanced operations.

SUM: Adding It All Together

The **SUM** function is used to add up numbers in a range of cells. It's particularly useful when you need to calculate totals, such as project costs, sales figures, or task durations.

Syntax:
=SUM([Column Name]:[Column Name])

Example Use Case: Imagine you're managing a project budget in Smartsheet. Each row contains an expense item, and the "Cost" column lists the corresponding amounts. To calculate the total project cost:

1. Click on an empty cell where you want the total to appear.

2. Enter the formula: =SUM(Cost:Cost)

3. Press Enter, and Smartsheet will calculate the total for all values in the "Cost" column.

Pro Tips:

- Ensure all cells in the referenced column contain numeric data; otherwise, the formula will return an error.

- You can use specific cell references instead of entire columns. For example, =SUM([Cost]1:[Cost]10) adds only the first ten rows of the "Cost" column.

- Combine **SUM** with other formulas for dynamic calculations. For example, use it with **IF** to total only values meeting certain criteria: =SUM(IF([Status]1:[Status]10 = "Complete", [Cost]1:[Cost]10)).

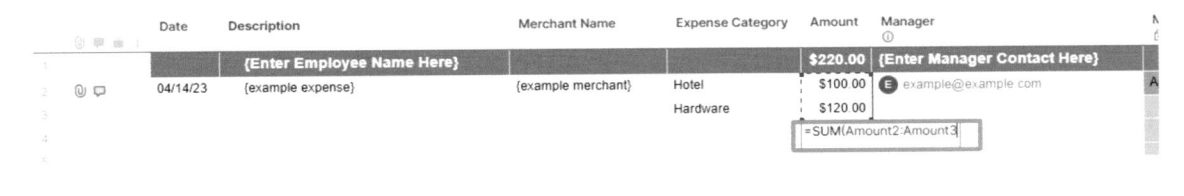

AVERAGE: Finding the Mean Value

The **AVERAGE** function calculates the mean (average) of a set of numbers. This function is helpful for finding trends, such as the average time to complete tasks or the average sales in a given period.

Syntax:
=AVERAGE([Column Name]:[Column Name])

Example Use Case: You're tracking task completion times in a project management sheet. Each row represents a task, and the "Completion Time" column records the number of hours taken to complete it. To find the average completion time:

1. Click on the cell where you want the average to appear.

2. Enter the formula: =AVERAGE([Completion Time]:[Completion Time]).

3. Smartsheet will return the average value of all numbers in the "Completion Time" column.

Pro Tips:

- Use the **AVERAGE** function to monitor performance trends over time.

- Pair **AVERAGE** with conditional statements for more focused analysis. For example:
  =AVERAGE(IF([Priority]1:[Priority]10 = "High", [Completion Time]1:[Completion Time]10)) calculates the average completion time for high-priority tasks only.

- Exclude blank cells to prevent skewing results. Smartsheet automatically ignores non-numeric and blank cells in its calculations.

COUNT: Counting Items

The **COUNT** function is used to count the number of cells containing numeric data in a specified range. It's great for tracking how many tasks have been completed, items have been sold, or goals have been achieved.

Syntax:
=COUNT([Column Name]:[Column Name])

Example Use Case: Suppose you're managing a sales pipeline, and the "Revenue" column contains numeric values for deals closed. To count the number of deals closed:

1. Select an empty cell where the result will display.
2. Enter the formula: =COUNT(Revenue:Revenue).
3. Smartsheet will count all cells with numeric values in the "Revenue" column.

Pro Tips:

- To count all cells (numeric or non-numeric), use the **COUNTA** function instead: =COUNTA([Column Name]:[Column Name]).

- Combine **COUNT** with **IF** for conditional counting. For example: =COUNT(IF([Status]1:[Status]10 = "Approved", [Revenue]1:[Revenue])) counts only approved deals.

- Use **COUNT** with date fields to analyze time-based metrics, such as counting tasks completed within a specific timeframe.

Practical Applications of Basic Formulas

1. **Budget Management:**

- Use **SUM** to calculate total expenses.
- Combine **AVERAGE** and **COUNT** to monitor spending trends and the frequency of transactions.

2. **Performance Tracking:**
   - Use **AVERAGE** to measure the average duration of completed tasks.
   - Use **COUNT** to determine how many tasks have been completed versus those still in progress.

3. **Sales and Revenue Analysis:**
   - Use **SUM** to calculate total sales revenue.
   - Use **COUNT** to track the number of successful sales or leads generated.

4. **Team Productivity:**
   - Use **AVERAGE** to evaluate average task completion times across team members.
   - Use **COUNT** to count completed milestones or deliverables.

Common Mistakes and Troubleshooting Tips

- **Error Messages:**
  - #UNPARSEABLE: This occurs when the formula syntax is incorrect. Double-check for typos or missing brackets.
  - #INVALID REF: This happens if you reference a deleted or renamed column. Update the formula to reflect the correct column name.

- **Data Mismatches:**
  - Ensure the data types in your columns match the requirements of the formula. For example, **SUM** and **AVERAGE** require numeric values.

- **Dynamic Data Updates:**
  - If you frequently add new rows, use column-wide references (e.g., Column:Column) to include new data automatically.

IF: Conditional Logic Made Simple

The **IF** function allows you to apply conditional logic to your data, enabling your sheets to make decisions based on the criteria you define. This is a versatile tool for creating dynamic and flexible workflows.

Syntax:
=IF(Logical Expression, Value if True, Value if False)

Example Use Case: Imagine you're tracking task statuses in a project management sheet. You have a column called "Status" with values like "Complete," "In Progress," and "Not Started." You want to create a new column that assigns a "1" for completed tasks and a "0" for incomplete tasks.

Steps:

1. Add a new column, e.g., "Task Score."
2. Enter the formula in the first cell of the new column: =IF([Status]1 = "Complete", 1, 0)
3. Drag the formula down to apply it to all rows.

Pro Tips:

- Combine **IF** with other functions for powerful calculations. For example: =IF([Cost]1 > 1000, "High", "Low") categorizes expenses into "High" or "Low" based on the cost.

- Nest multiple **IF** statements to handle more complex scenarios. Example: =IF([Score]1 >= 90, "A", IF([Score]1 >= 80, "B", "C")).

COUNTIF: Conditional Counting

The **COUNTIF** function counts the number of cells that meet a specific condition. It's particularly useful for tracking data subsets, such as completed tasks, high-priority items, or overdue deadlines.

Syntax:
=COUNTIF(Range, Condition)

Example Use Case: You're managing a to-do list and want to count how many tasks have the status "Complete."

1. Select a blank cell where you want the result to appear.
2. Enter the formula:
   =COUNTIF([Status]:[Status], "Complete")
3. Smartsheet will return the count of all rows where the "Status" column contains "Complete."

Pro Tips:

- Use operators for conditions. For example, count tasks with high priority: =COUNTIF([Priority]:[Priority], "High").
- Combine **COUNTIF** with date fields to analyze time-specific data: =COUNTIF([Due Date]:[Due Date], TODAY()) counts tasks due today.

VLOOKUP: Searching for Data

The **VLOOKUP** function searches for a value in the first column of a range and returns a corresponding value from another column in the same row. This is useful for creating relationships between data sets.

Syntax:
=VLOOKUP(Search Value, Range, Column Number, [Exact Match])

Example Use Case: You have a sheet with employee IDs in one column and their names in another. On a separate sheet, you want to retrieve employee names based on their IDs.

Steps:

1. On the second sheet, enter the employee ID in a column, e.g., "Lookup ID."
2. In the next column, enter the formula:
   =VLOOKUP([Lookup ID]1, {Employee Database}, 2, false)
   - Replace {Employee Database} with the range or reference to your employee data sheet.
3. Smartsheet will return the employee's name corresponding to the ID.

Pro Tips:

- Use exact match (false) to avoid errors when the value isn't found.
- Ensure the range is sorted by the first column for approximate matches (true).

MAX and MIN: Finding Extremes

The **MAX** and **MIN** functions identify the highest and lowest values in a range of data, respectively. These functions are perfect for tracking performance metrics, such as highest sales or lowest expenses.

Syntax:

- **MAX:** =MAX([Column Name]:[Column Name])
- **MIN:** =MIN([Column Name]:[Column Name])

Example Use Case:
You're tracking monthly sales data in a sheet and want to find the highest sales figure for the year.

1. Select a blank cell where you want the maximum value.
2. Enter the formula:
   =MAX([Sales]:[Sales])
3. Smartsheet will return the highest value in the "Sales" column.

Pro Tips:

- Pair **MAX** or **MIN** with conditional logic. For example:
  =IF(MAX([Sales]:[Sales]) > 10000, "Great Month", "Needs Improvement").
- Use these functions for comparisons. For instance, to find the difference between the highest and lowest values:
  =MAX([Sales]:[Sales]) - MIN([Sales]:[Sales]).

LEN: Measuring Text Length

The **LEN** function calculates the number of characters in a text string, including spaces. It's useful for text analysis or data validation.

Syntax:
=LEN(Text)

Example Use Case: You're creating a form where each entry has a unique identifier. You want to ensure that all IDs are exactly eight characters long. Use **LEN** to validate:
=IF(LEN([ID]1) = 8, "Valid", "Invalid").

CONCATENATE (or JOIN): Combining Text

The **CONCATENATE** or **JOIN** functions allow you to merge text from multiple cells into one. This is ideal for creating full names, addresses, or other combined data.

Syntax:

- **CONCATENATE:** =CONCATENATE(Text1, Text2, ...)
- **JOIN:** =JOIN(Delimiter, Range)

Example Use Case: To combine first and last names in separate columns into a "Full Name" column:
=CONCATENATE([First Name]1, " ", [Last Name]1)

SUMIF: Conditional Summing

The **SUMIF** function allows you to sum values in a range based on specific criteria. It's perfect for cases where you need to add up values that meet certain conditions, such as summing all costs above a certain threshold or calculating total sales for a specific product.

Syntax:
=SUMIF(Range, Criteria, [Sum Range])

Example Use Case: You want to calculate the total cost of all items in your inventory that are marked as "High Priority."

1. In a new cell, enter the formula:
   =SUMIF([Priority]:[Priority], "High", [Cost]:[Cost])
2. This will sum all values in the "Cost" column where the corresponding "Priority" column is marked "High."

Pro Tips:

- Use **SUMIF** with wildcards to match partial text. For example: =SUMIF([Product Name]:[Product Name], "Widget*", [Sales Amount]:[Sales Amount]) sums sales for all products that start with "Widget."
- Combine **SUMIF** with dates to calculate total sales within a specific time range.

AVERAGEIF: Conditional Averaging

The **AVERAGEIF** function works similarly to **SUMIF**, but instead of summing values, it averages them based on specific conditions. This is useful for tracking performance metrics, such as calculating the average score for completed tasks or the average sales amount for a specific product.

Syntax:
=AVERAGEIF(Range, Criteria, [Average Range])

Example Use Case: You want to calculate the average cost of all "High Priority" items in your inventory.

1. In a new cell, enter the formula:
   =AVERAGEIF([Priority]:[Priority], "High", [Cost]:[Cost])
2. This will return the average value of all items marked as "High Priority" in the "Cost" column.

Pro Tips:

- You can use **AVERAGEIF** for date ranges as well. For example: =AVERAGEIF([Due Date]:[Due Date], ">=TODAY()", [Task Duration]:[Task Duration]) calculates the average duration for tasks that are due today or later.
- To find the average of cells containing numeric values greater than a threshold: =AVERAGEIF([Sales Amount]:[Sales Amount], ">500") averages sales greater than 500.

INDEX and MATCH: Powerful Lookup Combination

While **VLOOKUP** is useful for looking up data from the leftmost column, **INDEX** and **MATCH** combined give you more flexibility and power when it comes to retrieving data from any column, regardless of its position.

Syntax:

- **INDEX:** =INDEX(Array, Row Number, [Column Number])
- **MATCH:** =MATCH(Search Value, Search Range, [Match Type])

Example Use Case: You have a table of products with their corresponding prices, but you want to look up the price based on the product name.

1. Use **MATCH** to find the row number of the product: =MATCH("Product A", [Product Name]:[Product Name], 0)
2. Use **INDEX** to retrieve the price from the corresponding row: =INDEX([Price]:[Price], MATCH("Product A", [Product Name]:[Product Name], 0))
3. This returns the price of "Product A" from the price column, even if the price column is not the first column.

Pro Tips:

- **MATCH** can be used to look for approximate matches (use 1 or -1 for **Match Type**) when the list is sorted.
- **INDEX/MATCH** is often more efficient than **VLOOKUP**, especially in larger data sets, because it allows for left-to-right and right-to-left lookups.

TODAY: Returning the Current Date

The **TODAY** function returns the current date, which is useful for date-based calculations such as tracking deadlines, overdue tasks, or comparing today's date to scheduled dates.

Syntax:
=TODAY()

Example Use Case: You want to track if tasks are overdue. You can use **TODAY** in a formula to check if a task's due date has passed.

1. In a new cell, enter the formula:
   =IF([Due Date]1 < TODAY(), "Overdue", "On Time")
2. This will return "Overdue" if the task's due date is before today and "On Time" if it's not.

Pro Tips:

- **TODAY** is dynamic, so it updates automatically every day.
- Combine **TODAY** with conditional logic for effective deadline tracking:
  =IF([Due Date]1 < TODAY(), "Past Due", IF([Due Date]1 = TODAY(), "Due Today", "Upcoming")).

NOW: Current Date and Time

The **NOW** function returns the current date and time. This is useful when you need a timestamp for logging or tracking changes. It is particularly useful for time-sensitive calculations.

Syntax:
=NOW()

Example Use Case: You want to track when a task was last updated. You can use **NOW** to record the exact timestamp:

1. In a new column, enter the formula:
   =NOW()
2. Every time the sheet recalculates, the timestamp will update to the current date and time.

Pro Tips:

- **NOW** also updates automatically, making it perfect for tracking real-time data changes.
- Combine **NOW** with conditional logic to track project milestones or time-sensitive tasks:
  =IF([Due Date]1 < NOW(), "Past Due", "Upcoming").

TEXT: Formatting Numbers and Dates

The **TEXT** function formats numbers, dates, or times in a specific way. It's perfect for changing how your data appears without altering the underlying values, such as formatting numbers as currency, percentages, or dates.

Syntax:
=TEXT(Value, Format)

Example Use Case: You want to display a numeric value as currency.

1. Enter the formula in a cell:
   =TEXT([Amount]1, "$#,##0.00")

2. This will display the value in the "Amount" column as currency.

Pro Tips:

- Use the **TEXT** function to format dates in different styles. For example: =TEXT([Date]1, "MM/DD/YYYY").

- Combine **TEXT** with other functions for customized results, such as formatting a combined date and time string:
  =TEXT([Date]1, "MM/DD/YYYY") & " " & TEXT([Time]1, "h:mm AM/PM").

COUNTIF: Conditional Counting

The **COUNTIF** function is used to count the number of cells that meet a certain condition. It's perfect for counting items that meet specific criteria, such as counting the number of tasks marked as "Completed" or the number of products above a certain price.

Syntax:
=COUNTIF(Range, Criteria)

Example Use Case: You want to count how many tasks are marked as "Completed" in a "Task Status" column.

1. In a new cell, enter the formula:
   =COUNTIF([Task Status]:[Task Status], "Completed")

2. This will return the number of tasks in the "Task Status" column that are marked as "Completed."

Pro Tips:

- Use **COUNTIF** with wildcards to match partial text. For example: =COUNTIF([Product Name]:[Product Name], "Widget*") counts all products starting with "Widget."

- Combine **COUNTIF** with dates to count tasks due in the future: =COUNTIF([Due Date]:[Due Date], ">=TODAY()") counts tasks with a due date today or later.

IFERROR: Handling Errors in Formulas

The **IFERROR** function is used to return a custom message or value if a formula results in an error. This is useful when you expect errors in calculations (like division by zero or missing data) and want to handle them gracefully without breaking your sheet.

Syntax:
=IFERROR(Value, Value_if_error)

Example Use Case: You have a formula that divides two numbers, but if the divisor is zero, it results in an error. You want to display a custom message instead.

1. In a new cell, enter the formula:
   =IFERROR([Total Sales]1 / [Units Sold]1, "Error: Division by Zero")
2. This will display "Error: Division by Zero" if the formula tries to divide by zero.

Pro Tips:

- **IFERROR** is particularly useful for managing large datasets where errors might occur in specific rows.
- You can use it with formulas like **VLOOKUP** or **INDEX/MATCH** to handle cases where a match is not found.

RANK: Ranking Values

The **RANK** function is used to rank values in a data set, such as ranking sales figures or employee performance. You can rank values in ascending or descending order based on how they compare to others.

Syntax:
=RANK(Number, Range, [Order])

Example Use Case: You want to rank the sales performance of different employees based on their sales figures.

1. In a new cell, enter the formula:
   =RANK([Sales]1, [Sales]:[Sales], 0)

2. This will rank the value in the "Sales" column (in this case, the value of cell 1) against all other values in the "Sales" column in descending order (largest to smallest).

Pro Tips:

- Use 1 for **Order** if you want to rank in ascending order (smallest to largest).
- The **RANK** function can be particularly useful for generating leaderboards, performance tracking, or sales comparisons.

VLOOKUP: Vertical Lookup

The **VLOOKUP** function is one of the most widely used functions in Smartsheet for looking up values in a vertical table. It searches for a value in the first column of a range and returns a value from a specified column in the same row.

Syntax:
=VLOOKUP(Search_Value, Range, Column_Index, [Exact_Match])

Example Use Case: You want to look up a product's price based on its name.

1. In a new cell, enter the formula:
   =VLOOKUP("Widget", [Product List]:[Price List], 2, FALSE)

2. This will return the price of the product named "Widget" from the second column of the "Product List" to "Price List" range.

Pro Tips:

- Use FALSE for **Exact_Match** when you want to find an exact match.
- **VLOOKUP** is ideal for looking up data when the value you're searching for is in the first column of your range.

CONCATENATE: Combining Text Values

The **CONCATENATE** function allows you to combine multiple text strings into one cell. This can be useful for creating full names, combining addresses, or merging other fields into a single column.

Syntax:
=CONCATENATE(Text1, Text2, ...)

Example Use Case: You want to combine the first name and last name of employees into a single column.

1. In a new cell, enter the formula:
   =CONCATENATE([First Name]1, " ", [Last Name]1)

2. This will combine the "First Name" and "Last Name" fields, with a space between them, into a single cell.

Pro Tips:

- You can also use the **&** operator to concatenate: =[First Name]1 & " " & [Last Name]1 achieves the same result as the **CONCATENATE** function.

- **CONCATENATE** is helpful when you need to create a full name or combine multiple text fields (such as adding a title or suffix).

Summary

Here are some of the most commonly used functions in Smartsheet that will help you with your daily tasks and make your data manipulation more efficient. Each of these functions is designed to save time and increase the accuracy of your work. Whether you're summing values conditionally, looking up data, handling errors, or combining text, these formulas can be used in a wide variety of scenarios.

2.3.2 Linking Data Across Sheets

Linking data across sheets in Smartsheet is an essential skill for creating robust and dynamic workflows. By establishing relationships between different sheets, you can ensure that your data is consistent, up-to-date, and accurate across your entire system. This section will explain how linking works, different methods to link data, and how to use this feature effectively to optimize your work in Smartsheet.

Why Link Data Across Sheets?

Before we dive into the technicalities of how to link data across sheets, it's essential to understand **why** you should link data. There are several key benefits to linking data across sheets:

1. **Centralized Management**: By linking data, you can keep all your information in one place. This is particularly helpful when managing large projects, where you might need to access data from multiple sheets but don't want to maintain duplicate records.

2. **Automatic Updates**: When you link data between sheets, changes made to one sheet will automatically be reflected in the other. This ensures data consistency and reduces the need for manual updates, saving time and minimizing errors.

3. **Increased Efficiency**: Linking allows you to reference data from multiple sheets, helping you make decisions more efficiently. This is especially useful when creating reports or dashboards that pull data from various sheets.

4. **Advanced Reporting**: Linking is essential for more advanced reporting capabilities. By pulling data from different sheets, you can create comprehensive reports that reflect the current state of all aspects of your project.

Types of Links You Can Create in Smartsheet

Smartsheet provides multiple ways to link data between sheets. The two most common methods are:

- **Cell Linking**: This is the most straightforward method, where you link a single cell from one sheet to a cell in another sheet. Any changes made to the original cell are automatically reflected in the linked cell.

- **Cross-Sheet Formulas**: A more advanced method that allows you to use formulas to pull data from other sheets. This can include functions like VLOOKUP, INDEX, and MATCH, among others.

We will dive into both methods in detail below.

---

1. Cell Linking in Smartsheet

Cell linking is a powerful feature that allows you to connect a specific cell in one sheet to another cell in a different sheet. This method is ideal when you want to reference a single piece of information, like a due date or budget figure, across multiple sheets.

How to Create a Cell Link

1. **Select the Cell to Link**: In the sheet where you want to create the link, click the cell where you want the linked data to appear.

2. **Open the Linking Dialog**: Right-click on the cell and select **Link from Cell in Another Sheet**. Alternatively, you can use the **Cell Linking** option in the toolbar.

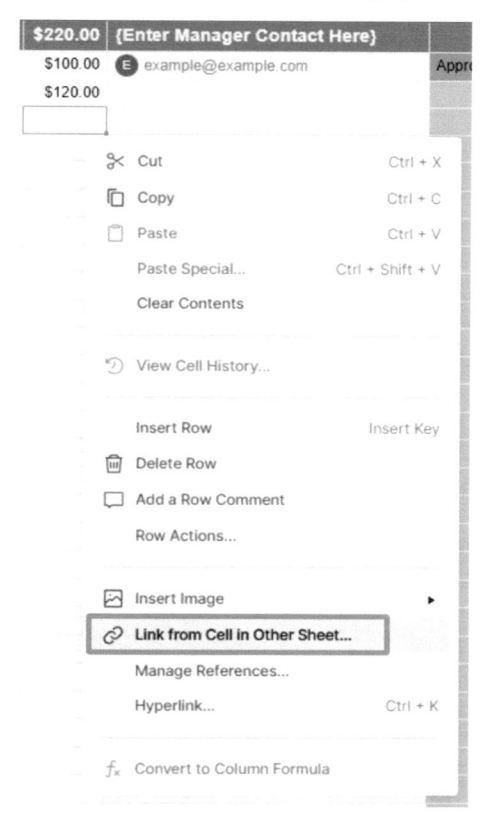

3. **Choose the Source Sheet**: A dialog box will appear, allowing you to choose the source sheet that contains the data you want to link to.

4. **Select the Source Cell**: Once you've selected the sheet, navigate through it to find the specific cell you want to link. After selecting it, click **OK** to establish the link.

5. **Confirm the Link**: The linked data will now appear in the selected cell. If the original data changes, the linked cell will automatically update.

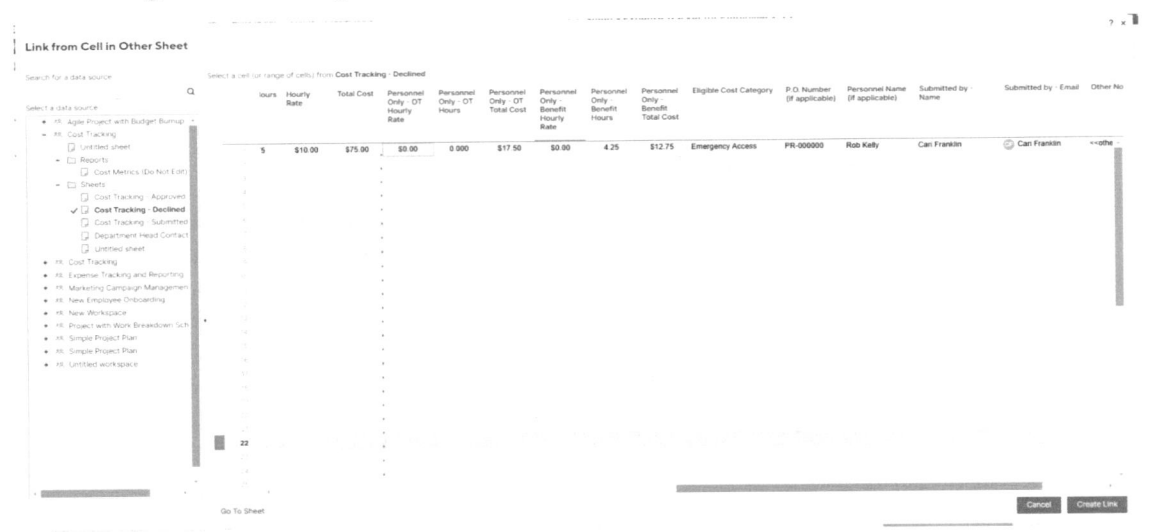

Benefits of Cell Linking

- **Easy to Set Up**: This is a quick and intuitive way to link data without needing to write complex formulas.

- **Real-Time Updates**: Since cell linking is a direct connection, any updates made to the original cell are reflected in real time.

- **Simplifies Data Access**: You can consolidate data from different sheets into a central location, making it easier to track key metrics.

Limitations of Cell Linking

While cell linking is an excellent tool for referencing individual data points, it is not as powerful when you need to work with large datasets or perform more complex operations. For that, you may want to explore using cross-sheet formulas.

---

2. Cross-Sheet Formulas in Smartsheet

Cross-sheet formulas allow you to pull data from one sheet into another by using formulas. This method is much more flexible and powerful than cell linking because it enables you to create dynamic relationships between sheets, automate calculations, and generate reports.

Creating Cross-Sheet Formulas

To create a cross-sheet formula, follow these steps:

1. **Open the Formula Dialog**: In the sheet where you want to display the linked data, select the cell and click on the **Formula** button in the toolbar.

2. **Reference the Other Sheet**: In the formula dialog, click on the **Reference Another Sheet** button. This will allow you to select a sheet from which to pull data.

3. **Choose the Data Range**: After selecting the source sheet, you can either choose a specific range of cells or use an entire column. This allows you to pull large sets of data into your formula.

4. **Write the Formula**: Once the range is selected, you can write the desired formula, such as VLOOKUP, INDEX, or SUM. For example, if you want to pull a value based on a unique identifier, you might use a formula like this:

5. =VLOOKUP([Project ID]@row, {Project Data Range}, 2, false)

In this example, the formula looks for a **Project ID** in the current sheet and pulls the corresponding value from another sheet.

6. **Finish and Save**: After completing the formula, click **OK** to apply it. The cell will now display the linked data from the other sheet.

Popular Cross-Sheet Formulas

- **VLOOKUP**: This is one of the most commonly used formulas for linking data across sheets. It searches for a value in one sheet and returns a corresponding value from another sheet.
  Example:

- =VLOOKUP([Task ID]@row, {Task Data Range}, 3, false)

- **INDEX & MATCH**: This combination is often used as a more flexible alternative to VLOOKUP. INDEX returns a value from a specified row and column, while MATCH searches for a value within a range. Example:

- =INDEX({Task Names}, MATCH([Task ID]@row, {Task IDs}, 0))

- **SUMIF**: This formula allows you to sum values in one sheet based on criteria from another sheet. Example:

- =SUMIF({Project Status}, "Completed", {Project Budget})
- **COUNTIF**: Similar to SUMIF, but instead of summing values, it counts the number of cells that meet a specific condition.

Using Cross-Sheet Formulas for Reporting

Cross-sheet formulas are particularly useful for creating dynamic reports that aggregate data from multiple sheets. For example, you might have separate sheets for individual projects, and you want to create a report that pulls key data from all those sheets into one central dashboard.

Example Use Cases

1. **Project Budget Overview**: If you have separate sheets for each project and want to pull in the total budget from each, you can use a formula like SUMIF or VLOOKUP to pull the budget data from each project sheet into your main reporting sheet.

2. **Tracking Task Status**: If you maintain task sheets for different teams or departments, you can link them using VLOOKUP or INDEX & MATCH to track the status of each task across various projects.

3. **Aggregating Data for Management**: Cross-sheet formulas are great for creating executive dashboards that show real-time progress across multiple sheets. By linking data from various sources, you can have a centralized view of performance, budgets, deadlines, and more.

3. Tips and Best Practices for Linking Data Across Sheets

While linking data across sheets is powerful, there are some best practices to keep in mind to avoid common pitfalls and ensure your system runs smoothly.

Best Practices

1. **Keep Sheet References Consistent**: When creating links, always use consistent naming conventions for your sheet references. This will make it easier to maintain links and formulas, especially as your project scales.

2. **Avoid Circular References**: Be mindful when creating links and formulas. Circular references (where Sheet A links to Sheet B, and Sheet B links back to Sheet A) can lead to errors and performance issues.

3. **Limit the Use of Complex Formulas**: While Smartsheet can handle complex formulas, it's a good idea to limit their use, especially in large sheets, to avoid performance slowdowns. Break down complex formulas into simpler ones if possible.

4. **Test Your Links**: Always test your links and formulas before relying on them for reporting or decision-making. This ensures that your data is accurate and up-to-date.

Conclusion

Linking data across sheets in Smartsheet is a powerful way to create a dynamic, interconnected system for managing projects, tracking tasks, and generating reports. Whether you use cell linking for quick references or cross-sheet formulas for more advanced operations, mastering these features will help you make the most of Smartsheet's capabilities. By following best practices and using the right formulas, you can ensure that your data is always accurate and up-to-date, allowing you to focus on what matters most: delivering successful projects.

2.3.3 Using Advanced Functions

Smartsheet provides a robust formula editor that allows users to apply a wide range of functions to manage their data efficiently. While basic formulas like SUM, AVERAGE, and COUNT are useful, there are numerous advanced functions that can take your data analysis and project management to the next level. In this section, we'll dive into several advanced functions you can use in Smartsheet to streamline your workflows and enhance your project management efforts.

Understanding Advanced Functions

Advanced functions in Smartsheet are designed to handle complex data relationships, automate calculations, and create dynamic reports that evolve based on changing data. These functions can include conditional logic, data lookups, and text manipulation, among others.

1. IF Statements: Conditional Logic

One of the most powerful advanced functions in Smartsheet is the IF statement. It allows you to implement conditional logic by specifying different results based on whether a condition is true or false. This function is invaluable when you need to make decisions based on specific criteria within your data.

Syntax:

IF(logical_test, value_if_true, value_if_false)

Example:
Let's say you have a column for project completion percentage and another column for project status. You could use an IF function to automatically assign a status based on the completion percentage.

=IF([Completion %]@row >= 80%, "Completed", "In Progress")

This formula will check if the value in the "Completion %" column is greater than or equal to 80%. If true, it will return "Completed"; otherwise, it will return "In Progress."

You can also nest IF statements to create more complex logic.

Example:
If you want to label projects as "Completed", "In Progress", or "Not Started" based on percentage ranges, you can nest multiple IF functions:

=IF([Completion %]@row >= 80%, "Completed", IF([Completion %]@row >= 50%, "In Progress", "Not Started"))

This will evaluate the completion percentage and return the appropriate status.

2. VLOOKUP: Searching for Data Across Sheets

The VLOOKUP function is one of the most commonly used advanced functions in Smartsheet, especially when you need to look up and retrieve data from another sheet. This is essential for scenarios where you have separate sheets for different tasks or projects, but you want to consolidate data in one location.

Syntax:

VLOOKUP(lookup_value, range, column_index, [is_sorted])

- **lookup_value**: The value you are searching for.
- **range**: The range of cells that contains the data you want to search through.

- **column_index**: The column in the range from which to retrieve the value.
- **is_sorted**: Optional argument, TRUE if the range is sorted, FALSE if it is not.

Example:

Suppose you have two sheets: one contains employee names and their IDs, and another contains their project assignments. If you want to retrieve the project assignment for an employee by their ID, you could use VLOOKUP.

=VLOOKUP([Employee ID]@row, {Project Assignments Range}, 2, FALSE)

This formula will search for the employee ID in the "Project Assignments Range" and return the corresponding project from the second column.

3. INDEX and MATCH: A More Flexible Alternative to VLOOKUP

While VLOOKUP is useful, it has limitations, particularly when it comes to looking up data in columns to the left of the reference column. For more flexibility, you can use the combination of INDEX and MATCH. This pair allows you to look up values in any column, not just those to the right of the reference column.

Syntax for INDEX:

INDEX(range, row_number, [column_number])

- **range**: The range of cells you want to return a value from.
- **row_number**: The row number in the range from which to retrieve the value.
- **column_number**: The column number within the range from which to retrieve the value.

Syntax for MATCH:

MATCH(lookup_value, lookup_range, [match_type])

- **lookup_value**: The value to search for.
- **lookup_range**: The range of cells to search through.
- **match_type**: 0 for an exact match, 1 for the largest value less than or equal to the lookup value, -1 for the smallest value greater than or equal to the lookup value.

Example:

Let's say you have a sheet of employees with their names in column 1 and their sales figures in column 2. If you want to find the sales figure of a particular employee, you can use the INDEX and MATCH combination.

=INDEX([Sales]@row, MATCH([Employee Name]@row, [Employee List]@row, 0))

This formula searches for the employee's name in the "Employee List" and retrieves the corresponding sales figure from the "Sales" column.

4. JOIN: Combining Text Values

The JOIN function in Smartsheet allows you to combine or concatenate values from multiple cells into one single cell, separated by a specified delimiter. This is particularly useful when you want to combine first and last names, list items, or dates.

Syntax:

JOIN(range, delimiter)

- **range**: The range of cells you want to join.
- **delimiter**: The character or string to use as a separator (e.g., a comma, space, or hyphen).

Example:
Suppose you have separate columns for the first and last names of employees, and you want to combine them into one full name. You can use JOIN to concatenate the values:

=JOIN([First Name]@row, " ", [Last Name]@row)

This formula combines the first name and last name with a space in between.

5. TODAY and NETWORKDAYS: Date Calculations

Smartsheet provides several useful date functions, such as TODAY and NETWORKDAYS, that can help you track project timelines and deadlines.

- **TODAY:** Returns the current date.
- **NETWORKDAYS:** Returns the number of working days between two dates, excluding weekends and holidays.

Example for TODAY:
If you want to calculate the number of days left until a project deadline, you can use TODAY in combination with simple subtraction:

=[Deadline]@row - TODAY()

This formula will calculate the number of days remaining until the deadline.

Example for NETWORKDAYS: To calculate the number of working days between two dates, you can use the NETWORKDAYS function. For instance, if your project has a start and end date, you can calculate the number of workdays between them:

=NETWORKDAYS([Start Date]@row, [End Date]@row)

This function will return the number of weekdays (excluding weekends) between the start and end dates.

6. DATE and TIME Functions: Manipulating Dates and Times

Smartsheet also offers several functions to manipulate date and time values, such as DATE, MONTH, YEAR, and DAY. These functions help you extract specific components from a date or create new date values.

Example:
To extract the month from a given date:

=MONTH([Project Start Date]@row)

This formula will return the month number from the "Project Start Date" column.

You can also calculate the difference between two dates in days, months, or years:

=DATEDIF([Start Date]@row, [End Date]@row, "D")

This formula calculates the difference between the start and end dates in days.

Conclusion

Mastering advanced functions in Smartsheet is a powerful way to manage your data, automate workflows, and improve decision-making. Functions like IF, VLOOKUP, INDEX/MATCH, JOIN, and date calculations allow you to create sophisticated and dynamic reports, track progress, and streamline processes.

By understanding and implementing these advanced functions, you can unlock the full potential of Smartsheet and make your projects more efficient and organized. Experiment with these functions in your own projects, and soon you'll be using them intuitively to manage your team and tasks with greater ease.

CHAPTER III
Collaborating in Smartsheet

3.1 Sharing Your Sheets and Workspaces

3.1.1 Inviting Collaborators

Collaboration is one of the most powerful features of Smartsheet. By inviting others to work on your sheets and workspaces, you can streamline teamwork, improve communication, and ensure everyone has access to the most up-to-date information. This section will walk you through the process of inviting collaborators, setting permissions, and ensuring a secure and efficient collaborative experience.

Understanding the Role of Collaborators

Before diving into the steps for inviting collaborators, it's important to understand what collaboration means in Smartsheet. Collaborators are individuals who you grant access to your sheets or workspaces. Depending on the permissions you set, they can view, edit, comment on, or even manage the sheet or workspace.

Collaboration in Smartsheet is ideal for:

- **Team Projects**: Sharing tasks and deadlines with team members.
- **Client Updates**: Giving clients access to reports or progress updates.
- **Cross-Department Coordination**: Enabling different teams to contribute to a single source of truth.

Steps to Invite Collaborators

Step 1: Open Your Sheet or Workspace

Begin by navigating to the specific sheet or workspace you want to share. Ensure that the content is ready to be shared and contains no confidential information you do not wish to disclose.

Step 2: Click on the "Share" Button

In the top-right corner of your Smartsheet interface, you'll find the **"Share"** button. Click on it to open the sharing menu.

Step 3: Add Collaborators' Email Addresses

A pop-up window will appear, prompting you to enter the email addresses of the people you wish to invite. Smartsheet allows you to invite multiple collaborators at once by separating email addresses with commas.

Tip: If your collaborators are already part of your organization's Smartsheet account, their names may auto-complete as you type.

Step 4: Set Permissions

Once you've entered the email addresses, you'll need to set the permissions for each collaborator. Smartsheet provides several permission levels:

1. **Viewer**: Can only view the sheet but cannot make changes. Ideal for clients or stakeholders who need updates without editing access.
2. **Editor - Can Share**: Can make changes to the sheet and also share it with others. Use this option sparingly to prevent unintended sharing.
3. **Editor - Cannot Share**: Can edit the sheet but cannot share it. This is a safer option for most collaborators.
4. **Admin**: Has full control over the sheet, including the ability to change permissions and delete the sheet. Reserve this level for trusted team members or managers.

Note: Permissions can also be set for entire workspaces, which will apply to all sheets within that workspace.

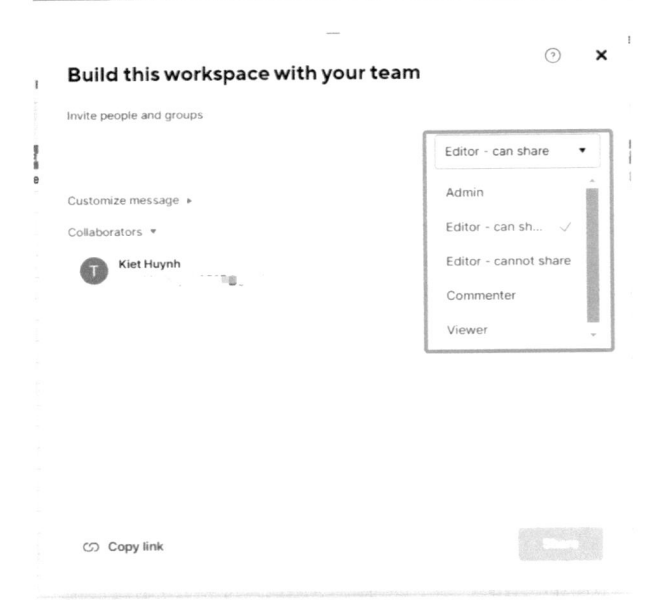

Step 5: Add a Personal Message (Optional)

To ensure your collaborators understand the purpose of the sheet, include a brief personal message. For example:

"Hi [Name],
I've shared this Smartsheet with you to track our project progress. Please review the tasks assigned to you and let me know if you have any questions."

Step 6: Click "Share"

Once everything is set, click the **"Share"** button to send invitations. Your collaborators will receive an email with a link to the sheet or workspace.

Best Practices for Inviting Collaborators

1. **Invite Only What's Necessary**: Avoid overwhelming collaborators by sharing only the sheets they need to work on.

2. **Use Groups for Efficiency**: If you frequently collaborate with the same group of people, consider creating a group in Smartsheet. This allows you to share sheets with the group instead of adding individual emails every time.

3. **Double-Check Permissions**: Always verify the permissions you're granting to collaborators. Providing too much access can lead to unintended changes or data loss.

Troubleshooting Common Issues When Inviting Collaborators

While inviting collaborators is straightforward, you may encounter a few common challenges:

Issue 1: The Invitee Didn't Receive the Email

- **Solution**: Ask the invitee to check their spam or junk folder. If the issue persists, resend the invitation or provide a direct sharing link.

Issue 2: The Invitee Can't Access the Sheet

- **Solution**: Ensure the email address was entered correctly and verify that the invitee has a Smartsheet account.

Issue 3: Collaboration Permissions Are Incorrect

- **Solution**: Revisit the sharing settings and adjust the permissions as needed. Remember, you can update permissions at any time.

Leveraging Smartsheet's Collaboration Features

Beyond basic sharing, Smartsheet offers advanced collaboration tools that can enhance team productivity:

1. **Sharing Links**: For temporary or view-only access, generate a sharing link instead of inviting collaborators directly.
2. **Embed Options**: Embed your Smartsheet into websites or intranets for easier access by large teams.
3. **Activity Log**: Use the activity log to track who accessed or edited the sheet.

Security Considerations When Inviting Collaborators

Sharing your Smartsheet is convenient, but it's important to prioritize security:

- Use **password protection** for sensitive sheets.
- Regularly review who has access to your sheets and remove outdated collaborators.
- Avoid sharing sheets with public links unless absolutely necessary.

By following these steps and best practices, you'll ensure a smooth and secure collaboration experience for your team. Next, we'll explore how to set permissions effectively in **3.1.2 Setting Permissions**.

3.1.2 Setting Permissions

Smartsheet offers a robust system for setting permissions, ensuring that you can control who has access to your sheets and workspaces and what they can do with them. This flexibility is essential for collaboration, particularly in larger teams or projects where sensitive data or task ownership needs to be carefully managed. In this section, we'll dive deep into the different types of permissions available, how to assign them, and best practices for maintaining control over your data.

Understanding Smartsheet Permission Levels

In Smartsheet, there are several permission levels that define what a user can and cannot do with a sheet or workspace. Understanding these levels is the first step to ensuring your collaborators have the appropriate access:

1. **Owner**
    - The owner has full control over the sheet or workspace. They can edit, delete, and share it with others. By default, the creator of a sheet or workspace is the owner. Ownership can also be transferred to another user if needed.
    - **Key Actions Allowed:**
        - Add, edit, and delete content
        - Change sharing settings

- Set permissions for collaborators

2. **Admin**
    - Admins have nearly the same permissions as the owner but cannot delete the sheet or transfer ownership. Admin access is ideal for trusted team members who need to help manage the sheet or workspace.
    - **Key Actions Allowed:**
        - Add, edit, and delete content
        - Manage sharing settings
        - Apply advanced features like automation

3. **Editor**
    - Editors can modify the content of a sheet but cannot change its structure or share it with others. This level is ideal for team members who need to update or manage data without altering the overall setup.
    - **Key Actions Allowed:**
        - Edit rows and cells
        - Attach files and comments

4. **Viewer**
    - Viewers can only view the content in a sheet or workspace. They cannot make any changes, making this the best option for stakeholders or clients who only need to review progress.
    - **Key Actions Allowed:**
        - View data
        - Export data (if enabled by the owner)

5. **Commenter**
    - Commenters can view the sheet and add comments but cannot edit the data. This role is useful for reviewers who need to provide feedback without changing the content.

- **Key Actions Allowed:**
    - View data
    - Add comments

Assigning Permissions to Users

Assigning permissions in Smartsheet is straightforward and can be done in just a few steps:

1. **Open the Sheet or Workspace**
    - Navigate to the sheet or workspace you want to share. Click on the "Share" button in the top-right corner.

2. **Add Collaborators**
    - In the sharing dialogue box, enter the email addresses of the people you want to share with. Smartsheet allows you to add multiple collaborators at once by separating their email addresses with commas.

3. **Set the Permission Level**
    - For each collaborator, choose the appropriate permission level from the dropdown menu. Options include **Admin**, **Editor**, **Viewer**, and **Commenter**.

4. **Customize Sharing Options**
    - You can choose to allow collaborators to reshare the sheet or prevent them from sharing it further. To do this, toggle the "Allow Resharing" option on or off.

5. **Send an Invitation**
    - Once you've configured the permissions, click the "Share" button to send an email invitation to the selected users. They will receive a link to access the sheet or workspace.

Best Practices for Setting Permissions

To maximize efficiency and minimize risks, follow these best practices when setting permissions in Smartsheet:

1. **Use the Principle of Least Privilege**
   - Assign the minimum level of access necessary for each collaborator to complete their tasks. For example, give editors access only if they need to make changes; otherwise, assign viewer or commenter roles.

2. **Regularly Review Permissions**
   - Periodically review who has access to your sheets and workspaces. Remove users who no longer need access and downgrade permissions if necessary.

3. **Use Workspaces for Large Projects**
   - If you're managing multiple sheets for a project, organize them in a workspace. This allows you to set permissions for the entire workspace instead of managing each sheet individually.

4. **Limit Resharing**
   - Disable the "Allow Resharing" option for sensitive sheets to prevent collaborators from granting access to unauthorized users.

5. **Train Your Team**
   - Ensure that collaborators understand their roles and responsibilities within Smartsheet. Provide training or documentation on how to use the platform effectively.

6. **Monitor Revision History**
   - Regularly check the revision history to ensure that no unauthorized changes have been made. If necessary, restore a previous version to revert unwanted modifications.

Common Scenarios and How to Handle Them

Here are some common scenarios where setting permissions becomes critical and tips on how to handle them:

1. **Collaborating with External Stakeholders**

- When working with clients or vendors, assign them **Viewer** or **Commenter** roles to ensure they can only see or provide feedback without modifying the content.

2. **Managing a Team Project**
    - Assign **Admin** roles to project managers who need to oversee the entire sheet. Give team members **Editor** roles to update their tasks and progress.

3. **Handling Sensitive Data**
    - For sheets containing sensitive or confidential information, limit access to trusted team members only. Consider using **Admin** and **Viewer** roles for additional control.

4. **Preventing Unauthorized Changes**
    - If you notice unexpected changes in a sheet, check the revision history to identify the collaborator responsible. Adjust their permissions if necessary to prevent further issues.

Advanced Permission Features

Smartsheet also offers advanced features to enhance permission management:

1. **Restricted Sharing Settings**
    - Owners can restrict sharing options, preventing collaborators from inviting others or exporting data. This is especially useful for confidential projects.

2. **User Groups**
    - For large organizations, consider creating user groups to streamline permission management. Instead of assigning permissions individually, you can grant access to entire groups at once.

3. **Access Reports**
    - Use Smartsheet's built-in reporting tools to track who has access to your sheets and what changes they've made. This feature is particularly useful for audits or compliance purposes.

Conclusion

Setting permissions in Smartsheet is an essential skill for effective collaboration. By understanding the different permission levels, assigning access appropriately, and following best practices, you can ensure that your data remains secure while enabling your team to work efficiently. Permissions aren't just a technical feature—they're a powerful tool for managing trust, responsibility, and productivity in any project.

3.1.3 Sharing Links and Embedding Sheets

Smartsheet offers several ways to share your work with others, and one of the most efficient methods is by sharing links or embedding sheets into external platforms. This functionality is particularly useful for collaborating with stakeholders who may not have direct access to Smartsheet but need to view or interact with your data. In this section, we'll explore how to generate sharing links, embed sheets into other tools, and make the most of these features to streamline your workflows.

Why Share Links and Embed Sheets?

Sharing links and embedding sheets provide a seamless way to:

- Allow stakeholders to access information without needing a Smartsheet account.
- Integrate Smartsheet into other tools, such as websites, intranets, or third-party applications.
- Enhance collaboration by providing live data views.
- Reduce the need for exporting or duplicating data across platforms.

These methods are ideal for organizations with diverse teams or external collaborators who rely on shared information to make decisions.

How to Share Links in Smartsheet

Sharing links is one of the easiest ways to allow others to view or edit your sheet. Here's how to do it:

1. **Access the Sharing Menu**

    o   Open the Smartsheet you want to share.

    o   Click the **"Share"** button located in the upper-right corner of the sheet.

    o   In the sharing panel, you'll see several options for inviting people, generating links, and managing permissions.

2. **Generate a Sharing Link**

    o   Click on **"Get Link"** in the sharing menu.

    o   Choose the type of access you want to provide:

        - **View Only:** Allows users to see the sheet but not make any changes.
        - **Editor – Can Share:** Grants users the ability to edit the sheet and share it with others.
        - **Admin Access:** Provides full control, including the ability to manage sharing settings.

3. **Customize Link Settings** Smartsheet allows you to customize link settings to ensure the right level of security:

    o   **Expiration Date:** Set a date after which the link will no longer work. This is helpful for time-sensitive projects.

    o   **Password Protection:** Add a password to restrict access to the link.

    o   **Domain Restrictions:** Limit access to users within a specific domain (e.g., @company.com).

4. **Copy and Share the Link**

    o   Once the link is generated, click **"Copy Link"** and share it via email, chat, or any other communication channel.

    o   The recipients can open the link in their browser and access the sheet based on the permissions you've set.

Best Practices for Sharing Links

While sharing links is convenient, it's essential to follow best practices to maintain data security and efficiency:

- **Limit Permissions:** Always provide the minimum level of access required. For example, use "View Only" links if recipients don't need to edit the sheet.

- **Use Expiration Dates:** For sensitive projects, set an expiration date to ensure the link is only accessible during the relevant period.

- **Monitor Access:** Regularly review the sharing settings of your sheets to ensure that no unauthorized users have access.

- **Communicate Instructions:** Include instructions with your shared link to guide recipients on how to use it effectively.

Embedding Sheets into External Platforms

Embedding a Smartsheet into an external platform allows you to display live data in real-time, creating a unified experience for your team or stakeholders. Here's how you can embed Smartsheet into different platforms:

Embedding into Websites or Intranets

1. **Generate Embed Code**
    - Open the Smartsheet you want to embed.
    - Click the **"File"** menu and select **"Publish to the Web"**.
    - In the publishing options, enable the "Embed Code" option.
    - Copy the generated HTML embed code.

2. **Customize Display Settings**: Smartsheet provides options to adjust the appearance of the embedded sheet:
    - **Default View:** Choose how the sheet will appear (e.g., Grid, Gantt, or Card view).
    - **Visible Columns:** Select specific columns to display in the embed.

- o **Interactivity Settings:** Decide whether viewers can sort, filter, or interact with the sheet.

3. **Add the Embed Code to Your Platform**
    - o Paste the embed code into the HTML section of your website or intranet.
    - o Adjust the size and layout to fit seamlessly with your platform's design.
    - o Save and preview the embedded sheet to ensure it looks and functions correctly.

Embedding into Third-Party Tools

Smartsheet integrates with various third-party tools, such as Microsoft Teams, Google Sites, and more. Here's how to embed a sheet into some popular platforms:

- **Microsoft Teams**
    - o Open Microsoft Teams and navigate to the channel where you want to embed the sheet.
    - o Click the **"+"** icon to add a new tab.
    - o Select **Smartsheet** from the list of apps.
    - o Sign in to your Smartsheet account and choose the sheet you want to embed.
    - o The sheet will now appear as a tab in your Teams channel.

- **Google Sites**
    - o Open your Google Site and click **"Embed"** in the editing toolbar.
    - o Paste the Smartsheet sharing link or embed code.
    - o Adjust the size and layout as needed.
    - o Publish your Google Site to make the embedded sheet accessible to viewers.

Embedding into PowerPoint Presentations

Smartsheet data can also be embedded into PowerPoint slides to enhance presentations:

1. Export a portion of your Smartsheet data as a chart or visual.
2. Use PowerPoint's "Insert" feature to embed the chart or link the sheet dynamically.
3. Alternatively, use third-party integrations to connect Smartsheet with your presentation tools.

Common Issues and Troubleshooting

When sharing links or embedding sheets, you may encounter some challenges. Here are solutions to common problems:

1. **Link Not Working**
    - Verify that the link is active and hasn't expired.
    - Ensure that recipients have the necessary permissions to access the link.
2. **Embedded Sheet Not Displaying Properly**
    - Check if the platform supports HTML embed codes.
    - Adjust the size or layout settings to resolve display issues.
3. **Data Security Concerns**
    - Use password protection and domain restrictions to enhance security.
    - Regularly audit your sharing settings to identify potential risks.

Tips for Effective Sharing and Embedding

- **Provide Context:** When sharing or embedding sheets, include a brief explanation of what the sheet contains and how recipients can use it.
- **Test Before Sharing:** Always test links and embedded sheets to ensure they function as intended.
- **Update Regularly:** If the data in your Smartsheet changes frequently, inform recipients so they're aware of updates.

By using Smartsheet's sharing links and embedding features, you can make your data more accessible, interactive, and valuable for your team and stakeholders. These tools empower you to extend the reach of your Smartsheet projects beyond the platform, driving collaboration and efficiency in every project.

3.2 Communicating with Team Members

3.2.1 Using Comments and Notes

Effective communication is critical for the success of any project, and Smartsheet provides robust tools to facilitate team collaboration. The **Comments** and **Notes** features in Smartsheet allow users to provide context, share updates, and discuss tasks directly within the platform. This section will explore the functionality, benefits, and best practices for using comments and notes effectively.

What Are Comments and Notes in Smartsheet?

- **Comments** are threaded discussions tied to specific rows, tasks, or the sheet as a whole. They are designed for real-time collaboration, enabling team members to ask questions, provide feedback, or update the team on the status of a task.

- **Notes**, on the other hand, are often used as static text fields within a sheet to document additional details or instructions related to a specific row. While less dynamic than comments, notes provide essential contextual information for tasks or data entries.

Key Features of Comments in Smartsheet

1. **Threaded Discussions**:
    - Comments are organized in a thread-like format, making it easy to track the flow of conversations. This structure ensures that all relevant discussions about a particular task or data point are grouped together.

2. **Mentions and Notifications**:
    - By using the "@" symbol followed by a team member's name, you can tag individuals in a comment. Tagged users receive notifications, ensuring they are immediately aware of the conversation.
    - Example: *"@JohnSmith Can you confirm the delivery date for this order?"*

3. **File Attachments:**

    o   Comments can include file attachments, such as documents, images, or spreadsheets, allowing users to share supporting materials directly within the conversation.

4. **Time Stamps and User Tags:**

    o   Every comment is automatically tagged with the commenter's name and a time stamp, providing accountability and a clear timeline of communication.

Adding and Managing Comments

1. **Adding a Comment to a Row or Sheet:**

    o   Navigate to the desired row or the comments section of the sheet.

    o   Click the speech bubble icon to open the comments pane.

		Date	Description
1			{Enter Employee Name Here}
2		04/14/23	{example expense}
3			
4		Add a comment	
5			

    o   Type your message and click **Send** to post the comment.

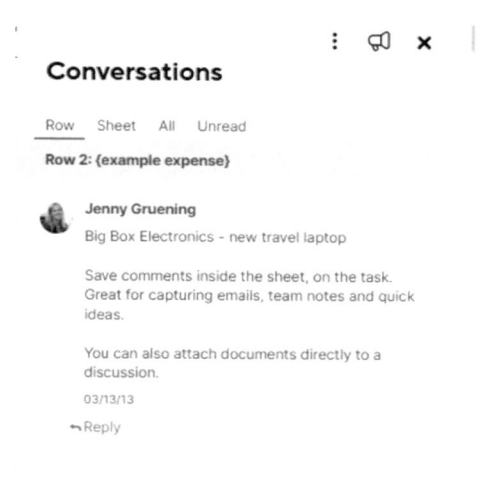

2. **Replying to a Comment**:

    o   Open the existing comment thread by clicking the speech bubble icon.

    o   Click **Reply** under the comment to add your response.

3. **Editing or Deleting Comments**:

    o   Users can edit their own comments to correct errors or provide additional details.

    o   To delete a comment, hover over it, click the ellipsis (...), and select **Delete**.

4. **Viewing All Comments in a Sheet**:

- The comments pane displays all discussions related to the sheet. Users can scroll through the history or search for specific keywords to locate relevant conversations.

Benefits of Using Comments

1. **Centralized Communication**:
    - Comments eliminate the need for email threads or external messaging platforms. All discussions are centralized within the sheet, making it easier for team members to access the information they need.

2. **Real-Time Collaboration**:
    - Comments facilitate real-time updates and responses, ensuring that teams can resolve issues quickly and efficiently.

3. **Accountability and Transparency**:
    - The time-stamped and user-tagged nature of comments ensures that all team members are accountable for their contributions to the discussion.

4. **Contextual Conversations**:
    - Comments tied to specific rows or tasks ensure that discussions remain relevant to the work at hand, reducing confusion and miscommunication.

Best Practices for Using Comments

1. **Be Clear and Concise**:
    - Keep your comments focused and to the point. Include only the necessary details to ensure your message is understood.

2. **Use Mentions Wisely**:
    - Tag only the individuals who need to be involved in the conversation to avoid overwhelming team members with unnecessary notifications.

3. **Attach Supporting Documents**:

- When discussing complex tasks or decisions, include relevant files to provide additional context and clarity.

4. **Follow Up**:
   - If a comment requires action, follow up to ensure that tasks are completed or questions are answered.

5. **Review Comments Regularly**:
   - Make it a habit to review recent comments to stay updated on project discussions and developments.

Using Notes for Additional Context

While comments are ideal for discussions, **notes** serve a different purpose. Notes are typically used to document critical information about a task or data point. For example, in a project management sheet, a note might include the step-by-step instructions for completing a task or additional details about a client requirement.

1. **Adding Notes**:
   - Notes can be added as a column in the sheet. Simply click on the cell within the notes column and type the necessary information.

2. **Formatting Notes**:
   - While Smartsheet's notes field supports plain text, you can use consistent formatting conventions (e.g., bullet points or numbering) to make notes easier to read.

3. **Updating and Editing Notes**:
   - Notes can be edited at any time to reflect changes or provide new information.

Examples of Effective Comments and Notes Usage

- **Scenario 1: Task Clarification** *Comment*: "@JaneDoe Could you provide an update on the client meeting scheduled for Friday? Also, do we need additional materials for the presentation?"

Note: "Client prefers visual-heavy slides. Ensure all graphs are updated with Q3 data."

- **Scenario 2: Status Updates** *Comment*: "The shipment is delayed due to weather. @MichaelBrown, can you inform the client about the revised timeline?" *Note*: "Revised delivery date: January 15, 2025. Awaiting confirmation from logistics."

Common Challenges and How to Address Them

1. **Overuse of Comments**:
    - Problem: Excessive comments can make it difficult to locate critical information.
    - Solution: Use notes for static information and comments for discussions. Archive old comment threads when no longer relevant.

2. **Missed Notifications**:
    - Problem: Team members might miss tagged comments if notifications are turned off.
    - Solution: Encourage team members to enable notifications and check the comments section regularly.

3. **Lack of Clarity**:
    - Problem: Vague or incomplete comments can lead to confusion.
    - Solution: Provide clear, actionable details in every comment.

Conclusion

The **Comments** and **Notes** features in Smartsheet are powerful tools for fostering collaboration and ensuring that all team members are aligned. By using these tools effectively, teams can streamline communication, enhance accountability, and keep all project-related discussions organized in one central location. Remember to use comments for dynamic conversations and notes for static, reference-worthy information. Together, these features form the foundation of efficient and effective teamwork in Smartsheet.

3.2.2 Assigning Tasks to Team Members

In Smartsheet, assigning tasks to team members is a fundamental aspect of project management. It allows you to delegate responsibilities clearly, ensure accountability, and keep everyone informed about their roles in the project. This section will guide you through the entire process of assigning tasks, provide best practices, and explain how to make the most of Smartsheet's features to optimize team collaboration.

Understanding Task Assignments in Smartsheet

Assigning tasks in Smartsheet revolves around the "Assigned To" column, which is a specialized column type designed to designate ownership of tasks. This column can be linked to team members' email addresses, enabling seamless communication and automated notifications.

- **Why Assign Tasks?** Assigning tasks ensures clarity about who is responsible for what. This reduces confusion, enhances accountability, and helps streamline workflows. It also empowers team members by providing them with a clear understanding of their responsibilities.

- **What Happens When You Assign a Task?** When a task is assigned to a team member in Smartsheet, they are automatically notified via email (if notifications are enabled). They can also see the task in their Smartsheet dashboard or email alerts, ensuring they're aware of their responsibilities.

How to Assign Tasks to Team Members

Assigning tasks in Smartsheet is straightforward. Follow these steps to assign tasks effectively:

1. **Create an "Assigned To" Column**

    - Open your sheet and navigate to the column headers.
    - Add a new column by clicking the "+" sign.
    - Choose "Contact List" as the column type. This ensures the column is optimized for task assignment and allows linking to email addresses.

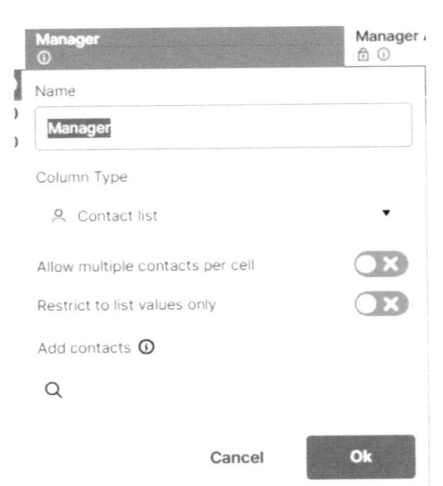

o   Name the column "Assigned To" or something similar for clarity.

2. **Add Team Members to the Contact List**

    o   In the "Assigned To" column, click on a cell and select or type the email address of the team member you want to assign the task to.

    o   Smartsheet will auto-suggest previously added contacts, or you can manually input new ones.

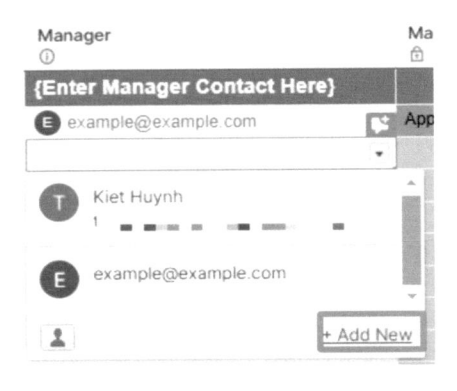

3. **Assign Tasks**

    o   Navigate to the task row you want to assign.

    o   In the "Assigned To" cell for that task, select or input the team member's email.

    o   Once assigned, the team member will receive an automated email notification (if enabled).

4. **Enable Notifications (Optional)**

    o   To ensure the assigned team member is alerted, enable notifications in the sheet settings.

    o   Go to the "Automation" tab and create a rule like "Notify someone when a task is assigned."

Advanced Task Assignment Features

Smartsheet provides additional features to enhance task assignment and tracking:

1. **Assigning Multiple Team Members**
   - In some cases, a task may require collaboration between multiple people. Smartsheet allows you to assign multiple contacts to a single task.
   - Simply separate email addresses with a comma in the "Assigned To" column.

2. **Adding Deadlines**
   - Enhance task clarity by combining task assignments with deadlines. Use the "Due Date" column to set specific timelines for each task.
   - This helps the assigned team member prioritize their workload and ensures timely completion.

3. **Color Coding Assignments**
   - Use conditional formatting to color-code tasks based on the assigned team member. For example, tasks assigned to "John Doe" can appear in blue, while those assigned to "Jane Smith" appear in green.
   - This visual aid is especially helpful for managers overseeing multiple team members.

4. **Combining Assignments with Dependencies**
   - If a task is dependent on another task's completion, use the "Predecessors" column to establish relationships.
   - This ensures that team members are aware of tasks they need to complete before others can start.

Best Practices for Assigning Tasks

To maximize productivity and collaboration, follow these best practices:

1. **Be Clear and Specific**

- When assigning a task, ensure the description is detailed and actionable. Avoid vague instructions.
- For example, instead of "Update report," specify "Update the sales report for Q1 with the latest figures."

2. **Set Realistic Deadlines**
    - Collaborate with team members to set achievable deadlines. Unrealistic timelines can lead to stress and poor performance.

3. **Communicate Context**
    - Provide the context or background for the task in the comments section. This helps the assignee understand why the task is important and how it fits into the larger project.

4. **Regularly Monitor and Follow Up**
    - Use Smartsheet's reporting and dashboard features to track task progress.
    - If a deadline is missed, follow up with the team member to identify and resolve bottlenecks.

Common Challenges and Solutions

Assigning tasks isn't always straightforward. Here are some common challenges and tips to overcome them:

1. **Challenge: Overlapping Responsibilities**
    - **Solution:** Clearly define roles and avoid assigning the same task to too many people. If collaboration is necessary, specify the role of each team member in the task description.

2. **Challenge: Miscommunication**
    - **Solution:** Use the comments feature to clarify task requirements and answer questions. Ensure team members have access to the necessary resources.

3. **Challenge: Missed Deadlines**

- **Solution:** Enable automated reminders for approaching deadlines. Regularly check the task's progress and provide support when needed.

Integrating Task Assignments with Other Smartsheet Features

1. **Task Tracking with Dashboards**
   - Create a dashboard that displays assigned tasks for each team member. Include widgets like task status, due dates, and priority levels for an at-a-glance view.

2. **Task Reporting**
   - Generate reports to summarize all tasks assigned to a specific team member. This is useful for weekly check-ins or performance reviews.

3. **Using Workspaces for Team Projects**
   - If your team is working on a large project, consider using a workspace. Assign tasks within sheets in the workspace to centralize communication and tracking.

Final Thoughts

Assigning tasks effectively in Smartsheet is a key skill for successful project management. By following these steps and best practices, you can ensure clarity, accountability, and streamlined workflows for your team. Smartsheet's powerful collaboration tools make it easy to assign tasks, monitor progress, and communicate effectively. As you continue using Smartsheet, experiment with its advanced features to customize task management for your team's specific needs.

3.2.3 Notifications and Alerts

Effective communication within a team is crucial for collaboration and project success, and notifications and alerts in Smartsheet serve as vital tools to keep everyone informed, aligned, and responsive. This section delves into the functionalities, customization options, and best practices for using notifications and alerts effectively in Smartsheet.

What Are Notifications and Alerts in Smartsheet?

Notifications and alerts are automated messages sent to users to inform them about changes, updates, or actions required in a Smartsheet. These tools ensure that critical information reaches the right people at the right time without manual follow-up. Alerts and notifications can be delivered through email, push notifications on mobile devices, or directly within the Smartsheet interface.

Notifications typically inform users of actions they need to take or updates that have occurred, such as task assignments, approaching deadlines, or completed approvals. Alerts, on the other hand, are more urgent and focus on notifying users of significant changes or issues requiring immediate attention.

Types of Notifications and Alerts in Smartsheet

1. **Row Alerts**: Row alerts notify users when a change occurs in a specific row, such as an update to a task's status, priority, or due date. These alerts are particularly useful in project management scenarios where individual tasks are assigned to team members.

2. **Column-Based Alerts**: These alerts are triggered when data in specific columns meets certain criteria, such as a deadline being marked as "overdue" or a task reaching a specific status.

3. **Reminders**: Reminders are a proactive form of notification sent before a task or milestone is due. They help ensure that team members stay on track and complete their work on time.

4. **Approval Requests**: Notifications for approval requests inform users when their input is needed to approve or reject a specific item or decision.

5. **Automated Updates**: Automated notifications are generated when certain conditions or rules are met, such as when a new row is added, or a specific cell value changes.

Setting Up Notifications and Alerts

Creating and customizing notifications and alerts in Smartsheet is straightforward, but it's essential to tailor them to your team's needs to avoid overwhelming users with unnecessary messages.

1. **Access the Automation Menu**: Navigate to the sheet where you want to set up notifications or alerts, and click on the "Automation" menu in the toolbar.

2. **Choose a Trigger Type**

    o Select a trigger that determines when the notification or alert should be sent. Common triggers include changes in rows, updates to specific columns, or approaching due dates.

    o Example: If you want to notify a team member when their task is marked "Completed," set the trigger to monitor changes in the "Status" column.

3. **Define Conditions**: Add conditions to specify when the alert should be sent. For instance, you can configure an alert to trigger only when a task's priority is marked as "High."

4. **Set Recipients**: Select who should receive the alert. Options include:

    o Specific users or groups.

    o Users mentioned in an "Assigned To" column.

    o External collaborators or stakeholders.

5. **Customize the Message**: Personalize the content of the alert to ensure clarity and relevance. Include specific details like the task name, due date, or any required actions.

6. **Test and Activate**: Preview the notification setup to confirm that it works as intended, then activate it to begin automating updates.

Best Practices for Using Notifications and Alerts

While notifications and alerts are powerful, overusing them can lead to alert fatigue, where users begin to ignore or overlook important messages. Follow these best practices to maximize their effectiveness:

1. **Keep Alerts Relevant**: Only set up notifications for critical updates or actions that require immediate attention. Avoid notifying users about every minor change.

2. **Use Clear and Actionable Language**: Ensure that the message content is concise and includes actionable instructions. For example, instead of "Task updated," use "Task X is now due tomorrow – please review."

3. **Leverage Conditional Logic**: Utilize conditions to ensure that notifications are only sent when necessary. For instance, trigger reminders for overdue tasks rather than all tasks.

4. **Group Notifications When Possible**: Instead of sending multiple notifications for every small update, consider bundling updates into a single summary email or notification.

5. **Encourage Team Members to Customize Their Settings**: Team members can tailor their notification preferences to suit their workflow, such as opting for push notifications on mobile devices for urgent updates or daily summary emails for less pressing matters.

Examples of Notifications and Alerts in Action

1. **Task Assignment Alerts**: When a new task is assigned to a team member, Smartsheet automatically sends an email notification with details about the task, its due date, and any attached files or comments.

2. **Project Status Updates**: A project manager sets up an alert to notify stakeholders whenever the overall project status changes to "Delayed" or "On Hold."

3. **Deadline Reminders**: Team members receive reminders two days before a task's due date, ensuring they allocate enough time to complete their work.

4. **Budget Threshold Warnings**: Finance teams use column-based alerts to monitor budget thresholds. For example, when the "Spent" column exceeds 80% of the allocated budget, an alert is sent to the project manager.

Troubleshooting Notification Issues

Occasionally, team members may encounter issues with notifications. Here's how to address common problems:

1. **Missing Notifications**
    - Verify that the recipient's email address is correct.
    - Ensure the user's email provider isn't filtering Smartsheet notifications into the spam or junk folder.
2. **Duplicate Notifications**
    - Review the automation rules to ensure that overlapping triggers aren't causing duplicate messages.
3. **Overwhelming Alerts**
    - Adjust the frequency or scope of notifications to reduce the volume of updates.

Conclusion

Notifications and alerts in Smartsheet are essential tools for ensuring seamless communication and accountability within a team. By setting up tailored alerts and following best practices, you can keep your team informed, minimize delays, and enhance overall collaboration. Start experimenting with these features today to see how they can simplify your project management efforts!

3.3 Version Control and History

3.3.1 Accessing Revision History

Smartsheet provides a robust feature called "Revision History," which enables users to track changes made to sheets over time. This functionality is critical for maintaining transparency, ensuring accountability, and easily reverting unintended modifications. Whether you're collaborating on a project with a team or managing a sheet on your own, the Revision History can help you monitor and manage changes efficiently. In this section, we'll explore the importance of Revision History, how to access it, and practical scenarios where it can be invaluable.

What is Revision History?

Revision History in Smartsheet is a feature that logs and displays all changes made to a sheet. It records updates such as data entry, column modifications, and structural changes like adding or removing rows. This log includes details about who made the change, what was modified, and when the change occurred. With this detailed information, teams can ensure accountability and avoid confusion when collaborating.

Key benefits of Revision History include:

- **Tracking Changes**: Understand who made specific edits and why.
- **Reverting Mistakes**: Restore a previous version of the sheet if an error was made.
- **Improving Collaboration**: Encourage accountability by showing a clear record of contributions.

Why Use Revision History?

For any collaborative tool, managing and tracking changes is essential. Revision History in Smartsheet plays a significant role in improving the workflow of teams and ensuring data integrity. Let's break down some of the key reasons to use this feature:

1. **Error Recovery**: Mistakes are inevitable in any collaborative environment. A collaborator might delete crucial data, overwrite important content, or

misconfigure automation rules. Revision History allows you to identify these errors and revert to an earlier version of the sheet.

2. **Accountability**
Knowing who made a change and when it occurred can eliminate confusion in collaborative projects. This is particularly useful when working with large teams where multiple individuals are making edits.

3. **Audit and Compliance**: Many industries require a clear audit trail for compliance purposes. Revision History provides an easy way to track all changes, ensuring compliance with industry standards and regulations.

4. **Improved Communication**: Revision History facilitates better communication among team members by making it easier to identify the changes and contributions made by each individual.

How to Access Revision History

Accessing the Revision History in Smartsheet is a straightforward process. Follow these steps to view the change log for any sheet:

1. **Open the Sheet**: Begin by opening the Smartsheet you want to review. Ensure you have the appropriate permissions to view Revision History. Typically, sheet owners and collaborators with edit permissions can access this feature.

2. **Click on the "File" Menu**: In the top-left corner of the sheet interface, click the **"File"** menu to reveal a dropdown list of options.

3. **Select "View Activity Log"**: From the dropdown menu, choose the **" View Activity Log "** option. This will open a panel displaying the sheet's Revision History.

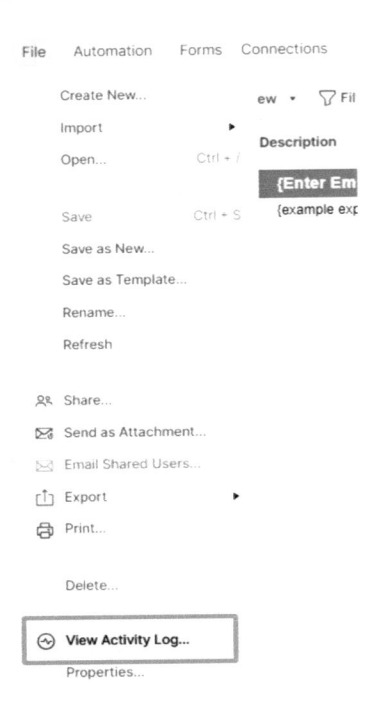

4. **Browse Through Changes**: The Revision History panel lists all changes chronologically, with the most recent changes displayed at the top. Each entry includes:

    o **Timestamp**: When the change occurred.

    o **Editor**: The user who made the change.

    o **Description**: Details of the change (e.g., "Row added," "Data updated").

![Activity Log screenshot]

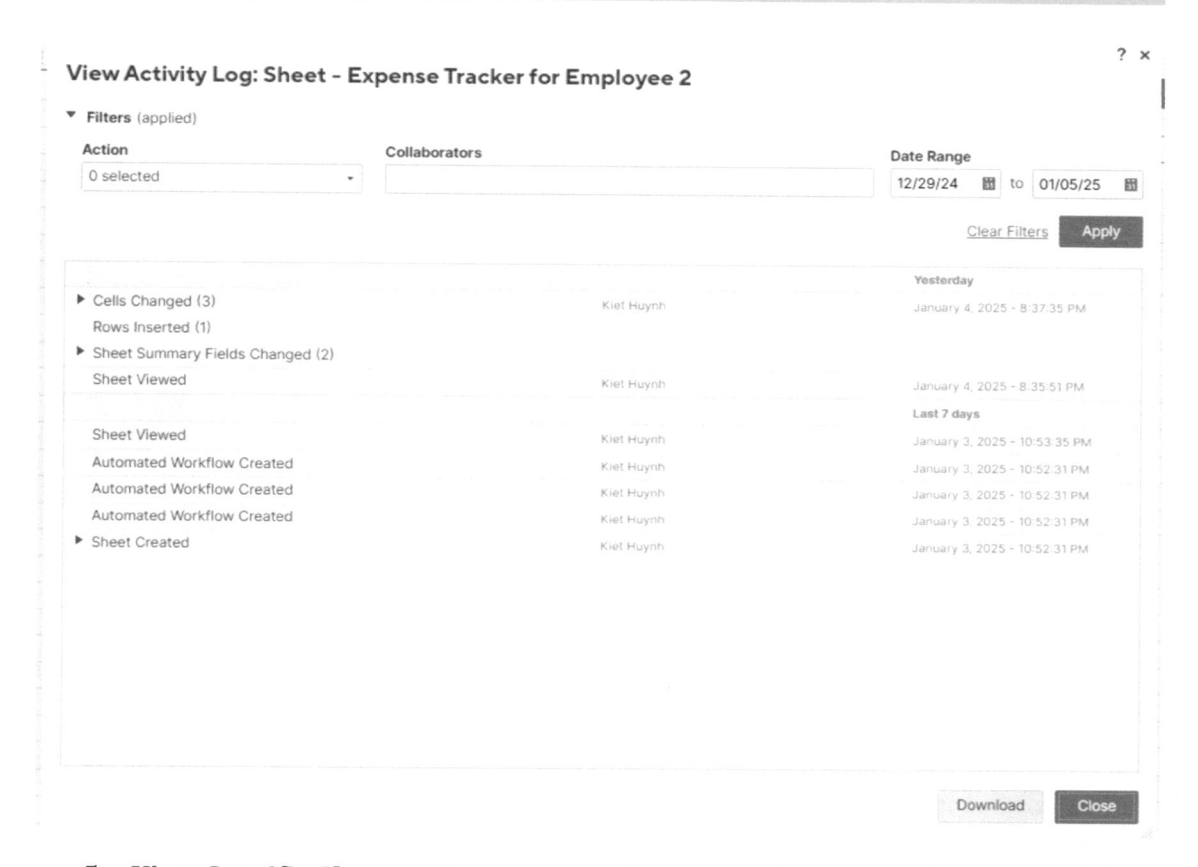

5. **View Specific Changes**: To get more information about a specific change, click on the entry in the Revision History. Smartsheet highlights the change directly on the sheet, allowing you to see exactly what was modified.

Best Practices for Using Revision History

While the Revision History feature is a powerful tool, using it effectively requires some best practices:

1. **Regular Monitoring**: Periodically check the Revision History, especially in sheets with high activity levels. This ensures you remain aware of all changes and can address potential issues promptly.

2. **Document Significant Changes**: For major updates, consider adding a comment or note within the sheet to explain the purpose of the change. This adds context to the Revision History and improves communication among team members.

3. **Set Permissions Wisely**: Limit editing permissions to essential collaborators. This reduces the likelihood of unintended changes and makes the Revision History easier to navigate.

4. **Use Filters**: Smartsheet allows you to filter the Revision History by specific dates or users. Use this feature to narrow down your search when investigating a particular issue.

5. **Communicate with Team Members**: When reverting to a previous version or addressing changes, inform the team members involved. Transparency ensures everyone stays on the same page and avoids confusion.

Practical Scenarios for Revision History

To better understand the value of Revision History, let's explore a few scenarios where this feature proves indispensable:

Scenario 1: Recovering Deleted Data: Imagine a team member accidentally deletes a critical row containing project deadlines. By accessing the Revision History, you can identify when the deletion occurred and restore the data to its previous state.

Scenario 2: Resolving Disputes: Two collaborators might disagree about when and why a particular change was made. Revision History provides a definitive record, helping resolve the dispute objectively.

Scenario 3: Auditing for Compliance: For organizations in regulated industries, maintaining a detailed record of changes is essential. Revision History simplifies audits by providing a transparent log of all modifications.

Scenario 4: Learning from Mistakes: Suppose a formula was incorrectly altered, causing calculation errors across the sheet. By reviewing the Revision History, you can pinpoint the source of the error, correct it, and communicate best practices to the team.

Conclusion

The Revision History feature in Smartsheet is a vital tool for ensuring data accuracy, accountability, and effective collaboration. By providing a detailed log of changes, it empowers users to recover from mistakes, resolve disputes, and maintain an organized workflow. Whether you're working solo or as part of a team, mastering this feature can greatly enhance your Smartsheet experience.

In the next section, **3.3.2 Restoring Previous Versions**, we'll dive deeper into how to use the Revision History to revert your sheet to an earlier state and explore strategies for minimizing disruption during this process.

3.3.2 Restoring Previous Versions

In any collaborative environment, maintaining data accuracy and preventing mistakes is crucial. Smartsheet's version control feature is a lifesaver, allowing users to restore previous versions of a sheet in case of accidental deletions, unintended edits, or even corrupted data. This section will walk you through the importance, the step-by-step process, and the best practices for restoring previous versions in Smartsheet.

Why Restore Previous Versions?

Restoring previous versions can be critical in several scenarios:

1. **Accidental Changes**: Team members may unintentionally overwrite important data, delete rows, or make incorrect edits. Having the ability to roll back changes ensures no valuable information is permanently lost.

2. **Testing and Experimentation**: During the trial phase of a project, you might implement new formulas or workflows. If these changes do not work as intended, reverting to a previous version ensures that you don't lose progress.

3. **Collaboration Missteps**: In collaborative projects, multiple people may edit the sheet simultaneously, which increases the risk of conflicting changes. Version control helps mitigate such issues.

4. **Audit and Compliance**: Some organizations are required to maintain historical records of changes for compliance purposes. Restoring older versions ensures the availability of necessary data for audits.

Understanding Version Control in Smartsheet

Smartsheet automatically saves changes made to a sheet, creating a record of every significant update. While it doesn't maintain an infinite record of every minor change, it provides access to key milestones in your sheet's history.

Key Points About Version Control:

- Smartsheet saves a version whenever major changes occur (e.g., adding/deleting multiple rows, significant column updates).

- Historical versions are stored for 30 days (or longer, depending on your Smartsheet plan).

- You can restore entire sheets or retrieve specific data manually from the previous version.

How to Restore Previous Versions in Smartsheet

Follow these steps to restore a previous version of your sheet:

1. **Access the Sheet History**

    o Open the sheet you want to restore.

    o Click on the **Menu** (three-dot icon) in the upper right corner of your sheet.

    o Select **View History** from the dropdown menu.

2. **Browse Through Version History**

    o The version history window will open, displaying a list of past versions.

    o Each version is tagged with a **timestamp** and the **name of the user** who made the changes.

    o Click on any version to preview its contents. This helps you confirm which version to restore.

3. **Preview the Version**

- When you click a version, a detailed view of the sheet as it appeared at that time is displayed.
- Carefully review the data, ensuring it matches the version you need.

4. **Restore the Version**
    - Once you've identified the correct version, click the **Restore** button.
    - Smartsheet will prompt you to confirm your choice. Restoring will replace the current sheet with the older version.
    - After restoration, the replaced version becomes the new "current" version, and you can continue making edits as usual.

Best Practices for Restoring Previous Versions

To use the version restoration feature effectively, consider these best practices:

1. **Communicate with Your Team**: Before restoring a previous version, inform all collaborators. Abruptly overwriting the current version might disrupt ongoing work. Discuss with the team to ensure restoration is necessary and agree on the version to be restored.

2. **Backup the Current Version**: Always create a backup of the current version before restoring an older one.
    - Download the current version as an Excel file or save it as a new sheet within Smartsheet.
    - This ensures you have a fallback option if the restored version is not as expected.

3. **Identify the Correct Version**: Avoid restoring multiple versions unnecessarily. Preview the history carefully to locate the most accurate version for your needs.

4. **Use Notes or Descriptions**: When restoring a version, include notes or comments explaining why the restoration was performed. This is especially useful for audit trails or if other team members need to understand the context of changes.

5. **Minimize Disruption**: If possible, schedule restoration during non-peak hours to avoid interruptions to your team's workflow.

Limitations of Restoring Versions

While the version restoration feature is powerful, it's important to be aware of its limitations:

- **Timeframe for Version History**: Smartsheet retains version history for a limited time (typically 30 days). If you need to maintain older records, consider exporting data regularly.

- **Partial Restoration**: Smartsheet does not support partial restorations (e.g., restoring specific rows or columns). To recover specific data, you might need to manually copy it from the older version.

- **Loss of Current Edits**: When a previous version is restored, all current edits are overwritten. Always ensure recent changes are not critical or are backed up elsewhere.

Case Study: Practical Example

Scenario: A project team working on a marketing campaign accidentally deletes an important set of data while restructuring their sheet.

Steps Taken:

1. The team accesses the version history and identifies the version from the previous day when the data was intact.

2. Before restoring, they export the current version as a backup to avoid losing recent updates unrelated to the deleted data.

3. They restore the older version and manually integrate recent changes from the backup.

4. Moving forward, they implement naming conventions and better collaboration protocols to avoid future errors.

Outcome: The restored version saves the team hours of work, and the incident highlights the importance of utilizing Smartsheet's collaborative tools effectively.

Tips for Preventing the Need to Restore Versions

1. **Use Locked Columns or Rows**: Lock critical sections of your sheet to prevent accidental edits by team members.

2. **Enable Notifications**: Set up alerts for significant changes to be informed about edits in real-time.

3. **Implement Access Controls**: Restrict editing permissions for collaborators who only need to view or comment on data.

Conclusion

Restoring previous versions in Smartsheet is an indispensable feature for maintaining data integrity and resolving errors in collaborative environments. By understanding how to navigate version history and implementing best practices, you can ensure a smooth and efficient workflow for your team. Always remember to back up your data, communicate with collaborators, and take preventive measures to minimize disruptions.

3.3.3 Best Practices for Collaboration

Collaboration is a cornerstone of effective project management, and Smartsheet offers a robust set of tools to facilitate seamless teamwork. However, the true power of these tools comes from adopting best practices that ensure smooth and efficient collaboration among team members. This section explores essential strategies for leveraging Smartsheet's collaboration features to maximize productivity and minimize errors.

---

1. Define Clear Roles and Responsibilities

Before diving into a project, it's essential to assign clear roles and responsibilities to each collaborator. Smartsheet allows you to specify who can edit, view, or comment on a sheet, making it easier to control access and avoid confusion.

Tips for Defining Roles:

- **Owner:** Assign one person as the sheet owner who will have full control over the content, structure, and permissions. This ensures accountability for the overall project.

- **Editors:** Grant editing permissions to team members responsible for updating specific sections. Be sure to communicate their specific areas of responsibility to avoid overlapping efforts.

- **Viewers:** For stakeholders or team members who need to stay informed but don't require editing capabilities, set their access to "View Only."

Practical Example: If you're managing a marketing campaign, assign roles such as "Content Lead" for editing the content calendar, "Graphic Designer" for updating design tasks, and "Campaign Manager" as the sheet owner to oversee the entire workflow.

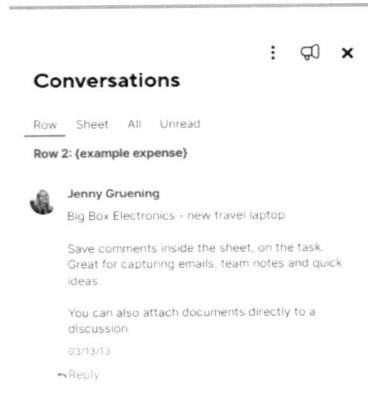

2. Use Comments to Centralize Communication

One of the biggest challenges in collaboration is managing scattered conversations across emails, messaging apps, and meetings. Smartsheet's comment feature centralizes communication within the sheet, keeping discussions tied to specific tasks or rows.

How to Use Comments Effectively:

• **Be Specific:** When leaving a comment, tag the relevant team member (@username) and clearly describe the issue or request.

• **Attach Files:** Use the attachment feature to provide context, such as images, documents, or other supporting files.

• **Follow Up:** Regularly check the "Comments" section to ensure all queries are addressed promptly.

Best Practice: Avoid using comments for unrelated or lengthy discussions. Instead, keep comments concise and focused on actionable items related to the sheet.

3. Regularly Review Revision History

Version control is critical for maintaining data integrity in collaborative environments. Smartsheet's revision history feature allows you to track changes, identify who made updates, and revert to previous versions if necessary.

Tips for Managing Revision History:

- **Audit Regularly:** Schedule weekly or bi-weekly reviews of the revision history to ensure the sheet's data remains accurate and relevant.

- **Identify Patterns:** Use the history log to identify recurring errors or areas where team members may need additional training.

- **Revert with Caution:** Before reverting to a previous version, communicate with the team to confirm the need for this action and document the reason for the change.

4. Maintain a Consistent Structure Across Sheets

Consistency is key to successful collaboration, especially when managing multiple projects or workspaces. By standardizing the structure and layout of your Smartsheet projects, team members can easily navigate and understand the workflow.

Best Practices for Consistency:

- **Use Templates:** Create and share templates for common projects, such as project timelines, task trackers, or resource plans.

- **Follow Naming Conventions:** Establish clear naming conventions for sheets, columns, and files to make searching and filtering data easier.

- **Standardize Columns:** Use uniform column names and types (e.g., "Assigned To," "Due Date," "Priority") across sheets for a consistent user experience.

5. Set up Automated Notifications and Alerts

Automation can significantly enhance collaboration by reducing the need for manual follow-ups and reminders. Smartsheet offers robust automation tools to keep everyone informed about updates and deadlines.

How to Use Automation for Collaboration:

- **Reminders:** Schedule reminders for upcoming deadlines or overdue tasks to ensure accountability.
- **Alerts:** Set up alerts for when changes are made to critical sections of the sheet, such as budget updates or project milestones.
- **Approval Requests:** Use automated approval workflows to streamline decision-making processes.

Example Scenario: In a product development project, you can automate notifications to alert the design team when the marketing team updates the product specifications.

6. Foster Transparency with Dashboards and Reports

Transparency is essential for building trust and alignment within a team. Dashboards and reports in Smartsheet can provide collaborators with real-time insights into the project's progress.

Best Practices for Dashboards and Reports:

- **Create Role-Specific Dashboards:** Tailor dashboards for different roles, such as team members, managers, or external stakeholders, to provide relevant information.
- **Highlight Key Metrics:** Use charts, graphs, and KPIs to focus on critical data points like task completion rates or budget usage.
- **Update Frequently:** Ensure that dashboards and reports reflect the latest data by linking them to live sheets.

7. Document Collaboration Guidelines

To avoid misunderstandings and ensure smooth teamwork, document collaboration guidelines and share them with all contributors.

What to Include in Collaboration Guidelines:

- **Communication Protocols:** Define when to use comments versus emails or meetings.
- **Update Schedules:** Establish regular times for updating the sheet (e.g., daily by 5 PM).
- **Conflict Resolution:** Outline how to address conflicts or discrepancies in data entries.

8. Encourage Regular Feedback

Collaboration is an evolving process, and feedback helps teams identify opportunities for improvement.

Strategies for Gathering Feedback:

- **Schedule Check-Ins:** Hold weekly or bi-weekly meetings to review the sheet and address any issues.
- **Use Surveys:** Collect anonymous feedback on the usability of the sheet and collaboration processes.
- **Iterate and Improve:** Continuously refine your sheets and workflows based on feedback.

Conclusion

Adopting best practices for collaboration in Smartsheet not only improves efficiency but also strengthens team dynamics. By defining roles, centralizing communication, leveraging automation, and fostering transparency, you can create a collaborative environment that empowers your team to achieve its goals. With these strategies, Smartsheet becomes not just a tool, but a cornerstone of your team's success.

CHAPTER IV
Automating Your Workflows

4.1 Introduction to Automation in Smartsheet

4.1.1 Why Automate?

Automation has become an essential tool in modern work environments, and Smartsheet offers a suite of features to streamline repetitive tasks, enhance productivity, and reduce human error. Whether you're managing a project, tracking deliverables, or coordinating across teams, automation allows you to focus on what truly matters: strategy, creativity, and problem-solving. In this section, we'll dive into the key reasons why automating your workflows in Smartsheet is a game-changer.

1. Save Time and Reduce Repetitive Work

Manual tasks can be a significant drain on your time and energy. Think about activities like sending reminders, updating statuses, or tracking deadlines—these are repetitive yet critical components of any workflow. Without automation, these tasks require constant attention and manual effort.

Smartsheet automation eliminates the need to micromanage these repetitive tasks. For instance, setting up an automated notification can ensure that team members are alerted when their tasks are due, freeing you from having to send emails or messages manually. Similarly, approvals that once required multiple follow-ups can now be handled automatically.

By saving time, you can allocate resources to higher-value activities, such as strategic planning, team building, or innovating new ideas. Automating small yet repetitive processes allows you to scale your workflows without adding unnecessary effort or overhead.

2. Minimize Human Error

No matter how diligent your team is, manual workflows are prone to human error. Forgetting to send a critical email, overlooking a deadline, or making mistakes in data entry are all risks associated with manual processes. These errors can cause delays, damage relationships with stakeholders, and even lead to financial losses.

With automation, Smartsheet ensures that processes run smoothly and consistently. Automated workflows don't forget deadlines, skip tasks, or misinterpret instructions. For example:

- Notifications and reminders ensure tasks are not missed.
- Approval workflows guarantee that requests are routed to the right people without errors.
- Conditional logic ensures that specific actions are triggered only when predefined criteria are met.

By relying on automation to handle routine processes, you reduce the likelihood of errors and build more robust, reliable workflows.

3. Enhance Team Collaboration and Accountability

In team settings, keeping everyone on the same page can be challenging. Miscommunication, missed updates, and a lack of transparency are common issues that can derail projects. Automation fosters better collaboration by creating a shared system of accountability.

Here are some ways automation in Smartsheet enhances collaboration:

- Automated task assignments: When a task moves to the next phase, Smartsheet can automatically assign it to the appropriate team member.
- Status updates: Automation can notify the team when a task is completed or when changes are made to the project timeline.
- Alerts for dependencies: If one task depends on another, automation ensures that team members are notified when dependencies are completed, keeping workflows moving seamlessly.

With these features, everyone is aware of their responsibilities and can stay updated on the project's progress, reducing bottlenecks and improving efficiency.

4. Improve Workflow Consistency and Scalability

One of the biggest challenges for growing teams and businesses is maintaining consistency in workflows. As the volume of tasks increases, manual processes can become unmanageable, leading to inconsistencies and inefficiencies.

Smartsheet automation ensures that workflows are executed consistently every time. For example:

- Approval requests are always routed to the correct approver, regardless of project size.
- Standardized templates ensure that processes follow the same structure and sequence across teams.
- Alerts and updates occur at predictable intervals, ensuring no steps are skipped.

Automation also makes scaling your workflows easier. As your projects grow, automated rules can handle the increased workload without additional resources. Whether you're managing a team of five or a global operation, Smartsheet provides the tools to scale your processes efficiently.

5. Increase Productivity and Focus on Strategic Tasks

Time-consuming, repetitive tasks can prevent teams from focusing on their core responsibilities. When team members spend too much time on administrative work, their productivity and creativity suffer.

By automating these routine processes, Smartsheet enables your team to focus on strategic priorities, such as:

- Developing innovative solutions
- Strengthening client relationships
- Improving team dynamics and communication

For example, instead of manually tracking task completion, a manager can set up automated workflows to monitor progress and receive updates. This allows them to spend more time on performance reviews, coaching, and team development.

6. Build Smarter, Data-Driven Workflows

Data is at the heart of every successful project. However, manually managing and analyzing data can be cumbersome. Automation in Smartsheet not only saves time but also ensures that your data is accurate and actionable.

For example:

- Automating data collection through forms ensures that input is consistent and error-free.

- Using automated reports, you can aggregate data from multiple sheets to get a real-time view of your project's performance.

- Alerts and reminders ensure that critical data points are not overlooked.

Automation allows you to make informed decisions based on real-time insights, empowering you to take proactive steps to keep your projects on track.

7. Ensure Compliance and Standardization

Many industries require strict compliance with policies, regulations, or standards. Manual processes can leave room for inconsistencies, which may lead to non-compliance.

Smartsheet automation helps ensure that workflows adhere to established standards. For example:

- Automating approval workflows ensures that requests are reviewed by the appropriate authority.

- Compliance checklists can be integrated into workflows to ensure all necessary steps are followed.

- Audit trails provide a history of all automated actions, offering transparency and accountability.

With these features, automation minimizes the risks associated with non-compliance and ensures that your processes meet regulatory requirements.

8. Adapt to a Hybrid and Remote Work Environment

In today's hybrid and remote work setups, automation is critical to maintaining productivity and communication across distributed teams. Without automation, it can be challenging to coordinate tasks, share updates, and maintain transparency.

Smartsheet automation ensures that remote and hybrid teams stay connected and aligned by:

- Automatically sending updates to team members, regardless of time zones.
- Creating shared dashboards to track project progress in real time.
- Generating reminders and notifications to ensure everyone is on track.

By automating workflows, you create a system where team members can focus on their work without worrying about coordination or communication gaps.

Conclusion

Automation is not just a convenience—it's a necessity in today's fast-paced work environments. By saving time, reducing errors, and enhancing collaboration, Smartsheet automation empowers teams to work smarter, not harder. Whether you're managing a small project or a complex operation, automation ensures that your workflows are efficient, scalable, and consistent.

In the next section, we'll explore **Automation Basics**, providing you with the foundational knowledge to start building automated workflows in Smartsheet. Let's get started!

4.1.2 Automation Basics

Automation in Smartsheet is a powerful feature designed to streamline your workflows, reduce manual tasks, and save time. By automating repetitive actions, you can focus on higher-value tasks and ensure your projects run smoothly without constant manual oversight. In this section, we'll cover the essential components of automation in Smartsheet, including triggers, actions, and conditions, as well as provide step-by-step guidance on how to create your first automated workflow.

What is Automation in Smartsheet?

Automation in Smartsheet refers to a set of tools and rules that allow you to automatically perform certain actions based on specific triggers. Whether it's sending notifications, updating data, or requesting approvals, automation ensures tasks are executed consistently without human intervention.

For example, if a task's due date is approaching, Smartsheet can automatically notify the assigned team member. Similarly, when a form is submitted, Smartsheet can create a new row in your sheet and alert the relevant person.

By understanding the basics of how automation works, you can simplify complex processes and achieve more efficiency in your projects.

Key Components of Automation

Automation in Smartsheet is built on three key components: triggers, actions, and conditions. Let's break each of these down in detail:

1. **Triggers**
   A trigger is the event that starts the automation. Triggers are the "when" in your automation rule. Examples of triggers include:

   - When a new row is added to a sheet.
   - When a specific date is reached (e.g., a due date or a reminder date).
   - When a row is updated (e.g., status changes to "Completed").

2. **Actions**
   Actions are the tasks Smartsheet performs once the trigger occurs. Actions are the "what" in your automation rule. Examples of actions include:

   - Sending an alert to a team member.
   - Requesting approval for a task.

- Moving or copying rows to another sheet.
- Changing cell values or updating statuses.

3. **Conditions**
Conditions are optional filters that refine when actions should be performed. Conditions are the "if" in your automation rule. For example:

- Perform the action **only if** the task status is "In Progress."
- Send an alert **only if** the assigned person is the team leader.

By combining these components, you can create dynamic and highly customizable automation workflows.

How to Access Automation Tools in Smartsheet

Smartsheet provides a user-friendly interface for creating and managing automation rules. Follow these steps to access and start working with automation tools:

1. Open the sheet where you want to set up automation.
2. Click the **Automation** menu at the top of your screen.
3. Select **Manage Rules** to view existing rules or create new ones.
4. Use the **Create Rule** button to start building a new automation.

The automation builder interface is intuitive, with guided options for choosing triggers, actions, and conditions.

Setting Up Your First Automation Rule

Let's walk through a simple example of setting up an automation rule: sending a notification when a task's due date is approaching.

CHAPTER IV: AUTOMATING YOUR WORKFLOWS

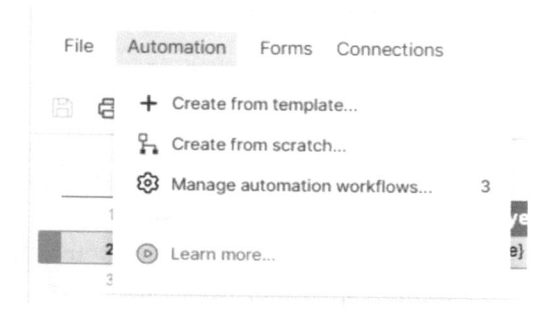

1. **Step 1: Define the Trigger**

    o Go to the **Automation** menu and select **Create From scratch**.

    o Choose the trigger: "When a date is reached."

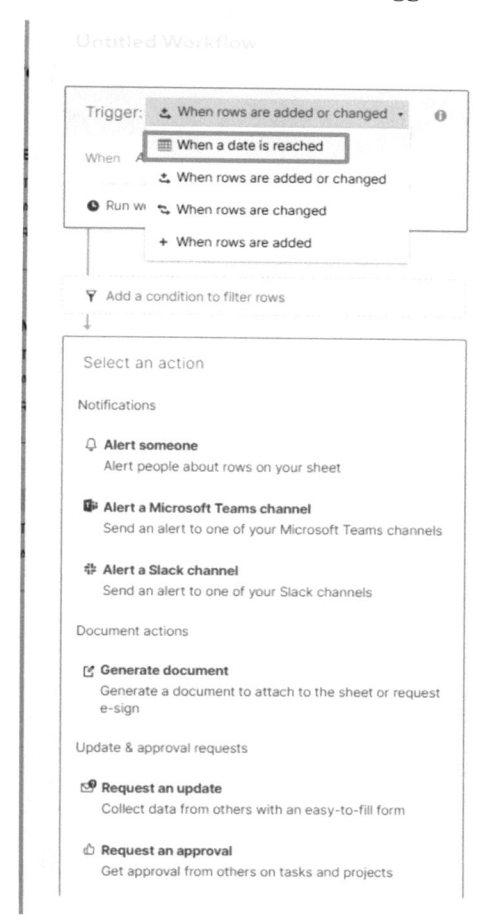

- Specify the date column in your sheet (e.g., "Due Date").
- Set the timing for the trigger, such as "1 day before the due date."

2. **Step 2: Define the Action**
    - Select the action: "Send an alert."
    - Choose the recipients for the alert. You can select a specific team member, the person listed in the "Assigned To" column, or an external email address.
    - Customize the message to include relevant details, such as the task name, due date, and priority level.

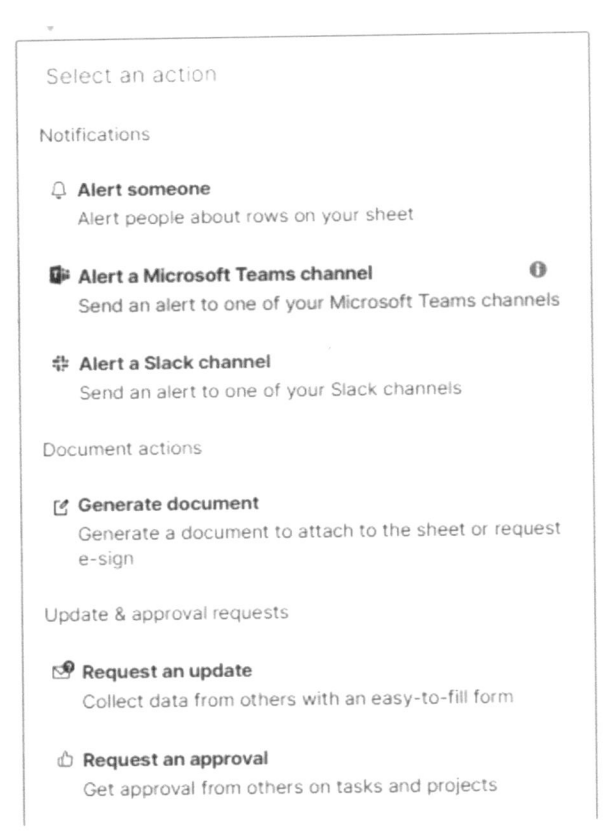

```
Select an action

Notifications

🔔 Alert someone
   Alert people about rows on your sheet

📢 Alert a Microsoft Teams channel                    ⓘ
   Send an alert to one of your Microsoft Teams channels

# Alert a Slack channel
   Send an alert to one of your Slack channels

Document actions

📝 Generate document
   Generate a document to attach to the sheet or request
   e-sign

Update & approval requests

💬 Request an update
   Collect data from others with an easy-to-fill form

👍 Request an approval
   Get approval from others on tasks and projects
```

3. **Step 3: Add Conditions (Optional)**
    - If you only want the notification to be sent for high-priority tasks, add a condition: "Priority = High."

4. **Step 4: Save and Activate**
   - Review your rule and click **Save**.
   - Activate the rule, and Smartsheet will begin executing it immediately.

Best Practices for Creating Automation

To maximize the efficiency of your automation workflows, consider the following best practices:

1. **Start Simple**: If you're new to automation, begin with straightforward rules such as sending notifications or updating statuses. As you become more comfortable, you can experiment with advanced features like multiple conditions or cross-sheet automation.

2. **Use Clear Naming Conventions**: Name your automation rules descriptively, such as "Notify Assigned Person - 1 Day Before Due Date." This makes it easier to manage and troubleshoot rules later.

3. **Test Your Rules**: Before relying on automation for critical tasks, test your rules to ensure they work as intended. Use sample data to simulate triggers and verify that the actions execute correctly.

4. **Avoid Overlapping Rules**: Be cautious about creating multiple rules that could conflict or trigger the same action. For example, two rules that update the same cell value could result in unexpected outcomes.

5. **Monitor and Adjust**: Regularly review your automation rules to ensure they are still relevant and effective. Deactivate or update outdated rules as your workflows evolve.

Examples of Common Automation Use Cases

Here are some common scenarios where automation can significantly improve efficiency:

1. **Task Reminders**: Send automatic reminders to team members as task deadlines approach or when tasks are overdue.

2. **Approval Requests**: Automatically request approvals for project milestones, budget changes, or deliverables.

3. **Status Updates**: Automatically update task statuses based on changes in other fields (e.g., when "Percent Complete" reaches 100%, update status to "Completed").

4. **Row Movement**: Move rows to a different sheet when tasks are completed, such as archiving finished projects or transferring issues to a resolution tracker.

5. **Cross-Sheet Data Sync**: Link data across multiple sheets and automate updates to ensure consistency. For example, when a sales order is marked as "Fulfilled" in one sheet, update the inventory status in another sheet.

Advanced Features to Explore

Once you're comfortable with the basics, you can explore advanced automation features in Smartsheet:

1. **Multi-Step Automation**: Combine multiple actions in a single rule, such as sending notifications and updating statuses simultaneously.

2. **Cross-Sheet Automation**: Create rules that span multiple sheets, enabling seamless data synchronization across your workspace.

3. **Integration with External Tools**: Use Smartsheet's integration capabilities to trigger automation based on external events, such as form submissions or CRM updates.

4. **Workflow Insights**: Leverage Smartsheet's reporting tools to monitor the performance of your automated workflows and identify opportunities for further optimization.

Conclusion

Automation in Smartsheet is a game-changer for anyone looking to reduce manual tasks and improve efficiency. By understanding the basics of triggers, actions, and conditions, you can start creating powerful automation workflows tailored to your specific needs. As you gain experience, you'll unlock even greater potential by exploring advanced features and integrating Smartsheet with other tools in your workflow.

Take some time to experiment with the automation tools in your own projects. You'll be amazed at how much time and effort you can save by letting Smartsheet handle the repetitive tasks for you.

4.2 Creating Automation Rules

4.2.1 Setting Up Alerts and Notifications

Automation is a key feature in Smartsheet that allows users to stay informed, streamline communication, and enhance collaboration. Among the most practical and widely used automation tools are alerts and notifications. These features ensure that the right people are informed about updates, changes, or tasks that require attention in a timely manner. In this section, we'll explore how to set up alerts and notifications, the different types available, and tips for effectively using them in your workflows.

What Are Alerts and Notifications in Smartsheet?

Alerts and notifications are automated messages triggered by specific actions or conditions within a sheet. These messages can be sent via email, push notifications, or directly within Smartsheet, keeping all team members informed without requiring manual updates.

- **Alerts**: Notifications triggered by specific changes in the sheet, such as the completion of a task, an updated status, or a due date approaching.
- **Notifications**: Messages sent when a change directly impacts a user, such as being assigned a task or added to a sheet.

Both alerts and notifications ensure that users are aware of key developments, reducing the risk of missed deadlines or overlooked updates.

How to Set Up Alerts and Notifications in Smartsheet

Setting up alerts and notifications in Smartsheet is a straightforward process. Here's a step-by-step guide to help you get started:

Step 1: Access Automation Options

1. Open the Smartsheet sheet you want to automate.
2. Click on the **Automation** tab located in the toolbar.

3. From the dropdown menu, select **Create From scratch**. This will open the automation editor where you can define the rules for alerts and notifications.

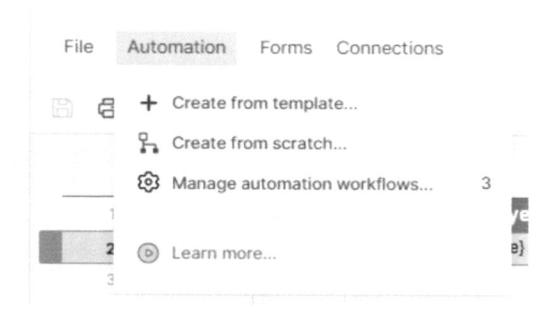

Step 2: Choose a Trigger for Alerts

A trigger is the condition that activates the alert or notification. Common triggers include:

- **When a row is added or updated**: Ideal for tracking changes made to the sheet.
- **When a date is reached**: Perfect for reminding team members about upcoming deadlines.
- **When a specific condition is met**: Useful for monitoring status changes, such as when a task is marked as "Complete" or "In Progress."

For example, if you want to notify your team when a task's due date is within three days, select "When a date is reached" as your trigger.

Step 3: Define Conditions

Conditions refine the trigger by specifying which rows or data points should activate the alert. You can set conditions such as:

- **Specific column values**: For instance, send an alert only when the status column is set to "Pending."
- **Row-level changes**: Notify users only when changes are made to specific rows or columns.

To add conditions:

1. Click on **Add Condition** in the automation editor.
2. Define the criteria, such as "Status is not Complete" or "Priority is High."

Step 4: Specify Recipients

Decide who will receive the alert or notification. Smartsheet allows flexibility in assigning recipients:

- **Specific users or groups**: Notify individuals or teams responsible for the task.
- **Dynamic recipients**: Use cell-linked contacts to notify people listed in a specific column, such as an "Assigned To" column.
- **External recipients**: Notify people outside your Smartsheet account, such as clients or vendors.

To assign recipients:

1. Click on **Alert Specific People** or **Notify Specific People** in the workflow editor.
2. Choose recipients from the list or select a contact column.

Step 5: Customize the Message

Customizing the message ensures clarity and relevance. Smartsheet allows you to:

- **Add a subject line**: Make it concise and informative, such as "Upcoming Due Date: Task XYZ."
- **Include dynamic fields**: Personalize the message by including data from the sheet, such as task names, deadlines, or comments.
- **Add instructions**: Provide context or next steps, such as "Please review and mark as complete."

To customize the message:

1. Click on the **Customize Message** option.
2. Edit the subject and body of the notification to include relevant details.

Step 6: Test and Save the Workflow

Once you've configured the alert or notification, test the workflow to ensure it behaves as expected:

1. Use sample data or trigger the condition manually.

2. Check whether recipients receive the notification correctly.

After testing, click **Save** to activate the workflow. You can revisit and edit it anytime by going to the **Automation** tab.

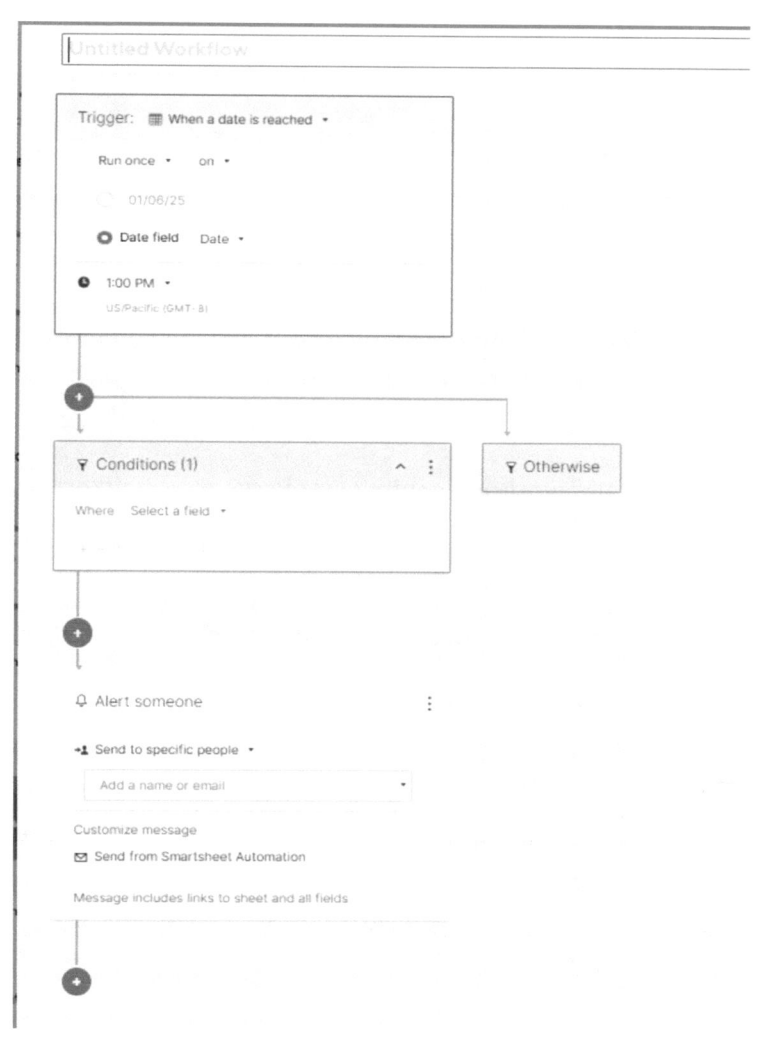

Best Practices for Setting Up Alerts and Notifications

While alerts and notifications are powerful, overusing them can lead to notification fatigue. Follow these best practices to ensure they remain effective:

1. Prioritize Key Updates

Focus on alerts for critical updates, such as deadlines, status changes, or approvals. Avoid triggering notifications for minor updates that don't require immediate attention.

2. Use Dynamic Recipients

Leverage contact columns to ensure notifications are sent to the right person without manual intervention. For example, if a task is reassigned, the alert will automatically go to the new assignee.

3. Schedule Digest Alerts

For non-urgent updates, consider scheduling a daily or weekly summary instead of real-time notifications. This reduces distractions and keeps recipients focused.

4. Test for Accuracy

Before rolling out alerts to the team, test the workflows with sample data to avoid errors or misdirected messages.

5. Monitor Workflow Performance

Regularly review and refine automation rules to ensure they align with changing project needs.

Examples of Alerts and Notifications in Action

Here are some practical examples to demonstrate how alerts and notifications can improve workflow management:

1. **Task Deadline Reminder**:
   Trigger: When a task's due date is within 3 days.
   Recipient: Assigned team member.

Message: "Reminder: The deadline for Task XYZ is approaching in 3 days. Please review and update progress."

2. **Status Change Notification**:
   Trigger: When the status changes to "Complete."
   Recipient: Project Manager.
   Message: "Task ABC has been marked as complete. Review the task for final approval."

3. **Approval Request**
   Trigger: When a new row is added to the "Approval" column.
   Recipient: Approver listed in the contact column.
   Message: "A new task requires your approval. Please review and confirm."

Common Issues and How to Resolve Them

Even with proper setup, you may encounter challenges with alerts and notifications. Here's how to address common issues:

- **Problem: Recipients Not Receiving Alerts**
    - Solution: Check recipient email addresses and ensure they have access to the sheet. Verify the automation rule's settings.

- **Problem: Alerts Triggering Too Frequently**
    - Solution: Add conditions to refine triggers or consolidate updates into a single daily notification.

- **Problem: Confusing Notification Messages**
    - Solution: Customize messages to provide clear and actionable information.

Conclusion

Setting up alerts and notifications in Smartsheet is a simple yet impactful way to enhance communication and stay on top of important updates. By leveraging these tools effectively, you can automate routine tasks, reduce manual follow-ups, and improve overall team collaboration. With a bit of planning and customization, alerts and notifications can become a powerful ally in your Smartsheet workflows.

4.2.2 Automating Approvals

Approvals are a critical component of workflow automation, especially in teams and organizations where decisions, reviews, or permissions must go through multiple layers of oversight. Smartsheet's automation features make it simple to set up approval workflows, ensuring that the process is efficient, traceable, and error-free. In this section, we will cover everything you need to know about automating approvals in Smartsheet—from understanding the benefits of approval automation to step-by-step instructions for creating approval rules, along with best practices and troubleshooting tips.

What is Approval Automation in Smartsheet?

Approval automation in Smartsheet allows you to create workflows where specific tasks or decisions are routed to individuals or teams for review and approval. This eliminates the need for manual follow-ups, reduces delays, and ensures a clear record of approvals. Whether you're working on project proposals, expense reimbursements, or contract approvals, automation streamlines the process and provides real-time visibility into approval status.

Key benefits include:

- **Speed:** Automated workflows eliminate delays caused by manual approval processes.
- **Clarity:** Everyone involved knows the status of an approval and their responsibilities.
- **Accountability:** Approval requests are tied to specific individuals, with timestamps for tracking.
- **Scalability:** Automating approvals ensures consistency, even as your team or organization grows.

Creating an Approval Workflow: A Step-by-Step Guide

Follow these steps to set up an automated approval workflow in Smartsheet:

Step 1: Define Your Workflow Requirements

Before setting up your approval automation, clearly outline the process. Answer the following questions:

- **What needs approval?** Identify the task, document, or process requiring approval.
- **Who is responsible for approving?** Specify the individual(s) or team(s) who will review and approve.
- **Are there conditions for approval?** Determine if certain criteria must be met before an item can proceed to the approval stage.
- **What happens after approval or rejection?** Plan for the next steps based on the outcome.

For example: If you're setting up a workflow for budget approvals, the approver might be the department manager. The approval condition could be that the budget does not exceed a predefined threshold.

Step 2: Create the Necessary Columns in Your Sheet

To automate approvals, you need to ensure your Smartsheet includes the right columns. Common columns include:

- **Approval Status:** Use a dropdown column to track the status (e.g., "Pending," "Approved," "Rejected").
- **Assigned To:** Indicate the person responsible for approving the task.
- **Comments/Notes:** Allow approvers to leave feedback or explanations for their decisions.
- **Due Date:** Set deadlines for the approval process.

Example:

Task Name	Approval Status	Assigned To	Due Date	Comments
Budget Proposal 1	Pending	John Smith	01/15/2025	
Contract Draft 2	Pending	Jane Doe	01/20/2025	

Step 3: Set Up the Automation Rule

Once your sheet is prepared, follow these steps to set up an approval workflow:

1. **Go to Automation Center:**
    - In your Smartsheet, click on the "Automation" menu at the top of the page.
    - Select "Create a Workflow."

2. **Choose a Trigger:**
    - Select the trigger that initiates the approval workflow. For example, choose "When a row is added or changed" if you want the workflow to activate when a new task is entered or when specific data changes.

3. **Add Conditions (Optional):**
    - Set conditions for when the approval process should begin. For example, you can specify that the "Approval Status" column must be set to "Pending" for the workflow to activate.

4. **Define Actions:**
    - Add the action "Request an approval" to send an automated approval request to the assigned person.
    - Specify the approver by selecting the "Assigned To" column.

5. **Customize Notifications:**
    - Write a clear and concise message for the approver. For example:

"You have a new approval request for [Task Name]. Please review the details and update the 'Approval Status' column to 'Approved' or 'Rejected.' Add comments if necessary."

6. **Specify Outcomes:**
    - Define what happens after the approver updates the "Approval Status." For example:
        - If "Approval Status" changes to "Approved," notify the task owner and move the row to a "Completed Tasks" sheet.
        - If "Approval Status" changes to "Rejected," notify the task owner with a request for revisions.

Step 4: Test and Refine the Workflow

Before rolling out the workflow to your team, test it to ensure it functions as expected:

- Add sample data to your sheet and trigger the workflow.
- Verify that the approval requests are sent correctly.
- Check that notifications and follow-up actions work as intended.

Best Practices for Automating Approvals

1. **Keep Approvers Informed:**
   - Use detailed notifications that include all relevant information, such as deadlines, links to documents, and comments.

2. **Set Deadlines:**
   - Specify due dates for approvals to avoid bottlenecks. Use Smartsheet's notification features to remind approvers of pending requests.

3. **Handle Multiple Approvals:**
   - If multiple approvals are required, use additional automation rules to route tasks sequentially or in parallel.

4. **Track Progress:**
   - Use Smartsheet's reporting tools to create a dashboard that tracks approval statuses across all projects.

5. **Optimize for Rejection Scenarios:**
   - Clearly define next steps for rejected tasks to prevent confusion and ensure quick resolution.

Common Challenges and How to Solve Them

1. **Approver Overload:**
   - If one individual is receiving too many approval requests, consider delegating tasks or setting up a team-based approval system.

2. **Missed Notifications:**
   - Ensure that all approvers have email notifications enabled and that the messages are clear and actionable.

3. **Inconsistent Updates:**
   - Train your team to use the correct dropdown options in the "Approval Status" column.

4. **Complex Workflows:**
   - Break down complex approval processes into smaller, manageable workflows. Use conditional logic to ensure smooth transitions between steps.

Conclusion

Automating approvals in Smartsheet is a powerful way to streamline processes, ensure accountability, and improve team productivity. By setting up well-structured workflows, you can eliminate delays, enhance transparency, and maintain a clear record of all approvals. With these tools and best practices, you're ready to create efficient, scalable approval workflows that meet the needs of your projects and organization.

4.2.3 Recurring Tasks and Updates

Automation in Smartsheet not only saves time but also ensures consistency and accuracy in managing repetitive processes. One of the most powerful automation features in Smartsheet is the ability to create **recurring tasks and updates**, which allow users to set up workflows that repeat at specified intervals or send updates automatically. This section dives deep into how to create and manage recurring tasks and updates to keep your projects and workflows on track.

Understanding Recurring Tasks and Updates

Recurring tasks are activities or events that happen regularly and need to be tracked in Smartsheet. Examples include weekly status updates, monthly financial reporting, or daily task reminders. Automating these recurring actions ensures you don't miss deadlines or overlook important deliverables.

Similarly, recurring updates notify stakeholders about project progress or remind them about upcoming deadlines. These updates can include emails, alerts, or changes to specific Smartsheet cells. Automating updates eliminates the need to manually send notifications, making your communication more efficient and timely.

Step-by-Step Guide to Automating Recurring Tasks

Step 1: Identify the Recurring Task

Before setting up automation, clearly define the task or process that needs to recur. Consider the following:

- **Frequency:** How often does the task occur (daily, weekly, monthly)?
- **Stakeholders:** Who needs to be involved or informed about the task?
- **Dependencies:** Are there any prerequisites or conditions for the task to repeat?

Step 2: Create the Initial Task

Start by creating the task in Smartsheet:

1. Open the relevant sheet where you want to track the recurring task.
2. Add a row for the task, including all necessary details (e.g., task name, owner, due date, status).
3. Use columns like **Assigned To**, **Start Date**, and **End Date** to provide clarity on responsibilities and timelines.

Step 3: Set Up an Automation Rule for Recurrence

Now, automate the task to repeat:

1. **Navigate to the Automation Menu:** Click on the "Automation" tab in the toolbar and select **Create from scratch**.
2. **Choose a Trigger:** Select **Date-Based Trigger** if the task recurrence is tied to specific dates. For example:
    - "Run this workflow every Monday at 9:00 AM."

- "Repeat this task on the 1st of every month."

3. **Set the Action:** Select **Create a Row** as the action. This will automatically generate a new row for the recurring task each time the workflow runs.

4. **Customize the Workflow:**
    - Add specific conditions (e.g., only create a row if the previous task is marked "Complete").
    - Include pre-filled information, such as the task owner, due dates, and priority levels.

5. **Save and Activate the Workflow:** Give your workflow a name (e.g., "Weekly Task Recurrence") and click **Save** to activate it.

Step-by-Step Guide to Automating Recurring Updates

Step 1: Identify Key Updates

Define the type of updates you need to send and their frequency. Common examples include:

- Project progress updates sent to stakeholders every week.
- Alerts for upcoming deadlines, sent three days before a due date.
- Notifications when a task's status changes to "In Progress" or "Completed."

Step 2: Set Up an Update Workflow

1. **Open the Automation Menu:** In the toolbar, click on **Automation** and select **Create from scratch**.
2. **Choose an Update Trigger:** Select a trigger for when the update should be sent. Triggers can include:
    - **Date-Based Triggers:** Send updates on specific dates or intervals.
    - **Change-Based Triggers:** Send updates when a task is marked as complete or when a deadline changes.
3. **Set the Action:**

- Select **Alert Someone** to send an email or Smartsheet notification.
- Customize the message to include relevant details about the update, such as task status, owner, and due date.

4. **Add Stakeholders:**
    - Choose the recipients of the update. This can be specific individuals, teams, or all collaborators on the sheet.
    - Optionally, add dynamic fields (e.g., Assigned To) to automatically notify the task owner.

5. **Save and Activate the Workflow:** Name your workflow (e.g., "Monthly Project Update") and click **Save**.

Best Practices for Managing Recurring Tasks and Updates

1. **Use Templates for Consistency:** Start with a template to ensure uniformity in your recurring tasks. Smartsheet offers various templates for task tracking, project management, and reporting that you can customize to fit your needs.

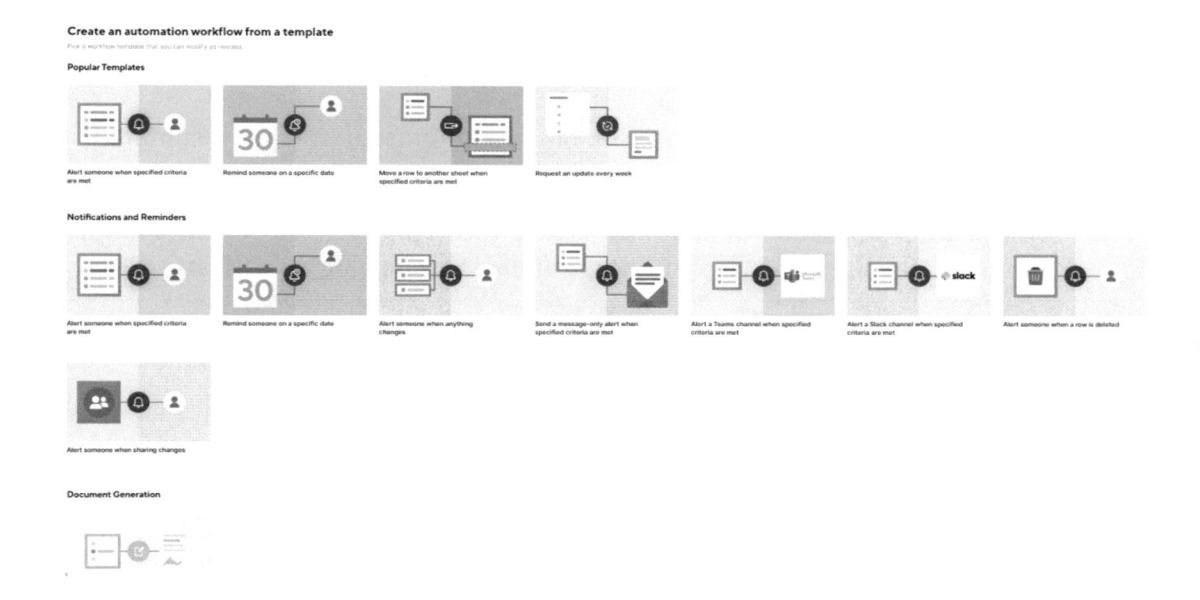

2. **Test Automation Rules:** Before rolling out a workflow, test it to ensure it behaves as expected. For instance, verify that rows are created at the correct intervals or that updates reach the right recipients.

3. **Review and Refine Workflows Regularly:** Periodically review your automation rules to ensure they remain relevant. For example, you may need to adjust the frequency of a recurring task or update the list of recipients as your team evolves.

4. **Combine Automation Rules for Efficiency:** Create workflows that handle multiple tasks at once. For instance, a single workflow can generate a recurring task and send an update to stakeholders about its progress.

5. **Monitor Workflow Activity:** Use the **Activity Log** in Smartsheet to track automation actions. This helps you troubleshoot issues and verify that workflows are functioning correctly.

Use Cases for Recurring Tasks and Updates in Smartsheet

1. **Weekly Team Meetings:** Automate the creation of agenda items for your weekly meetings. Each week, Smartsheet can generate a new row with predefined topics and due dates.

2. **Monthly Budget Reviews:** Set up a recurring task to remind team members to update financial data and prepare reports for monthly reviews.

3. **Client Updates:** Automate weekly or bi-weekly updates to clients, summarizing project progress, milestones, and next steps.

4. **Event Planning:** Use automation to create recurring tasks for event checklists, such as sending invitations, confirming venues, or following up with attendees.

5. **Performance Reviews:** Schedule recurring updates to remind managers and team members about upcoming performance reviews or feedback sessions.

Benefits of Automating Recurring Tasks and Updates

1. **Increased Productivity:** Automation frees up time by eliminating repetitive manual tasks, allowing you to focus on high-value activities.

2. **Improved Accuracy:** By pre-defining task details and updates, you reduce the likelihood of errors or omissions.

3. **Enhanced Collaboration:** Automated updates ensure that all stakeholders stay informed and aligned, fostering better teamwork.

4. **Consistency Across Projects:** Automation ensures that recurring tasks are handled the same way every time, maintaining consistency in your processes.

5. **Better Time Management:** Automating reminders and updates helps you stay on top of deadlines and deliverables, reducing the risk of delays.

By mastering recurring tasks and updates, you can unlock the full potential of Smartsheet's automation capabilities, streamlining your workflows and enhancing your productivity. This feature is a cornerstone of effective project management and will help you stay organized, efficient, and focused on your goals.

4.3 Workflow Optimization Tips

4.3.1 Identifying Repetitive Processes

Automation is one of the most powerful tools Smartsheet offers, and identifying repetitive processes is the first step toward leveraging its full potential. Repetitive tasks are not only time-consuming but also prone to human error. By systematically recognizing these tasks and addressing them with automation, teams can significantly enhance productivity, improve accuracy, and free up time for more strategic activities. In this section, we'll explore how to identify repetitive processes within your workflows, assess their automation potential, and set the stage for long-term efficiency improvements.

Why Identifying Repetitive Processes Matters

Repetitive processes are a natural part of any workflow. These include tasks such as sending reminders, updating status reports, assigning tasks to team members, or creating approvals for decision-making. While these activities are essential for keeping projects on track, they often consume a disproportionate amount of time and resources.

By identifying these recurring activities, you gain the opportunity to:

- **Streamline operations:** Automating repetitive tasks reduces the need for manual intervention, making processes faster and more consistent.
- **Minimize errors:** Automated workflows are less prone to oversight, ensuring tasks are completed accurately and on time.
- **Enhance focus:** Removing mundane tasks allows team members to concentrate on higher-value activities, such as brainstorming, strategizing, or problem-solving.
- **Improve accountability:** Smartsheet's automation features provide clear visibility into task ownership and progress, ensuring everyone stays aligned.

Step 1: Mapping Your Current Workflows

The first step in identifying repetitive processes is understanding how your current workflows operate. This involves mapping out the key steps in your projects and identifying areas where tasks are repeated frequently.

1. **Document Your Workflow:** Use a tool like Smartsheet itself, Lucidchart, or even pen and paper to create a visual map of your workflow. Break down each process into individual steps, noting where data is entered, tasks are assigned, or approvals are required.

Example:
For a project management workflow, you might document the following:

- Task is created.
- Task is assigned to a team member.
- Deadlines are set.
- Status updates are sent weekly.
- Approval is requested at key milestones.

2. **Identify Pain Points:** Look for areas in your workflow where tasks take longer than expected or where errors frequently occur. These are often signs of inefficiencies caused by manual processes.

3. **Highlight Repetitive Tasks:** Focus on activities that occur on a regular basis. Examples include:

- Sending follow-up emails or reminders.
- Approving expense reports or project milestones.
- Updating spreadsheets or reports with new data.
- Assigning similar tasks to different team members.

Step 2: Analyzing Automation Opportunities

Once you've mapped your workflows and identified repetitive tasks, the next step is to assess which of these tasks can be automated using Smartsheet.

1. **Categorize Your Tasks:** Group repetitive tasks into categories based on their type and complexity. Examples include:
    - **Communication tasks:** Sending notifications or reminders.
    - **Data entry tasks:** Updating fields or records.
    - **Approval processes:** Routing requests for review or sign-off.
2. **Match Tasks with Smartsheet Features:** Explore Smartsheet's automation tools to determine how each task can be streamlined. Key features include:
    - **Alerts and notifications:** Automatically send reminders or updates when specific triggers occur.
    - **Approval requests:** Automate the approval process with a structured workflow.
    - **Recurring tasks:** Set up recurring updates or tasks to ensure consistency.
    - **Cell linking and formulas:** Automate data updates across multiple sheets.
3. **Evaluate Time Savings:** Consider the amount of time saved by automating each task. Tasks with high frequency and low complexity are often the easiest to automate and deliver the most immediate benefits.

Step 3: Using Smartsheet to Identify Patterns

Smartsheet provides built-in tools that can help you analyze and identify repetitive processes within your workflows.

1. **Activity Logs:** Smartsheet's activity logs can help you track which tasks are performed frequently and by whom. By analyzing this data, you can pinpoint areas where automation could reduce workload.
2. **Usage Reports:** Run usage reports to understand how your team interacts with Smartsheet. For example, if you notice that a specific team member spends hours updating status reports each week, this could be a prime candidate for automation.
3. **Conditional Formatting Insights:** Use conditional formatting to highlight patterns in your data. For example, if certain tasks are consistently overdue, this may indicate the need for automated reminders or escalations.

Step 4: Communicating with Your Team

Effective automation begins with collaboration. Engage your team to gain insights into their workflows and identify repetitive tasks from their perspective.

1. **Conduct Surveys or Interviews:** Ask team members to share which tasks they find repetitive or time-consuming. Their input will help you uncover inefficiencies you might not have noticed.

2. **Collaborative Brainstorming:** Use team meetings or workshops to brainstorm automation opportunities. Encourage team members to suggest areas where automation could improve their productivity.

3. **Pilot Automation Ideas:** Start small by automating one or two processes. Gather feedback from your team to refine and expand your automation efforts.

Step 5: Monitoring and Refining Automation

Automation is not a one-and-done process. As workflows evolve, new opportunities for automation may arise. Regularly monitor your automated processes to ensure they continue to meet your team's needs.

1. **Review Automation Rules:** Periodically review your automation rules to identify areas for improvement. For example, you might adjust notification timing to better align with your team's working hours.

2. **Measure Success Metrics:** Use Smartsheet's reporting tools to track the impact of automation on key metrics, such as task completion rates, project timelines, and team productivity.

3. **Stay Updated on New Features:** Smartsheet frequently introduces new features and updates. Stay informed to ensure you're taking full advantage of the platform's capabilities.

Conclusion

Identifying repetitive processes is the cornerstone of successful workflow automation in Smartsheet. By carefully mapping your workflows, analyzing automation opportunities, and collaborating with your team, you can transform time-consuming tasks into streamlined, error-free operations. Remember, automation is not just about saving time—it's about creating a more efficient, productive, and empowered team.

In the next section, we'll dive deeper into **"Using Templates for Automation"**, where you'll learn how to leverage Smartsheet's pre-built templates to further optimize your workflows.

4.3.2 Using Templates for Automation

Introduction to Smartsheet Templates: Templates in Smartsheet are powerful tools that can save you time and effort by providing pre-designed structures tailored to specific tasks, industries, or workflows. They serve as a foundation for your projects, helping you set up sheets quickly without the need to build them from scratch. When combined with automation, templates can further optimize repetitive workflows, reduce manual errors, and increase overall efficiency.

This section explores how to select, customize, and effectively use templates in Smartsheet to automate your processes. Whether you are a beginner or an experienced user, mastering templates can transform the way you manage your tasks and projects.

Why Use Templates for Automation?

Templates streamline the process of setting up automation by pre-configuring essential columns, workflows, and structures. Here are some key benefits:

1. **Time-Saving**
   Templates eliminate the need to create sheets manually for recurring workflows. Instead, you can start with a ready-made structure that includes predefined automation rules, such as task reminders, approval processes, or recurring updates.

2. **Consistency Across Projects**

   By using a standard template, you ensure uniformity in your workflows. This is especially useful for teams managing multiple projects or clients, as it simplifies reporting and collaboration.

3. **Error Reduction**

   Pre-configured templates minimize the chances of missing critical elements, such as columns for due dates, assignees, or approval statuses. They also ensure that automation rules are applied consistently across projects.

4. **Scalability**

   Templates can be duplicated and adjusted for various projects, making it easier to scale operations without rethinking your workflows.

Exploring Smartsheet Template Options

Smartsheet provides a wide variety of templates for different industries and use cases, such as project management, marketing campaigns, IT workflows, and more. Some templates are specifically designed with automation in mind.

- **Project Tracking and Rollups**: Includes automation for task reminders and project status updates.
- **Content Calendars**: Automatically sends notifications to contributors when deadlines approach.
- **IT Service Management**: Features automated approval workflows and status tracking.
- **Employee Onboarding**: Uses automation to send welcome emails and track progress.

To access these templates:

1. Go to the Smartsheet homepage.
2. Click **"Solution Center"** (the "+" icon in the navigation bar).
3. Browse templates by category or search for specific use cases.
4. Select a template and click **"Use Template"** to get started.

Customizing Templates for Automation

While Smartsheet's templates are incredibly versatile, customizing them to suit your specific needs ensures they work seamlessly with your existing workflows. Here's how to adjust templates for automation:

1. Add or Modify Columns

- Identify key data points required for your workflow, such as "Task Priority," "Status," or "Assigned To."
- Add columns to capture this information if they're missing from the default template.
- Use column types (e.g., dropdown, checkbox, date) that align with your automation requirements.

2. Set Up Custom Automation Rules

- Navigate to **Automation > Create Workflow** to add rules tailored to your workflow.
- Examples of automation rules to include:
    - **Alerts**: Notify team members when tasks are assigned or deadlines are near.
    - **Approvals**: Automatically route approval requests to the right person.
    - **Recurring Updates**: Send reminders to review progress weekly or monthly.

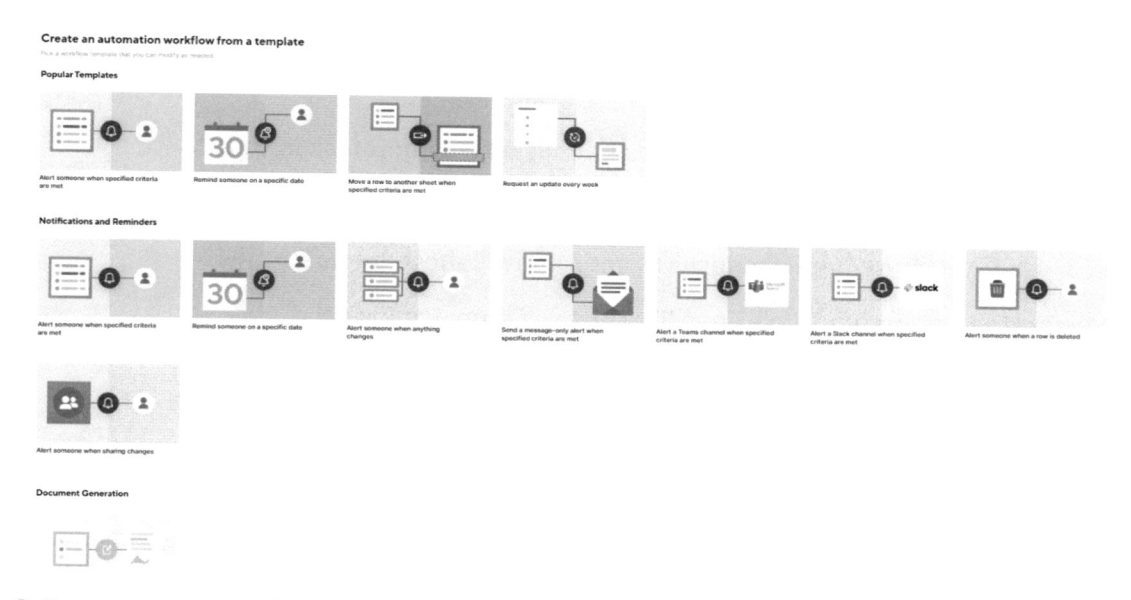

3. Incorporate Conditional Formatting

- Apply formatting rules to highlight overdue tasks, completed items, or high-priority activities.
- Conditional formatting helps ensure that team members can quickly identify critical issues.

4. Pre-define Roles and Permissions

- Assign default permissions for collaborators (e.g., editors, viewers, or admins) to ensure proper access levels.
- Set permissions for automation triggers to avoid accidental changes.

5. Align Templates with Reporting Needs

- Configure key metrics or summary fields to roll up data for dashboards or reports.
- Ensure the data captured in the sheet aligns with the automated reporting workflow.

Examples of Workflow Automation with Templates

1. Task Management Workflow: Template: "Task Tracker"

- Automation:
    - Send a notification to the assignee when a new task is added.
    - Alert the team lead if a task is marked as "Overdue."
    - Move completed tasks to an "Archive" sheet automatically.

2. Marketing Campaign Workflow: Template: "Campaign Tracker"

- Automation:
    - Notify the creative team when a new campaign is initiated.
    - Set up reminders for upcoming deadlines for content approval.
    - Send a weekly update to stakeholders summarizing campaign performance.

3. Employee Onboarding Workflow: Template: "Employee Onboarding Plan"

- Automation:
    - Automatically email welcome packets to new hires.
    - Notify HR to schedule orientation sessions.
    - Track the completion of onboarding tasks and alert managers for overdue items.

4. IT Support Workflow: Template: "IT Request Tracker"

- Automation:
    - Route IT support requests to the appropriate technician based on category.
    - Notify the requestor when their ticket is updated or resolved.
    - Escalate unresolved tickets to supervisors after 72 hours.

Best Practices for Using Templates with Automation

1. Start Simple

- Begin with a basic template and add complexity as needed. Avoid overloading your sheet with too many automation rules at once.

2. Test Your Automation

- Before rolling out a template to your team, test all automation rules to ensure they work as intended.

3. Name Templates Clearly

- Use descriptive names like "Client Onboarding - Automation" to help identify the purpose of the template quickly.

4. Maintain a Template Library

- Create a folder or workspace to store commonly used templates for easy access. Ensure they are updated regularly to reflect changes in your workflow.

5. Train Your Team

- Provide training to team members on how to use templates and automation effectively. Include a quick guide or documentation for each template.

Challenges and How to Overcome Them

While templates can greatly simplify workflows, there may be challenges in implementing them effectively:

1. Overcustomization

- Avoid making templates overly complex, as this can confuse team members. Focus on simplicity and functionality.

2. Template Misalignment

- Ensure that templates match the specific needs of your workflow. Modify templates as needed, but avoid straying too far from the intended structure.

3. Automation Errors

- Regularly review automation rules to ensure they trigger correctly. Use Smartsheet's logs to monitor activity and debug issues.

Conclusion

Templates are one of the most effective tools for automating workflows in Smartsheet. By selecting the right template, customizing it to meet your needs, and combining it with automation rules, you can significantly improve your team's productivity and collaboration. With practice and refinement, templates will become an integral part of your Smartsheet toolkit, enabling you to work smarter, not harder.

4.3.3 Monitoring Automated Workflows

Monitoring automated workflows is a critical step in ensuring that your Smartsheet automations function as intended and provide maximum efficiency. By consistently reviewing and refining your automated processes, you can identify issues, address inefficiencies, and optimize performance. This section will guide you through the best practices and strategies for monitoring your workflows effectively, providing tips and tools to ensure your automations stay on track.

The Importance of Monitoring Automated Workflows

Automated workflows are designed to reduce manual effort, eliminate repetitive tasks, and improve productivity. However, without proper monitoring, they can fail to deliver the desired results. Problems such as missed notifications, incorrect data inputs, or outdated automation rules can disrupt your processes and lead to inefficiencies. Monitoring your workflows allows you to:

- **Identify Errors Early:** Catch issues like broken automation rules or failed triggers before they escalate.

- **Ensure Accuracy:** Verify that the workflows are executing the correct tasks at the right time.

- **Maintain Relevance:** Update automations to match evolving business needs or process changes.

- **Improve Efficiency:** Spot opportunities for refinement to save even more time and resources.

Key Metrics to Monitor in Automated Workflows

When evaluating your workflows, there are specific metrics and indicators to track to ensure everything is running smoothly:

1. **Trigger Success Rates:** Monitor how often automation triggers (such as date-based or condition-based rules) execute successfully. A low success rate may indicate issues with trigger setup or underlying data.

2. **Notification Delivery:** Ensure that alerts and notifications are reaching the intended recipients. Check for undelivered messages, incorrect email addresses, or delays.

3. **Workflow Completion Times:** Measure how long automated tasks take to complete. Unexpected delays may signal inefficiencies or conflicts in the workflow.

4. **Error Logs:** Use Smartsheet's activity logs and workflow history to identify errors, such as missing data or invalid field references.

5. **User Feedback:** Gather feedback from collaborators to learn whether automations are meeting their needs or causing unintended problems.

How to Monitor Automated Workflows in Smartsheet

Smartsheet provides several built-in tools and features to help you monitor and refine your automated workflows:

1. **Activity Log:** The activity log in Smartsheet tracks all actions performed on a sheet, including automated processes. Use it to review who triggered an automation, when it occurred, and whether it executed successfully.

    o   Access the activity log by clicking the "Activity Log" icon in your sheet.

    o   Filter the log to display only automation-related actions for focused monitoring.

2. **Automation Summary:** The Automation Summary is a dedicated interface in Smartsheet where you can view all automation rules applied to a sheet. It allows you to see which workflows are active, when they were last updated, and if any rules have errors.

    o   Navigate to Automation > Manage Rules to access the summary.

- Check for warning icons indicating potential problems with rules.

3. **Alerts and Notifications Tracking:** Smartsheet allows you to track whether alerts and notifications are sent successfully. If users report missing notifications, revisit the rule setup and ensure recipient details are correct.

4. **Testing Automations Regularly:** Use test cases to simulate different scenarios and verify that workflows behave as expected. For example, create a test entry to see if alerts are triggered or approvals are processed.

5. **Auditing Workflow Performance:** Periodically review your workflows' performance by comparing results to original goals. For example, if a task was meant to save 2 hours per week, confirm if the automation achieves this consistently.

Best Practices for Workflow Monitoring

Effective monitoring involves proactive measures to ensure your workflows stay optimized. Here are some best practices:

1. **Set Review Schedules:** Automations should be reviewed on a regular basis. Set a schedule—weekly, monthly, or quarterly—depending on the complexity and importance of the workflow.

2. **Create a Monitoring Checklist:** Develop a checklist to review critical elements of your workflows, such as trigger accuracy, data integrity, and notification delivery.

3. **Involve Key Stakeholders:** Collaborate with team members who rely on the workflows. Their insights can help you uncover hidden issues or suggest improvements.

4. **Document Changes:** Keep a record of changes made to your workflows, including updates to triggers, conditions, and actions. This helps in troubleshooting and ensures transparency.

5. **Train Your Team:** Educate your team on how to use and monitor automations effectively. Provide them with the knowledge to identify issues and suggest enhancements.

6. **Leverage Templates:** If a particular workflow is effective, save it as a template for use in other projects. Templates reduce the risk of errors and ensure consistency.

Advanced Tips for Monitoring and Optimization

For advanced users, here are some additional techniques to enhance workflow monitoring:

1. **Use Reporting Dashboards:** Create dashboards to visualize workflow performance. Add widgets that display key metrics like task completion rates or pending approvals, making it easier to track trends and anomalies.

2. **Integrate Third-Party Tools:** Pair Smartsheet with tools like Zapier, Power Automate, or Tableau for enhanced monitoring and analytics. These tools can provide deeper insights and automate even more aspects of the process.

3. **Automate the Monitoring Itself:** Set up meta-automations to monitor your workflows. For example, create a rule that sends you a summary email whenever a critical automation rule fails.

4. **Analyze Historical Data:** Review historical data trends to identify recurring issues or bottlenecks. Use this information to fine-tune your workflows for better performance.

Troubleshooting Common Issues

Monitoring often reveals problems in your workflows. Here's how to troubleshoot some of the most common issues:

1. **Missed Triggers:**
   - Check the trigger conditions and ensure the required data is present.
   - Verify that the workflow is active and not paused or disabled.

2. **Incorrect Actions:**
   - Review the actions defined in the automation. Ensure they are configured to update the correct fields or send alerts to the right people.

3. **Overlapping Rules:**
   - If multiple automation rules overlap, they may conflict with each other. Consolidate similar rules or adjust trigger conditions to avoid duplication.

4. **Permission Issues:**
    - Ensure that all collaborators have the required permissions to interact with the automation, especially for shared sheets or workspaces.

Conclusion

Monitoring your automated workflows is not a one-time task—it's an ongoing process that requires vigilance, review, and refinement. By actively tracking performance, leveraging Smartsheet's built-in tools, and applying best practices, you can ensure that your automations deliver consistent, reliable results. Over time, this effort will pay off by saving you even more time, reducing errors, and maximizing the value of Smartsheet's automation features.

Remember: automation is only as good as its implementation. A well-monitored and optimized workflow will keep your team operating efficiently, freeing you to focus on higher-value tasks and strategic goals.

CHAPTER V
Visualizing Data

5.1 Creating and Customizing Reports

5.1.1 Generating a New Report

Reports in Smartsheet are powerful tools that allow you to consolidate, filter, and display data from one or multiple sheets in a way that best suits your needs. Whether you're tracking project progress, managing team assignments, or preparing updates for stakeholders, reports provide a dynamic way to organize and present information. In this section, we will walk you through the step-by-step process of generating a new report, covering all the essential aspects to ensure you create effective and meaningful reports.

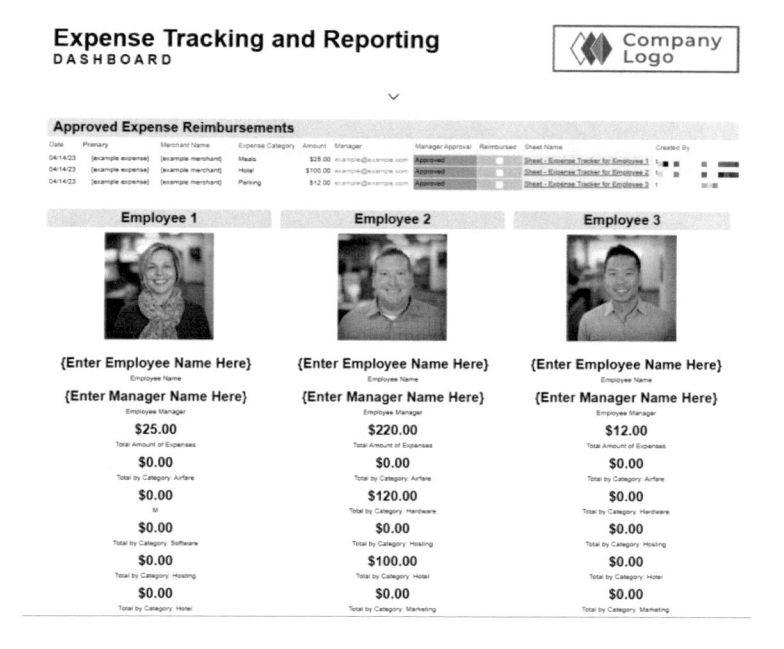

Step 1: Understanding the Types of Reports

Before diving into creating a report, it's crucial to understand the two main types of reports available in Smartsheet:

1. **Row Reports**: These reports focus on the data stored in rows across one or more sheets. For example, you can create a report to display tasks assigned to a specific person or tasks that are overdue.

2. **Sheet Summary Reports**: These reports pull data from the Sheet Summary fields in one or more sheets, providing a high-level overview of key metrics or project details.

Depending on your goal, choose the type of report that aligns with your data needs.

Step 2: Accessing the Report Builder

To start creating a new report:

1. Navigate to the Smartsheet homepage.
2. Click the **+ Create** button located in the left panel.
3. Select **Report** from the dropdown menu.
4. Choose the type of report you want to create: **Row Report** or **Sheet Summary Report**.

The Report Builder will open, allowing you to configure the settings for your report.

Step 3: Adding Data Sources

Reports in Smartsheet are built by pulling data from existing sheets. To specify the sheets you want to include:

1. In the **Report Builder**, click the **+ Select Sheets** button.
2. A window will appear listing all the sheets available in your account.
3. Use the search bar to quickly find specific sheets.

4. Check the boxes next to the sheets you want to include in your report.

5. Click **OK** to confirm your selection.

💡 Tip: If you're managing a large-scale project, consider selecting sheets related to a single department, project phase, or objective to keep your report focused.

Step 4: Configuring Columns

Once you've added your data sources, it's time to choose which columns to display in your report:

1. In the **Columns** section of the Report Builder, click **+ Add Columns**.

2. A list of available columns from your selected sheets will appear.

3. Check the boxes next to the columns you want to include.

4. Rearrange the column order by dragging and dropping them into your desired sequence.

5. Click **OK** to save your changes.

💡 Tip: Avoid clutter by only selecting columns relevant to your report's purpose. Too many columns can make the report overwhelming to read.

Step 5: Filtering Data

To ensure your report displays only the most relevant information, apply filters:

1. In the **Filters** section of the Report Builder, click **+ Add Condition**.

2. Choose a column, condition (e.g., equals, contains, is blank), and value for your filter. For example:
    - Column: **Status**
    - Condition: **Is not**
    - Value: **Completed**

3. Add additional conditions as needed. You can use **AND** or **OR** logic to combine filters.
4. Preview the filtered data in the Report Builder to ensure it matches your expectations.

💡 **Example Use Case**: Create a report that displays all tasks assigned to a specific team member that are due this week and have a status of "In Progress."

Step 6: Sorting and Grouping Data

Sorting and grouping help organize your report for better readability:

1. In the **Sort** section of the Report Builder, click **+ Add Sort**.
2. Select a column to sort by and choose ascending or descending order. For example:
   - Column: **Due Date**
   - Order: **Ascending** (to display the earliest due dates first)
3. To group data, select a column to group by in the **Group by** section. For example, group tasks by **Assigned To** for a clear breakdown of responsibilities.

Step 7: Customizing Report Appearance

Smartsheet allows you to customize the appearance of your report to match your needs:

1. Use the **Grid View** or **Card View** options to change how data is displayed.
   - **Grid View**: Ideal for detailed reports with multiple columns.
   - **Card View**: Best for visualizing tasks and workflows.
2. Apply Conditional Formatting rules to highlight key information. For example, set up a rule to display tasks with a **High Priority** in red text.
3. Resize and align columns to ensure the report looks polished and professional.

Step 8: Saving and Naming Your Report

Once you're satisfied with your report, save it for future use:

1. Click **Save** in the top-right corner of the Report Builder.
2. Enter a descriptive name for your report, such as "Weekly Project Tasks" or "Team Assignments Overview."
3. Choose a location in your Smartsheet workspace or folder to save the report.

💡 **Tip**: Use consistent naming conventions for your reports to make them easy to find later.

Step 9: Sharing Your Report

Collaboration is a key strength of Smartsheet. Share your report with stakeholders by:

1. Clicking the **Share** button in the top-right corner of the Report Builder.
2. Entering the email addresses of the people you want to share the report with.
3. Setting permissions, such as Viewer (read-only) or Editor (can make changes).
4. Adding a personalized message, if necessary.

💡 **Tip**: Use Smartsheet's automated sharing options to send reports to stakeholders at regular intervals, such as weekly or monthly updates.

Step 10: Testing and Refining Your Report

After creating your report, review it to ensure it meets your goals:

1. Test the filters to verify they're capturing the correct data.
2. Check the sorting and grouping to confirm the information is organized logically.
3. Solicit feedback from team members or stakeholders and refine the report accordingly.

💡 **Example**: If a stakeholder finds it challenging to identify overdue tasks, consider adding a filter or conditional formatting rule to highlight them.

Conclusion

Generating a new report in Smartsheet is a straightforward but highly customizable process that empowers users to organize and present data effectively. By following these steps, you'll be able to create reports that not only provide valuable insights but also enhance collaboration and decision-making across your team or organization.

In the next section, **5.1.2 Filtering and Grouping Data in Reports**, we'll dive deeper into fine-tuning your reports to extract the most relevant and actionable insights.

5.1.2 Filtering and Grouping Data in Reports

Reports in Smartsheet are powerful tools for extracting, organizing, and presenting data. Filtering and grouping allow you to customize how data is displayed, enabling you to focus on the most relevant information and create meaningful insights for stakeholders. This section provides a step-by-step guide to effectively filter and group data in Smartsheet reports, along with tips and best practices to maximize their utility.

Understanding Filtering and Grouping in Smartsheet Reports

Filtering helps you narrow down data by setting specific criteria, so only the information that meets those conditions appears in the report. For example, you might want to see only tasks assigned to a particular team member or projects due in the current month.

Grouping, on the other hand, allows you to organize data into categories or segments based on shared characteristics, such as project names, task statuses, or due dates. Grouping adds structure to your report, making it easier to analyze trends and relationships.

Step-by-Step Guide to Filtering Data

1. **Open the Report Builder**
    - To start, open an existing report or create a new one by navigating to the "Reports" section on your Smartsheet dashboard.
    - Select "Edit Report" to enter the Report Builder.

2. **Add Filters to Your Report**

- In the Report Builder, locate the **Filter** panel. This is where you'll set up conditions to narrow down your data.
- Click **Add New Filter** and choose the column you want to filter by. For example:
  - Column: **Assigned To**
  - Filter Condition: **is**
  - Value: Select a specific user (e.g., John Smith).
- You can add multiple filter conditions by clicking the **+Add Condition** button. For instance:
  - Filter 1: **Status is In Progress**
  - Filter 2: **Due Date is within the next 7 days**
- Use the **AND/OR** operators to refine your logic:
  - **AND** ensures that all conditions must be true.
  - **OR** allows the report to display rows that meet any of the conditions.

3. **Save and Apply Filters**
   - Once you've set your filters, click **Save** to apply them.
   - The report will immediately update to display only the rows that match the criteria.

4. **Refining Filters**
   - You can always return to the Filter panel to adjust conditions. For example, if you want to expand your report to include completed tasks, simply add a condition like **Status is Completed** and modify the logic.

Step-by-Step Guide to Grouping Data

1. **Open the Report Builder**
   - Access the report you want to edit, just as you did for filtering.

2. **Enable Grouping**
   - In the Report Builder, locate the **Group By** section, typically below the Filter panel.
   - Click **Add Grouping** and select a column to group by. For instance:
     - **Group By**: Project Name.
   - The report will instantly reorganize to show rows grouped under each project.

3. **Add Multiple Levels of Grouping**
   - Smartsheet allows up to three levels of grouping for more detailed organization. For example:
     - **First Group By**: Project Name
     - **Second Group By**: Assigned To
     - **Third Group By**: Task Status
   - This creates a hierarchical structure where data is grouped first by project, then by team member, and finally by task status.

4. **Customize Grouping Options**
   - Adjust how groups are displayed by clicking on the settings icon next to each grouping level. Options include:
     - **Sort Order**: Choose ascending or descending order.
     - **Expand/Collapse**: Decide whether groups should be expanded or collapsed by default.

5. **Save and Apply Grouping**
   - Once satisfied with your grouping setup, save the report. The grouped structure will be immediately visible.

Combining Filters and Grouping for Enhanced Reports

While filtering and grouping are useful individually, combining them unlocks the full potential of Smartsheet reports. Here's an example:

- **Scenario**: You're managing a team working on multiple projects. You need a report that shows tasks assigned to specific team members, grouped by project, and filtered to show only tasks due this week.

- **Steps**:
    1. Set up a filter:
        - Column: **Assigned To**
        - Condition: **is**
        - Value: Select team members (e.g., John Smith, Jane Doe).
    2. Add another filter:
        - Column: **Due Date**
        - Condition: **is within the next 7 days**.
    3. Enable grouping:
        - First Group By: Project Name.
        - Second Group By: Task Status.

The resulting report will display tasks for the specified team members, grouped by project, and filtered to include only tasks due this week.

Practical Use Cases for Filtering and Grouping

1. **Team Task Management**
    - **Filter**: Assigned To is "Team Member A."
    - **Group**: Group by Task Status (e.g., "In Progress," "Completed").
    - Use Case: Quickly review the progress of individual team members.

2. **Project Progress Overview**
    - **Filter**: Project Name is "Project X."

- **Group**: Group by Task Priority (e.g., "High," "Medium," "Low").
- **Use Case**: Identify critical tasks within a specific project.

3. **Deadline Monitoring**
    - **Filter**: Due Date is within the next 7 days.
    - **Group**: Group by Assigned To.
    - **Use Case**: Focus on upcoming deadlines and ensure accountability.

4. **Customer-Specific Reports**
    - **Filter**: Customer Name is "Customer A."
    - **Group**: Group by Project Name.
    - **Use Case**: Generate a report tailored to a specific client.

Tips for Effective Filtering and Grouping

- **Use Descriptive Column Names**: Ensure that your column names clearly describe the data they contain. This makes it easier to set up filters and groupings.
- **Limit the Number of Filters**: Too many filters can overcomplicate your report and make it difficult to interpret. Focus on the most critical criteria.
- **Prioritize Grouping Hierarchies**: When using multiple levels of grouping, arrange them in a logical hierarchy (e.g., project > team member > status).
- **Test and Iterate**: Regularly review your filters and grouping settings to ensure they still meet your needs as projects evolve.

Troubleshooting Common Issues

1. **No Data Appears in the Report**
    - **Cause**: Your filters may be too restrictive.
    - **Solution**: Review the filter conditions and ensure they align with the data in your sheets.

2. **Duplicate Groups in the Report**
    - **Cause**: Data inconsistencies, such as typos in column values.
    - **Solution**: Standardize your data entries to avoid duplicates.
3. **Incorrect Grouping Order**
    - **Cause**: Grouping settings may not reflect the desired hierarchy.
    - **Solution**: Reorder the grouping levels in the Report Builder.

Best Practices for Sharing Filtered and Grouped Reports

- **Provide Context**: When sharing a report, include a brief description of the filters and groupings used, so recipients understand the report's focus.
- **Export and Present**: Use the export feature to create PDFs or presentations, making it easier to share insights with stakeholders who may not use Smartsheet.
- **Automate Updates**: Set up automated notifications to ensure team members receive updated reports at regular intervals.

By mastering filtering and grouping, you can transform your Smartsheet reports into actionable insights that save time, enhance decision-making, and drive productivity. With these tools, your reports will no longer be static data displays but dynamic resources that empower your team and stakeholders.

5.1.3 Sharing Reports with Stakeholders

Sharing reports effectively is a crucial step in ensuring your stakeholders—whether they're team members, clients, or decision-makers—have the information they need to stay updated and make informed decisions. Smartsheet provides a variety of features to make sharing reports seamless, customizable, and secure. This section covers everything you need to know about sharing reports, including methods, permissions, and best practices.

Understanding the Importance of Sharing Reports

Sharing reports is not just about delivering information—it's about presenting data in a way that stakeholders can easily interpret and act upon. A well-shared report allows for:

- **Clear Communication:** Ensuring everyone has access to the same up-to-date information.
- **Accountability:** Assigning responsibility for tasks and tracking progress.
- **Efficient Decision-Making:** Providing real-time insights to stakeholders.

Before sharing your report, it's important to understand who your stakeholders are and tailor the report format and access levels to their needs.

Methods for Sharing Reports in Smartsheet

Smartsheet offers several ways to share reports, depending on your audience and requirements. Here are the most common methods:

1. **Sharing Directly via Smartsheet:**
    - Navigate to your report and click on the **Share** button in the top-right corner.
    - Add the email addresses of the people you want to share the report with.
    - Set their permission levels:
        - **Viewer:** Can view the report but cannot make changes.
        - **Editor:** Can view and edit the report.
    - Write an optional message to provide context or instructions, then click **Send**.

2. **Sending a Link to the Report:**
    - Use the **Share** button to generate a link to the report.
    - Choose the link's access level:
        - **Anyone with the link:** Allows anyone with the link to view or edit the report, depending on permissions.

- **Only specific users:** Restricts access to those invited via email.
    - Copy and send the link via email, messaging apps, or other communication tools.
3. **Exporting and Sharing as a File:**
    - Export the report as a PDF, Excel file, or another format (covered in detail in Section 5.3.1).
    - Share the file via email or upload it to a shared drive like Google Drive, OneDrive, or Dropbox.
4. **Embedding Reports into Other Tools:**
    - Use Smartsheet integrations to embed reports into tools like Microsoft Teams, Google Workspace, or Slack.
    - This approach is ideal for real-time collaboration within a specific platform.

Setting Permissions for Shared Reports

Smartsheet allows you to control who can access your reports and what they can do with them. Here's a detailed breakdown of permission levels and how to manage them:

1. **Viewer Permissions:**
    - Stakeholders with viewer permissions can only view the report without making any changes.
    - Ideal for stakeholders who need to stay informed but don't need to interact with the data.
2. **Editor Permissions:**
    - Editors can make changes to the report, including modifying filters, adjusting groupings, and even deleting the report (depending on their access level).
    - This is useful for team members collaborating on the same report.
3. **Admin Permissions:**

- Admins have full control over the report, including sharing it with others and setting permissions.
- This role is typically assigned to the report creator or a project manager.

4. **Public Access Settings:**
    - When sharing reports via a public link, you can choose whether recipients can only view the report or also edit it.
    - Use this option cautiously to avoid unauthorized access.

Customizing Shared Reports for Stakeholders

When sharing reports, consider tailoring them to meet the needs of different stakeholders. Here's how you can customize shared reports:

1. **Filter Data for Specific Audiences:**
    - Use Smartsheet's filtering options to show only the data relevant to each stakeholder group. For example, you can create a version of the report that displays only tasks assigned to a particular department or team.

2. **Use Conditional Formatting:**
    - Apply conditional formatting to highlight important metrics, deadlines, or potential risks. This makes the report easier to interpret and draws attention to key points.

3. **Adjust Layout and Columns:**
    - Remove unnecessary columns or rearrange them to prioritize the most important data for your audience.

4. **Add Explanatory Notes or Comments:**
    - Use the comments feature to provide context for specific data points or to outline next steps for stakeholders.

Best Practices for Sharing Reports

1. **Define the Purpose of the Report:**

- Before sharing, clarify the report's purpose and what actions you expect stakeholders to take based on the data.

2. **Ensure Data Accuracy:**
   - Double-check that all data in the report is up-to-date and accurate. Sharing incorrect information can lead to confusion and misinformed decisions.

3. **Use Clear Naming Conventions:**
   - Name your reports descriptively (e.g., "Q1 Sales Overview - Team A") so stakeholders can easily identify their purpose.

4. **Share Regular Updates:**
   - For ongoing projects, set a schedule for sharing updated versions of the report (e.g., weekly or monthly). Use automation features in Smartsheet to send scheduled updates automatically.

5. **Train Stakeholders on How to Use the Report:**
   - Provide a brief overview or training session for stakeholders unfamiliar with Smartsheet to ensure they can navigate and interpret the report effectively.

6. **Monitor Access and Engagement:**
   - Use Smartsheet's activity log to track who has accessed the report and whether they've interacted with it. This helps you identify engagement issues and follow up with stakeholders as needed.

Troubleshooting Common Issues When Sharing Reports

1. **Stakeholders Can't Access the Report:**
   - Ensure you've shared the report with the correct email addresses and that they have the required permissions.
   - Confirm that recipients have a Smartsheet account if access is restricted to specific users.

2. **Outdated Data in Reports:**

- If stakeholders are viewing outdated data, verify that the report is pulling live data from the source sheets. Check the report's settings to ensure it updates automatically.

3. **Collaboration Conflicts:**
    - If multiple stakeholders are editing the report simultaneously, use the comments feature to communicate and avoid overwriting changes.

Summary

Sharing reports in Smartsheet is a powerful way to ensure transparency, improve collaboration, and drive informed decision-making. By leveraging Smartsheet's sharing features, customizing reports for your audience, and following best practices, you can ensure your reports deliver maximum impact.

Next, we'll explore how to visualize data even further by creating and using dashboards in Chapter 5.2!

5.2 Using Dashboards

Dashboards in Smartsheet are powerful tools that allow users to visualize, analyze, and communicate critical information in real-time. A well-designed dashboard provides a centralized view of your project, helping you track progress, monitor KPIs, and share insights with stakeholders effectively.

Cost Tracking DASHBOARD

Welcome to the Cost Tracking Dashboard.
Use this dashboard to track and manage incoming requests for business reimbursements so that you can stay organized, even when the unexpected happens. Scroll down for an at-a-glace view of expenditures per department, as well as information regarding approved and declined requests.

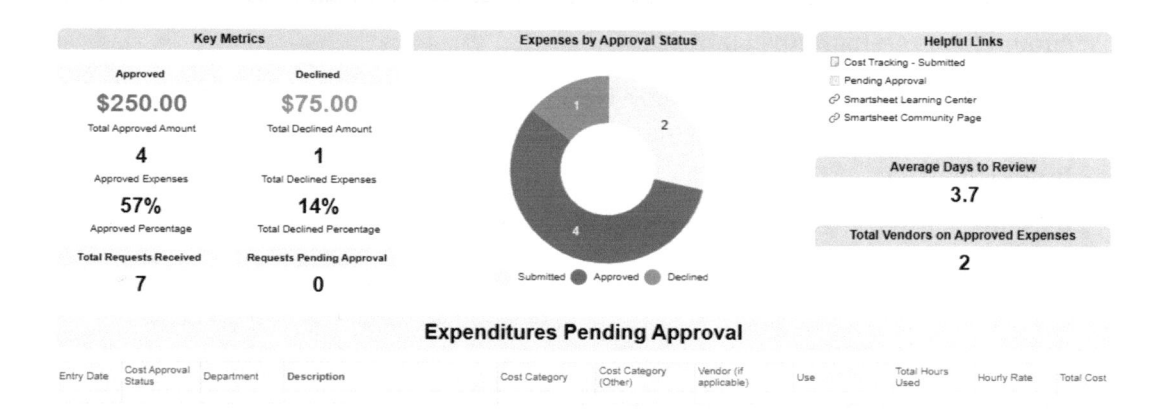

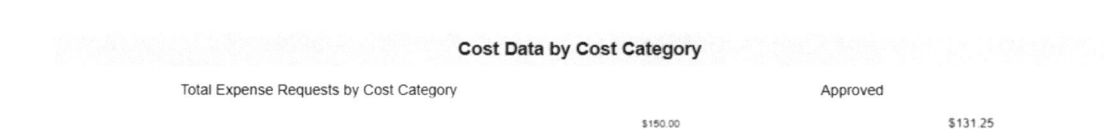

Key Metrics

Approved	Declined
$250.00	$75.00
Total Approved Amount	Total Declined Amount
4	1
Approved Expenses	Total Declined Expenses
57%	14%
Approved Percentage	Total Declined Percentage
Total Requests Received	Requests Pending Approval
7	0

Expenses by Approval Status

Submitted: 1, Approved: 4, Declined: 2

Helpful Links
- Cost Tracking - Submitted
- Pending Approval
- Smartsheet Learning Center
- Smartsheet Community Page

Average Days to Review
3.7

Total Vendors on Approved Expenses
2

Expenditures Pending Approval

Entry Date | Cost Approval Status | Department | Description | Cost Category | Cost Category (Other) | Vendor (if applicable) | Use | Total Hours Used | Hourly Rate | Total Cost

Cost Data by Cost Category

Total Expense Requests by Cost Category — $150.00
Approved — $131.25

5.2.1 Building a Dashboard from Scratch

Building a Smartsheet dashboard from scratch may seem daunting at first, but by following a structured process, you can create an effective and visually appealing tool. This section will guide you step by step to help you design, build, and optimize your dashboard.

Step 1: Understand Your Purpose

Before you start building, it's essential to understand the purpose of your dashboard. Ask yourself:

- **What is the goal of this dashboard?** Is it to track project progress, monitor team performance, analyze sales data, or provide a summary for executives?
- **Who will use this dashboard?** Identify your audience. A dashboard for team members may require task-specific details, while a dashboard for executives should focus on high-level metrics.
- **What data needs to be included?** Decide what information is critical. Including too much data can make your dashboard cluttered, while too little may leave it uninformative.

Clearly defining these factors will ensure your dashboard meets its objectives and serves its intended audience.

Step 2: Prepare Your Data

Smartsheet dashboards rely on data from existing sheets and reports. Properly organizing your data before starting the dashboard is crucial.

1. **Identify Relevant Sheets and Reports**: Gather the data sources you'll use in your dashboard. These might include project sheets, sales reports, or team schedules.
2. **Clean Your Data**: Ensure the data is accurate, up-to-date, and well-organized. Remove unnecessary rows, fix errors, and standardize formats.
3. **Use Reports to Summarize Data**: If your data is spread across multiple sheets, create Smartsheet reports to consolidate and summarize it. Reports make it easier to pull key metrics into your dashboard.

4. **Establish Key Metrics and KPIs**: Decide which metrics you want to highlight, such as project completion percentage, budget status, or task count.

Step 3: Create Your Dashboard

Once your data is ready, follow these steps to create a dashboard from scratch:

Step 3.1: Access the Dashboard Creation Tool

1. Navigate to your Smartsheet workspace or folder.
2. Click the **Create** button in the toolbar and select **Dashboard/Portal**.
3. Name your dashboard and click **OK** to open the dashboard editor.

Step 3.2: Add Widgets to Your Dashboard

Widgets are the building blocks of Smartsheet dashboards. They allow you to display various types of information such as charts, metrics, text, and images.

Here's how to add widgets:

1. **Click the "+ Add Widget" Button**: Located at the top-left corner of the editor, this button opens the widget menu.
2. **Select a Widget Type**: Choose the appropriate widget based on the data you want to display:
    - **Metric Widget**: Displays numerical KPIs like project completion percentage.
    - **Chart Widget**: Visualizes data using bar, line, or pie charts.
    - **Grid Widget**: Displays raw data in a table format.
    - **Rich Text Widget**: Adds context or instructions using formatted text.
    - **Image Widget**: Displays your company logo, visual elements, or charts.
    - **Shortcut Widget**: Links to other sheets, reports, or external resources.
3. **Customize Each Widget**: After adding a widget, configure it by linking it to your data source. For example, a metric widget needs a cell or report to pull data from.

Step 3.3: Arrange and Design Your Dashboard

The layout and design of your dashboard are crucial for usability and visual appeal.

1. **Drag and Drop Widgets**: Click and drag widgets to arrange them on the dashboard canvas. Resize widgets by dragging their edges to fit your layout.

2. **Organize Widgets Logically**:
   Group related information together. For example:
   - Place KPIs at the top for quick reference.
   - Group task-related widgets in one section.
   - Reserve the bottom area for detailed data or links.

3. **Use Consistent Colors and Fonts**:
   Apply a consistent theme to improve readability. Smartsheet allows you to customize widget colors and fonts to match your branding or project style.

4. **Add Titles and Labels**:
   Use text widgets to add titles, labels, or descriptions to each section of the dashboard. This helps users quickly understand the data presented.

Step 4: Link Data to Widgets

Each widget needs to be connected to a data source. Follow these steps to link your data:

1. **Open Widget Settings**:
   Click the gear icon on a widget to open its settings.

2. **Choose a Data Source**:
   Select a sheet, report, or cell as the data source for the widget. For example:
   - Use a report as the source for a chart widget.
   - Link a cell from a project sheet to a metric widget.

3. **Configure Display Options**:
   Customize how the data appears. For charts, choose the chart type, axis labels, and colors. For metrics, set thresholds to highlight values in red, yellow, or green.

Step 5: Test and Refine Your Dashboard

After adding and linking all widgets, it's time to test your dashboard.

1. **Check Data Accuracy**:
   Verify that each widget displays the correct data from your sheets and reports.

2. **Gather Feedback**:
   Share your dashboard with a few team members or stakeholders and ask for their input.

3. **Refine the Layout**:
   Adjust the size and positioning of widgets based on feedback to ensure the dashboard is easy to navigate.

Step 6: Share and Publish Your Dashboard

Once your dashboard is complete, make it accessible to your intended audience:

1. **Share with Specific Users**:
   Click the **Share** button, add users, and set their permissions (Viewer or Editor).

2. **Publish the Dashboard**:
   Generate a shareable link to allow access without requiring a Smartsheet account.

3. **Embed in Other Tools**:
   Embed your dashboard in external platforms like Microsoft Teams, intranet portals, or presentations for broader visibility.

Best Practices for Building Dashboards

- **Keep it Simple**: Avoid overcrowding the dashboard with too many widgets or data points.

- **Focus on Actionable Insights**: Highlight data that helps users make informed decisions.

- **Update Regularly**: Ensure the dashboard stays relevant by keeping the underlying data up to date.

By following these steps, you can build a Smartsheet dashboard that meets your needs and adds value to your projects and team. Dashboards are dynamic tools that evolve with your projects, so don't hesitate to revisit and refine them as necessary.

5.2.2 Adding Widgets (Charts, Metrics, etc.)

Dashboards in Smartsheet are powerful tools for visualizing data, tracking key metrics, and presenting information in an easily digestible format. Widgets are the building blocks of a dashboard, allowing users to customize and display data in various ways. This section will guide you through the process of adding widgets to your dashboard, explain the types of widgets available, and provide tips for making your dashboard both functional and visually appealing.

What Are Widgets in Smartsheet?

Widgets are customizable elements that you can add to a dashboard to display information such as charts, metrics, reports, or even external content. Each widget serves a specific purpose, and when combined effectively, they create a comprehensive overview of your data.

Types of widgets include:

- **Metric Widgets**: Highlight key performance indicators (KPIs) and summary data.
- **Chart Widgets**: Visualize data through graphs and charts (e.g., bar, pie, line charts).
- **Report Widgets**: Display data from reports created in Smartsheet.
- **Text Widgets**: Add titles, headers, or descriptions for context.
- **Image Widgets**: Add logos, photos, or other visual elements.
- **Web Content Widgets**: Embed external content like videos, websites, or other tools.

Steps to Add Widgets to Your Dashboard

Step 1: Open Your Dashboard

1. Navigate to your Smartsheet account and select the **"Dashboards"** tab from the home screen.
2. Open an existing dashboard or create a new one by clicking the **"+"** icon and selecting **"Dashboard"**.
3. Once in the dashboard editor, ensure you're in **edit mode** by clicking the **pencil icon** in the top-right corner.

Step 2: Add a Widget

1. Click the **"Add Widget"** button, typically located at the top of the dashboard editor.
2. A menu will appear showing all available widget types. Select the widget that best fits your data visualization needs.
   - For example, choose **Metric** for displaying numerical data or **Chart** for graphical representation.

Types of Widgets and How to Configure Them

Metric Widgets

Metric widgets are used to display specific numbers or calculations. These are ideal for showing KPIs like total sales, completed tasks, or pending items.

1. After selecting **Metric**, choose the source sheet or report where your data is stored.
2. Specify the cell or column that contains the data you want to display.
3. Customize the widget appearance by editing the title, font size, and colors.

Chart Widgets

Chart widgets allow you to represent data visually in formats such as bar charts, pie charts, or line graphs.

1. Select **Chart** from the widget menu.
2. Link your widget to a data source, such as a Smartsheet report or sheet.
3. Choose the chart type that best suits your data. For instance:
   - **Bar Chart**: Use for comparisons across categories (e.g., sales by region).

- **Pie Chart**: Ideal for showing proportions (e.g., percentage of tasks completed).
- **Line Chart**: Great for displaying trends over time (e.g., monthly revenue).

4. Adjust the settings, such as colors, labels, and axis titles, to make the chart more understandable.
5. Preview the chart and ensure the data is displayed accurately.

Report Widgets

Report widgets display data from existing reports in Smartsheet. These are especially useful for presenting real-time updates.

1. Select **Report** from the widget menu.
2. Link the widget to a report that you've created.
3. Adjust the display settings, such as sorting and filtering, to show only the relevant information.

Text Widgets

Text widgets add context to your dashboard by allowing you to include titles, instructions, or annotations.

1. Select **Text** from the widget menu.
2. Enter your desired text and customize the formatting (e.g., bold, italic, font size).
3. Position the text widget in a logical spot on your dashboard.

Image Widgets

Image widgets are perfect for adding logos or visuals to enhance the aesthetics of your dashboard.

1. Select **Image** from the widget menu.
2. Upload an image from your computer or link to an online image.
3. Resize and position the image widget as needed.

Web Content Widgets

Web content widgets enable you to embed external resources, such as YouTube videos, websites, or Google Maps.

1. Select **Web Content** from the widget menu.

2. Paste the URL of the content you want to embed.

3. Adjust the dimensions of the widget to ensure the embedded content fits your dashboard layout.

Best Practices for Adding Widgets

1. **Plan Your Layout First**

   Before adding widgets, outline your dashboard layout on paper or in your mind. Group similar widgets together to make navigation intuitive.

2. **Focus on Key Metrics**

   Avoid overcrowding your dashboard. Highlight the most important data to keep the focus clear and relevant.

3. **Use Consistent Colors and Fonts**

   Maintain a cohesive design by using consistent color schemes and font styles across all widgets.

4. **Test for Responsiveness**

   Ensure your dashboard looks good on both desktop and mobile devices. Adjust widget sizes and positions as needed.

5. **Refresh Data Sources Regularly**

   Keep your dashboard up-to-date by linking widgets to live data sources and enabling automatic updates.

Troubleshooting Widget Issues

- **Widget Not Displaying Data**: Check the data source to ensure it's correctly linked and contains the required data.

- **Chart Not Showing Properly**: Verify that the data is in the correct format (e.g., numerical data for bar charts).
- **Dashboard Layout Looks Cluttered**: Resize or rearrange widgets to improve readability.

By following these steps and tips, you can effectively add widgets to your Smartsheet dashboards, creating a powerful and visually engaging tool for data visualization. As you become more familiar with the process, experiment with different widget combinations to build dashboards that meet your unique needs.

5.2.3 Best Practices for Effective Dashboards

Creating dashboards in Smartsheet is a powerful way to present data and insights in a visual, easy-to-understand manner. Dashboards serve as a central hub where users can access key metrics, track project progress, and make informed decisions. While building a dashboard is relatively straightforward, creating an *effective* dashboard that communicates clearly and supports decision-making requires thoughtful planning and execution. Below is a detailed guide to best practices for designing and maintaining dashboards in Smartsheet.

1. Define the Purpose of the Dashboard

Before creating a dashboard, clarify its primary purpose. Dashboards can serve various functions, such as:

- Tracking project progress.
- Monitoring key performance indicators (KPIs).
- Presenting data for executive-level decision-making.
- Visualizing task status for team updates.

Ask yourself:

- **Who is the audience?** Is the dashboard intended for team members, stakeholders, or executives?
- **What information do they need?** Identify the most relevant data and metrics.
- **What actions will the audience take based on the dashboard?** Align your design to support these actions.

For example, a project manager may need a dashboard that highlights task statuses and deadlines, while an executive might prefer high-level metrics like budget utilization or ROI.

2. Keep It Simple and Focused

An effective dashboard delivers key information quickly and without clutter. Overloading your dashboard with too many widgets, data points, or graphics can confuse users and dilute the message.

Tips for Simplicity:

- Limit the number of widgets to those essential for the dashboard's purpose.
- Use concise titles and labels to describe data.
- Group related information together (e.g., team metrics in one section, financials in another).
- Avoid unnecessary visual elements like excessive colors or decorative images.

Example:

For a project tracking dashboard, include only task status, deadlines, budget usage, and team workload. Avoid adding unrelated information like historical data or other projects' KPIs.

3. Prioritize Data Visualization

Visual elements like charts and graphs are often easier to understand than raw numbers. Smartsheet dashboards allow you to use widgets for visualizing data effectively.

Key Principles for Data Visualization:

- **Use the right chart type:**

- Bar charts for comparing categories.
- Line charts for trends over time.
- Pie charts for showing proportions.
- **Highlight critical metrics:** Use larger widgets or bold colors to draw attention to KPIs.
- **Maintain consistency:** Use the same color schemes and formats across the dashboard to create a cohesive design.

Avoid Pitfalls:

- Avoid using 3D charts or overly complex visualizations that may distort data.
- Don't display too much data in a single chart; focus on clarity.

4. Leverage Widgets Effectively

Widgets are the building blocks of Smartsheet dashboards. Each widget serves a specific purpose and can be customized to meet your needs.

Common Widgets and Their Uses:

1. **Metric Widgets:** Display single values, such as total project budget or number of completed tasks.
2. **Chart Widgets:** Visualize trends, comparisons, and distributions.
3. **Grid Widgets:** Present raw data or summaries in a table format.
4. **Image Widgets:** Add logos or visual context, such as a map for location-based data.
5. **Shortcut Widgets:** Provide quick links to Smartsheet items, external resources, or other dashboards.

Customization Tips:

- Use headers to separate different sections of the dashboard.
- Resize widgets appropriately—don't let a small widget hold too much space.
- Test the layout on different devices to ensure readability.

5. Design for Your Audience

Different audiences have different needs. For example, a dashboard for executives should focus on high-level KPIs, while one for team members may need task-specific details.

Design Tips for Specific Audiences:

- **Executives:**
    - Keep dashboards simple, focusing on metrics like ROI, budget utilization, and milestone completion.
    - Use high-level charts and avoid granular task details.
- **Team Members:**
    - Include task progress, deadlines, and workload distribution.
    - Allow for detailed grids or charts showing day-to-day activities.
- **Clients or Stakeholders:**
    - Ensure data is easy to understand with minimal technical jargon.
    - Use visuals to highlight key achievements or project outcomes.

6. Ensure Real-Time Updates

Smartsheet dashboards can display real-time data, which is critical for decision-making. Ensure your data sources are set up correctly to provide up-to-date information.

How to Maintain Real-Time Data:

- Link widgets to live data sources, such as sheets or reports.
- Set up automatic updates for any data integrations.
- Use Smartsheet automation to notify users of changes.

Troubleshooting Tips:

- Check widget connections regularly to ensure they are pointing to the correct data.

- Test your dashboard to confirm updates are reflected accurately.

7. Optimize Layout and Usability

The layout of your dashboard significantly impacts how users interact with it. A well-structured layout ensures users can quickly locate the information they need.

Best Practices for Layout:

- Place the most important widgets at the top or in the center of the dashboard.
- Group related widgets together in logical sections.
- Leave enough white space to make the dashboard visually appealing and easy to read.
- Use consistent font sizes and styles for text widgets.

Responsive Design:

Smartsheet dashboards are accessible on both desktop and mobile devices. Ensure your dashboard is easy to navigate on smaller screens by avoiding overly complex layouts.

8. Test and Gather Feedback

Once your dashboard is complete, test it with the intended audience. User feedback is essential for identifying areas of improvement.

Testing Steps:

1. Share the dashboard with a small group of users.
2. Ask for feedback on layout, clarity, and functionality.
3. Observe how users interact with the dashboard and make adjustments as needed.

9. Maintain and Update the Dashboard

An effective dashboard is not a one-time project—it requires regular updates to remain relevant.

Maintenance Tips:

- Review dashboards periodically to remove outdated information.
- Update widgets and data sources as project needs evolve.
- Keep an archive of previous dashboard versions for reference.

10. Follow Smartsheet Best Practices

Smartsheet offers resources and best practices for dashboard design. Explore the Smartsheet help center, forums, and training materials to refine your skills further.

By following these best practices, you can create Smartsheet dashboards that not only look professional but also deliver meaningful insights to your team or stakeholders. A well-designed dashboard saves time, improves collaboration, and enhances decision-making processes.

5.3 Exporting and Presenting Data

5.3.1 Exporting to Excel, PDF, and Other Formats

Exporting data from Smartsheet allows users to share, analyze, and present their information in various formats. This functionality is essential for ensuring that data remains accessible and usable outside Smartsheet, whether for collaboration with stakeholders, offline access, or detailed reporting. In this section, we will cover the steps, tips, and use cases for exporting data to Excel, PDF, and other formats.

Why Export Data from Smartsheet?

Before diving into the technical steps, it's important to understand why exporting is a valuable feature:

- **Sharing Information with Non-SmartSheet Users**: Some team members or clients may not use Smartsheet but need access to the data. Exporting ensures that they can view the information in commonly used formats like Excel or PDF.

- **Detailed Data Analysis**: While Smartsheet provides robust reporting features, exporting to Excel enables users to perform advanced calculations, create pivot tables, or use Excel's powerful formulas and charting tools.

- **Creating Printable Documents**: PDF exports are ideal for creating polished, print-friendly versions of your data for presentations or meetings.

- **Archiving Data**: Exporting to a static format ensures that you can maintain a snapshot of your data at a specific point in time, even if the Smartsheet itself continues to evolve.

Step-by-Step Guide to Exporting Data

Exporting to Excel (.xlsx)

1. **Access the Sheet You Want to Export**
    - Navigate to the Smartsheet containing the data you wish to export.

CHAPTER V: VISUALIZING DATA

- Ensure that your data is up-to-date and properly formatted before proceeding.

2. **Open the Export Menu**

    - Click on the **File** menu in the top toolbar.
    - From the dropdown options, select **Export** and then choose **Export to Microsoft Excel (.xlsx)**.

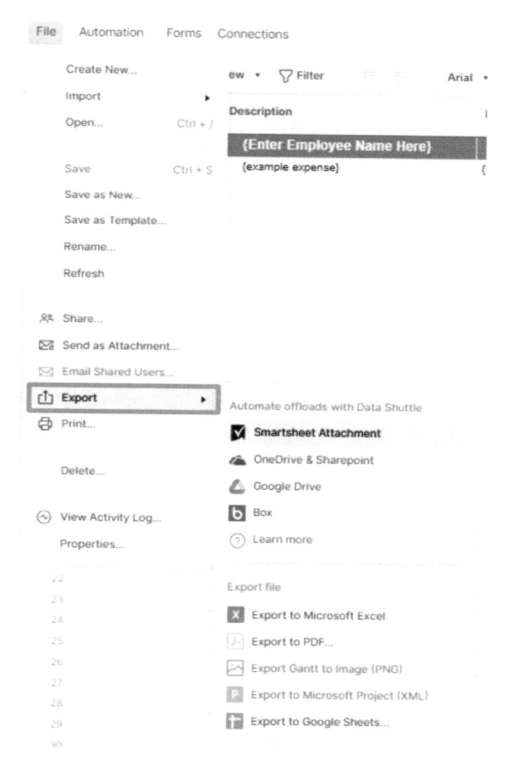

3. **Download the File**

    - A dialog box will appear, prompting you to save the file to your computer.
    - Choose the destination folder and click **Save**.

4. **Verify the Exported File**

    - Open the exported Excel file to ensure that the data has been transferred correctly.

Page 275 | 383

CHAPTER V: VISUALIZING DATA

- Review the formatting, column headers, and data integrity.

Tips for Exporting to Excel:

- Ensure that your columns in Smartsheet are properly named, as these names will appear as headers in Excel.

- If your Smartsheet contains formulas, only the results of those formulas will be exported (not the formulas themselves).

- Exported Excel files retain Smartsheet's structure, including cell colors, bold text, and date formats.

Exporting to PDF

1. **Prepare Your Sheet for Printing**

    - Before exporting to PDF, review how your data will appear.
    - Use the **Print Setup** feature (found under the File menu) to adjust page orientation, scaling, and margins.

2. **Open the Export Menu**

    - Click on the **File** menu.
    - Select **Export** and then choose **Export to PDF**.

3. **Customize the Export Settings**

    - In the Print Setup window, you'll see several options:
        - **Page Orientation**: Choose between portrait and landscape.
        - **Scaling**: Adjust how much of the sheet fits onto a single page. Use "Fit to Width" to avoid cut-off columns.
        - **Margins**: Set the size of margins for your PDF.
        - **Gridlines and Column Headings**: You can choose whether to include gridlines and headings in the exported PDF.

4. **Export and Save**

    - Once you've adjusted the settings, click **Export**.

o   Save the PDF file to your desired location.

Tips for Exporting to PDF:

- Use landscape orientation for wide sheets with many columns.
- Preview the PDF before saving to ensure that all critical information is visible and properly formatted.
- Include gridlines and column headers for better readability.

Exporting to Other Formats

In addition to Excel and PDF, Smartsheet supports exporting to other formats, such as CSV and Google Sheets. These formats are especially useful for specific use cases:

Exporting to CSV (Comma-Separated Values):

- **Use Case**: Ideal for transferring data to systems that support CSV imports, such as databases or other project management tools.
- **Steps**:
    1. Open the File menu and select **Export > Export to CSV (.csv)**.
    2. Save the file to your computer.
    3. Open the file in a text editor or spreadsheet application to review the data.
- **Limitations**: CSV exports do not retain formatting, such as colors or bold text. Only raw data is included.

Exporting to Google Sheets:

- **Use Case**: Perfect for teams using Google Workspace who want to collaborate on the exported data.
- **Steps**:
    1. Export your Smartsheet to Excel format first.
    2. Open Google Sheets, click **File > Import**, and upload the Excel file.
    3. Review and adjust formatting if necessary.

- **Note**: While Smartsheet does not have a direct export option to Google Sheets, this workaround is simple and effective.

Common Exporting Challenges and How to Solve Them

1. **Data Truncation**
   - **Issue**: Some columns or rows are cut off in the exported file.
   - **Solution**: Adjust the page scaling and margins in the Print Setup or reduce the number of visible columns in Smartsheet before exporting.

2. **Formatting Issues in Excel**
   - **Issue**: Exported data appears misaligned or disorganized.
   - **Solution**: Review your Smartsheet formatting before exporting and ensure consistent column widths and data types.

3. **File Size Limitations**
   - **Issue**: Large sheets may result in overly large export files.
   - **Solution**: Break the sheet into smaller sections or export filtered views of the data.

4. **Missing Data in PDF Exports**
   - **Issue**: Not all rows or columns are visible in the exported PDF.
   - **Solution**: Use the scaling feature in Print Setup to fit more data onto a single page or split the export into multiple PDFs.

Use Cases for Exported Data

- **Presentations**: Export reports and dashboards to PDF for use in meetings and presentations.
- **Data Integration**: Export to CSV for importing into CRM, ERP, or data analytics tools.

- **Collaboration**: Share Excel files with external stakeholders who do not use Smartsheet.
- **Documentation**: Save data snapshots in PDF format for auditing or compliance purposes.

By mastering the export functions of Smartsheet, you can ensure that your data remains flexible, accessible, and impactful in any context. Whether creating polished reports for stakeholders or preparing data for in-depth analysis, exporting is an essential skill for Smartsheet users at all levels.

5.3.2 Printing Sheets and Reports

Printing your Smartsheet sheets and reports is a vital feature for those who need to present their work in a physical format or share tangible copies with team members, stakeholders, or clients. Smartsheet provides a variety of options to print data with customizable layouts, ensuring that the final printed output aligns with your needs. This section will guide you step by step through the process of printing sheets and reports, offering tips and best practices to achieve professional-quality results.

Understanding the Printing Process in Smartsheet

Before diving into the steps, it's important to understand the nature of printing in Smartsheet. Since Smartsheet operates in a digital environment, its sheets and reports are optimized for online use. Printing is a way to translate this digital data into a physical or PDF format while preserving the structure and readability of the content.

The printing process involves three key steps:

1. **Configuring the sheet or report layout**: Adjusting the visible columns, rows, and data.
2. **Customizing print settings**: Choosing print options such as orientation, scaling, and margins.

3. **Exporting and printing**: Saving to a file format (like PDF) or sending directly to a printer.

Step-by-Step Guide to Printing Sheets and Reports

1. Preparing the Data for Printing

Before you print, ensure your data is well-organized and ready for a professional presentation:

- **Hide Unnecessary Columns or Rows**: If there are columns or rows that aren't relevant to the printed version, hide them to avoid clutter. To hide a column or row:
    - Right-click on the column header or row number.
    - Select **"Hide Column"** or **"Hide Row"**.
    - Note: This will only affect the current view, not the underlying data.
- **Adjust Column Widths and Row Heights**: Resize columns and rows to ensure the data fits neatly on the printed page. Use the drag handle on column or row borders to resize them manually.
- **Freeze Important Rows or Columns**: To keep headers or key information visible when scrolling, freeze them. This is especially useful when preparing large datasets for printing.
- **Sort and Filter Data**: Apply sorting or filtering to emphasize specific information. For instance, filter tasks by a particular status or sort data chronologically to make it easier to interpret.

2. Accessing the Print Menu

To access the print menu in Smartsheet:

1. Open the sheet or report you want to print.
2. Click on the **File** menu in the upper-left corner of the toolbar.
3. Select **Print** from the dropdown menu. This will open the print preview screen.

3. Customizing Print Settings

Once the print preview is open, you'll have several options to customize how your sheet or report is printed:

- **Page Layout**:
    - **Orientation**: Choose between portrait (vertical) or landscape (horizontal) mode based on the data layout. For example, landscape mode works better for sheets with many columns.
    - **Scaling**: Use the scaling options to fit your data to a specific number of pages. You can select:
        - **Fit to Width**: Scales the content to fit the page width.
        - **Fit to Page**: Scales the content to fit entirely on one page.
        - **Custom Scaling**: Manually adjust scaling percentages to control the size of the printed content.
- **Margins**:
Adjust the margins (top, bottom, left, and right) to control the whitespace around the printed content. Smaller margins are useful for fitting more data on a page.

- **Header and Footer Options**:
  - Add custom headers or footers to include details like the sheet name, report title, or date.
  - You can also include dynamic fields, such as page numbers or the current date, in the header/footer.

- **Gridlines and Colors**:
  - Toggle gridlines on or off based on your preference. Gridlines can make tabular data easier to read.
  - Choose whether to print in color or black-and-white. This is especially useful for reports with charts or conditional formatting.

4. Previewing Your Print Output

Always preview your document before printing to ensure it meets your expectations. The print preview window provides an accurate representation of how your sheet or report will look when printed. Check the following:

- Ensure all critical data fits within the page boundaries.
- Verify that the headers and footers are correctly displayed.
- Confirm that gridlines and formatting are consistent across pages.

5. Printing to PDF or Printer

Once you're satisfied with the preview:

- **Printing to PDF**:
  - Click the **Print to PDF** option to generate a PDF file. This is ideal for sharing electronically or preserving a digital copy.
  - Save the PDF to your preferred location.

- **Printing to a Physical Printer**:
  - Connect your device to a printer and click **Print**.

- Adjust printer-specific settings, such as paper size or print quality, in the printer dialog box.

Tips for Printing Professional-Quality Documents

- **Optimize for Readability**: Use consistent fonts, clear column headings, and appropriate spacing to ensure the data is easy to read.

- **Use Color Strategically**: If printing in color, leverage Smartsheet's conditional formatting to highlight important data points.

- **Include a Summary Page**: For reports, consider adding a summary or executive overview on the first page.

Troubleshooting Common Printing Issues

Even with the best preparation, printing issues can arise. Here are solutions to some common problems:

- **Data Cuts Off at Page Edges**:
    - Adjust the scaling options to fit data to the page width.
    - Ensure that columns aren't excessively wide, causing the content to spill over.

- **Blank Pages in the Output**:
    - Check the print preview for hidden rows or unnecessary whitespace.
    - Adjust margins to reduce excess spacing.

- **Poor Print Quality**:
    - Ensure the printer settings are configured for high-quality output.
    - Use a high-resolution PDF format if printing from a file.

By mastering the printing process in Smartsheet, you can create polished, professional outputs that effectively convey your data and insights. Whether you're presenting to stakeholders or simply archiving your work, the ability to customize and control your printed sheets and reports is an invaluable skill.

5.3.3 Integrating Smartsheet with Presentation Tools

Integrating Smartsheet with presentation tools can be a game-changer when it comes to communicating data, progress, and insights effectively to your team, stakeholders, or clients. This section will guide you through the process of linking Smartsheet with commonly used presentation tools like Microsoft PowerPoint, Google Slides, and other software. Additionally, you'll learn about best practices to ensure that your presentations are both visually appealing and impactful.

1. Why Integrate Smartsheet with Presentation Tools?

Smartsheet is a powerful tool for managing data and projects, but presentation tools are essential for delivering that information in an engaging way. By integrating the two, you can:

- **Save Time:** Automatically update slides with real-time data from Smartsheet.
- **Enhance Accuracy:** Reduce manual errors by linking data directly to your slides.
- **Streamline Communication:** Present live data, charts, and progress without needing to export or reformat.
- **Engage Your Audience:** Visualize complex data in an understandable format tailored to your audience.

2. Common Presentation Tools to Use with Smartsheet

Some of the most popular presentation tools that work well with Smartsheet include:

- **Microsoft PowerPoint:** Ideal for professional and corporate presentations.
- **Google Slides:** Great for cloud-based collaboration and sharing.
- **Canva:** A versatile tool for designing visually appealing slides.

- **Prezi:** Useful for creating dynamic, non-linear presentations.

Smartsheet's flexibility allows for integrations and compatibility with most of these tools, ensuring that you can share your data in a format that suits your needs.

3. Exporting Data for Integration

Before you can integrate Smartsheet with a presentation tool, you need to export the data you wish to present. Here are some steps to do this effectively:

3.1 Exporting Data from Smartsheet

- Open the sheet or report you want to use.
- Click the "File" menu and select **Export.**
- Choose your desired format, such as **Excel, PDF, or CSV.** For most integrations, Excel is the most compatible option.
- Save the exported file to your computer or cloud storage for easy access.

3.2 Cleaning the Data

- Review the exported data to ensure it is accurate and relevant to your presentation.
- Remove unnecessary columns, rows, or data points that may clutter your slides.
- Format the data for consistency, such as using uniform date formats or numerical precision.

3.3 Visualizing the Data

- Use Smartsheet's chart feature to generate bar charts, pie charts, or line graphs directly from your data.
- Export these visuals as PNG or JPEG files for seamless insertion into slides.

4. Linking Smartsheet Data to Presentation Tools

Once you've prepared your data, you can integrate it with your chosen presentation tool. Below are step-by-step guides for common tools:

4.1 Microsoft PowerPoint

- **Step 1: Embed Data Using Excel Links**
    - Export your Smartsheet data to Excel.
    - Open your PowerPoint presentation and navigate to the slide where you want to display the data.
    - Click "Insert" > "Object" > "Create from File," then browse for your Excel file.
    - Check the box for "Link" to ensure that the data updates automatically when changes are made in Smartsheet.

- **Step 2: Use Smartsheet Add-Ons**
    - Smartsheet offers add-ons that integrate directly with Microsoft Office.
    - Download the Smartsheet for Microsoft Office add-on and use it to pull data, charts, and reports directly into PowerPoint.

- **Step 3: Insert Charts and Graphs**
    - Use the Excel data to create charts within PowerPoint.
    - Customize the design to match your presentation theme.

4.2 Google Slides

- **Step 1: Import Data into Google Sheets**
    - Export your Smartsheet data as a CSV file.
    - Upload the file to Google Sheets and format the data as needed.

- **Step 2: Link Google Sheets to Google Slides**
    - Open your Google Slides presentation and go to the slide where you want to display the data.
    - Click "Insert" > "Chart" > "From Sheets."
    - Select the Google Sheet containing your Smartsheet data.

- ○ Choose the desired chart and click "Link to Spreadsheet" to enable real-time updates.
- **Step 3: Embed Smartsheet Dashboards as Images**
  - ○ Take a screenshot of a Smartsheet dashboard and upload it as an image in Google Slides for a quick visual representation.

4.3 Canva

- **Step 1: Upload Data Visuals**
  - ○ Export charts or graphs from Smartsheet as PNG files.
  - ○ Open Canva and choose a presentation template.
  - ○ Upload the visuals to your Canva design and adjust them for size and layout.
- **Step 2: Create Custom Graphics**
  - ○ Use Canva to enhance the Smartsheet data with icons, animations, or illustrations to make the presentation more engaging.

4.4 Prezi

- **Step 1: Import Smartsheet Data as Static Visuals**
  - ○ Export Smartsheet data or charts as images.
  - ○ Insert the visuals into your Prezi presentation for a dynamic, interactive experience.
- **Step 2: Link Real-Time Dashboards**
  - ○ Embed live dashboards from Smartsheet into Prezi using the "Insert Link" option.

5. Best Practices for Integrating Smartsheet with Presentations

To ensure your presentations are effective and professional, follow these best practices:

1. **Use Consistent Branding:** Ensure fonts, colors, and styles align with your organization's branding.

2. **Highlight Key Data:** Focus on the most relevant information and avoid overwhelming your audience with too much detail.

3. **Keep Visuals Simple:** Use clean and uncluttered charts or graphs to make data easier to interpret.

4. **Test for Accuracy:** Double-check that all links and integrations are working properly before presenting.

5. **Update Regularly:** If you're using live data from Smartsheet, confirm that it's up to date before sharing.

6. Benefits of Integration

By integrating Smartsheet with presentation tools, you can:

- **Increase Efficiency:** Automate data updates and reduce manual work.
- **Improve Collaboration:** Share consistent information across teams.
- **Enhance Engagement:** Deliver visually appealing presentations that keep your audience's attention.

Conclusion

Integrating Smartsheet with presentation tools is a straightforward process that can significantly enhance how you communicate and visualize data. Whether you're presenting project updates, financial summaries, or strategic plans, these integrations ensure that your presentations are impactful and aligned with your audience's needs. With the steps and tips provided, you're now equipped to confidently leverage Smartsheet's power in any presentation setting.

CHAPTER VI
Tips and Tricks for Beginners

6.1 Keyboard Shortcuts for Efficiency

Keyboard shortcuts are an essential part of maximizing your productivity in Smartsheet. By reducing reliance on the mouse and learning a set of powerful shortcuts, you can work faster, streamline repetitive tasks, and focus on what matters most. This section will guide you through the most useful Smartsheet shortcuts, categorize them by functionality, and provide practical examples to help you incorporate them into your workflow.

Why Use Keyboard Shortcuts?

Using keyboard shortcuts offers several advantages:

1. **Speed**: Shortcuts significantly reduce the time it takes to complete tasks.
2. **Efficiency**: You can execute commands quickly without navigating through menus.
3. **Focus**: Staying on the keyboard helps you avoid distractions caused by switching between the mouse and keyboard.
4. **Ergonomics**: Reducing mouse usage can prevent repetitive strain injuries over time.

Smartsheet is designed with a wide range of shortcuts that allow users to create, edit, navigate, and manage data seamlessly.

Basic Navigation Shortcuts

Smartsheet shortcuts for navigation help you move around your sheets effortlessly:

- **Arrow Keys**: Navigate between cells in all directions.

- **Tab**: Move to the next cell in the same row.
- **Shift + Tab**: Move to the previous cell in the same row.
- **Ctrl + Home** (Windows) or **Command + Home** (Mac): Jump to the top-left corner of the sheet.
- **Ctrl + End** (Windows) or **Command + End** (Mac): Jump to the bottom-right corner of the sheet.

Example in Action: If you're working with a sheet containing hundreds of rows, use **Ctrl + Home** to quickly return to the top without scrolling.

Editing Shortcuts

Editing data in Smartsheet becomes much faster with these shortcuts:

- **Enter**: Open the selected cell for editing.
- **Ctrl + C**: Copy the content of a selected cell.
- **Ctrl + X**: Cut the content of a selected cell.
- **Ctrl + V**: Paste content into the selected cell.
- **Delete**: Clear the content of a selected cell.
- **Ctrl + Z**: Undo the last action.
- **Ctrl + Y**: Redo the last undone action.

Pro Tip: When pasting data, you can copy multiple cells from Excel or Google Sheets and paste them directly into Smartsheet.

Example in Action: Suppose you accidentally delete an important entry in your sheet. Use **Ctrl + Z** to instantly recover it.

Formatting Shortcuts

Formatting shortcuts allow you to highlight important data quickly:

- **Ctrl + B**: Bold the text in a selected cell.

- **Ctrl + I**: Italicize the text in a selected cell.
- **Ctrl + U**: Underline the text in a selected cell.
- **Ctrl + Shift + C**: Copy formatting from one cell.
- **Ctrl + Shift + V**: Paste formatting into another cell.

Example in Action: If you want to highlight all deadlines in bold, select the cell, press **Ctrl + B**, and use **Ctrl + Shift + V** to apply the formatting to similar cells.

Row and Column Management Shortcuts

Managing rows and columns can be tedious without shortcuts. Here's how to speed things up:

- **Ctrl + Spacebar**: Select an entire column.
- **Shift + Spacebar**: Select an entire row.
- **Ctrl + Shift + "+"**: Add a new row below the selected row.
- **Ctrl + Shift + "-"**: Delete the selected row.
- **Ctrl + D**: Duplicate the selected row.

Example in Action: If you frequently add rows to a project plan, simply use **Ctrl + Shift + "+"** instead of navigating through the toolbar.

Navigating Between Sheets

If you work with multiple sheets in Smartsheet, these shortcuts can save time:

- **Ctrl + Tab** (Windows) or **Command + Tab** (Mac): Switch between open sheets.
- **Ctrl + W** (Windows) or **Command + W** (Mac): Close the current sheet.
- **Ctrl + Shift + T**: Reopen the last closed sheet.

Example in Action: When comparing data across multiple sheets, use **Ctrl + Tab** to toggle between them without interrupting your workflow.

Automation and Workflow Shortcuts

Smartsheet offers shortcuts for managing automated workflows and processes:

- **Ctrl + Shift + A**: Open the automation menu.
- **Ctrl + Shift + R**: Refresh the sheet to apply recent automation changes.

Example in Action:
If you've set up automation rules to notify team members, use **Ctrl + Shift + R** to ensure your updates trigger the rules immediately.

Shortcuts for Comments and Collaboration

Collaboration is central to Smartsheet, and these shortcuts make it easy:

- **Alt + C**: Open the comments panel for the selected cell.
- **Alt + Shift + N**: Add a new comment to the selected cell.
- **Ctrl + Shift + E**: Share the current sheet via email.

Example in Action: If you're reviewing tasks with a team member, use **Alt + C** to quickly pull up relevant comments and make updates in real time.

Advanced Shortcuts for Power Users

For users looking to take their efficiency to the next level:

- **Ctrl + K**: Insert a hyperlink into a selected cell.
- **Ctrl + Shift + L**: Lock or unlock a selected column or row.
- **Ctrl + P**: Print the current sheet.

Example in Action: If you need to link a task to an external resource, use **Ctrl + K** to add a clickable hyperlink directly to the cell.

Building a Custom Shortcut Routine

To truly benefit from shortcuts, it's essential to incorporate them into your daily workflow. Here's a step-by-step process:

1. **Learn in Categories**: Start with navigation shortcuts, then move to editing and formatting.

2. **Practice Regularly**: Dedicate time to practicing shortcuts until they become second nature.

3. **Combine Actions**: Use multiple shortcuts in sequence. For example:
    - Navigate with **Arrow Keys**, copy with **Ctrl + C**, paste with **Ctrl + V**, and format with **Ctrl + B**.

4. **Customize**: While Smartsheet doesn't currently allow custom shortcuts, you can use third-party tools like AutoHotkey to create personalized macros for repetitive tasks.

Summary of Keyboard Shortcuts

To make it easier to reference the shortcuts, here's a summary table:

Action	Shortcut (Windows)	Shortcut (Mac)
Navigate between cells	Arrow Keys	Arrow Keys
Edit a cell	Enter	Enter
Copy	Ctrl + C	Command + C
Paste	Ctrl + V	Command + V
Undo	Ctrl + Z	Command + Z
Bold	Ctrl + B	Command + B
Add a new row	Ctrl + Shift + "+"	Command + Shift + "+"
Open comments	Alt + C	Option + C

By adopting these shortcuts, you'll transform the way you work in Smartsheet. Practice regularly, and you'll soon notice a significant improvement in your productivity and ability to manage complex projects with ease.

6.2 Troubleshooting Common Issues

6.2.1 Resolving Login Problems

When using Smartsheet, login problems can occasionally occur, disrupting your workflow. This section offers a comprehensive guide to identifying, resolving, and preventing login issues, ensuring seamless access to your Smartsheet account.

Understanding Common Login Issues

Before troubleshooting, it's essential to understand the root causes of login problems. These issues typically fall into one of the following categories:

1. **Incorrect Credentials:**
    - Forgetting your email address or password.
    - Typographical errors in the login details.

2. **Account Status Issues:**
    - The account is locked due to multiple failed login attempts.
    - The account is inactive or deactivated.

3. **Browser-Related Problems:**
    - Outdated browser versions.
    - Cached data or cookies causing conflicts.

4. **Network Connectivity Issues:**
    - Poor internet connection or blocked access due to firewall settings.

5. **Technical Errors:**
    - Server downtime or technical glitches on Smartsheet's end.

By identifying which category your problem falls into, you can apply the appropriate solution quickly and effectively.

Step-by-Step Solutions for Login Problems

1. Verify Your Credentials

The most common reason for login failure is incorrect login credentials. Follow these steps:

- **Double-Check Your Email Address:** Ensure the email address you are entering matches the one you used to create your Smartsheet account. Check for accidental spaces or spelling errors.

- **Reset Your Password:** If you've forgotten your password or suspect it may be incorrect:

    - Click on the **"Forgot Password"** link on the login page.
    - Enter your registered email address.
    - Follow the instructions in the password reset email to create a new password.

Tip: Use a strong password that combines uppercase letters, lowercase letters, numbers, and special characters.

2. Address Account Lockouts

After multiple unsuccessful login attempts, Smartsheet may temporarily lock your account to protect it from unauthorized access. To resolve this:

- Wait for 15-30 minutes, as most locks are temporary.
- Reset your password to regain access if you believe you entered the wrong password multiple times.

If the issue persists, contact Smartsheet Support for assistance in unlocking your account.

3. Update Your Browser

An outdated browser may cause login failures or display issues. Ensure your browser is up to date by:

- Visiting the browser's settings or help menu to check for updates.
- Downloading the latest version of your preferred browser (e.g., Google Chrome, Mozilla Firefox, Microsoft Edge).

4. Clear Browser Cache and Cookies

Cached data or cookies may cause login conflicts. To clear them:

- Open your browser settings.
- Navigate to **Privacy and Security**.
- Select **Clear Browsing Data** and check the boxes for **Cookies** and **Cached Images and Files**.
- Reload the Smartsheet login page and try again.

5. Check Your Internet Connection

If you suspect a network issue:

- Test your internet speed using tools like Speedtest. https://www.speedtest.net/
- Restart your router or modem to refresh your connection.
- Connect to a different network to rule out firewall or ISP restrictions.

6. Disable Browser Extensions

Sometimes, browser extensions can interfere with Smartsheet. Disable all extensions and attempt to log in. If successful, re-enable extensions one by one to identify the culprit.

7. Ensure Smartsheet's Servers Are Online

Occasionally, Smartsheet may experience downtime or maintenance periods. Check the Smartsheet **Status Page** at status.smartsheet.com to verify if the platform is operational.

8. Use Incognito Mode

Login issues may be resolved by accessing Smartsheet in your browser's incognito or private browsing mode, which disables most extensions and ignores cached data.

9. Contact Smartsheet Support

If none of the above steps work, Smartsheet's customer support team can assist you further. Before reaching out:

- Note down any error messages you've encountered.
- Prepare details about the steps you've already taken to resolve the issue.

Contact support via the **Help & Learning Center** or through the email provided for your account type.

Preventing Login Problems

While login issues can be resolved, it's better to prevent them altogether. Here are some preventive measures:

1. Use a Password Manager

Password managers like LastPass or 1Password help you store and retrieve complex passwords, reducing the risk of entering incorrect credentials.

2. Enable Two-Factor Authentication (2FA)

Adding 2FA to your account enhances security and minimizes unauthorized access. Smartsheet supports 2FA through authentication apps like Google Authenticator or Authy.

3. Regularly Update Your Browser

Outdated browsers are vulnerable to security risks and may cause compatibility issues. Set your browser to update automatically.

4. Avoid Public Wi-Fi for Sensitive Logins

Logging in to Smartsheet on unsecured public networks increases the risk of unauthorized access. Use a Virtual Private Network (VPN) if you must connect via public Wi-Fi.

5. Regularly Clear Cache and Cookies

Prevent data conflicts by periodically clearing your browser's cache and cookies.

6. Monitor Smartsheet Announcements

Stay informed about scheduled maintenance or potential downtime by subscribing to Smartsheet's announcements or checking the status page regularly.

Common Scenarios and Solutions

Scenario 1: Forgotten Password

- **Problem:** You can't remember your password.
- **Solution:** Use the "Forgot Password" option to reset it.

Scenario 2: Locked Account

- **Problem:** Multiple failed login attempts have locked your account.
- **Solution:** Wait for 15-30 minutes and reset your password if necessary.

Scenario 3: Browser Compatibility

- **Problem:** Login page not loading properly.
- **Solution:** Update your browser, clear cache and cookies, or use incognito mode.

Scenario 4: Smartsheet Servers Down

- **Problem:** Login attempts fail due to server issues.
- **Solution:** Check the Smartsheet status page and wait for the issue to resolve.

Summary

Login problems can be frustrating, but they are usually straightforward to resolve with the right approach. By following the steps in this guide and implementing preventive measures, you can minimize disruptions to your Smartsheet workflow. Remember, Smartsheet's support team is always available to assist if you encounter persistent issues.

6.2.2 Fixing Formatting Errors

Formatting is a critical aspect of working in Smartsheet, as it ensures your data is presented in an organized and visually appealing manner. However, formatting errors can disrupt your workflow and lead to confusion among collaborators. In this section, we'll address common formatting issues, explain why they occur, and provide detailed step-by-step solutions to fix them.

Understanding Formatting in Smartsheet

Before diving into troubleshooting, it's essential to understand the types of formatting options Smartsheet offers:

- **Cell Formatting:** Includes text alignment, font styles, colors, borders, and conditional formatting.
- **Column Formatting:** Includes column types (e.g., Text/Number, Dropdown, Date, Checkbox) and default alignment.
- **Sheet-Level Formatting:** Includes overall sheet layout, gridlines, and row heights.

Each of these plays a role in how data is displayed and interpreted, and errors in any of these can lead to formatting problems.

Common Formatting Errors and How to Fix Them

Below are the most frequent formatting issues users encounter in Smartsheet and the steps to resolve them:

1. Misaligned Data (Text or Numbers Not Aligning Correctly)

Problem:

Text or numerical data may not align properly within cells, making the sheet difficult to read. This often occurs when column types are incorrectly configured or when alignment settings have been manually overridden.

Solution:

1. **Check Column Type:**
    - Right-click the column header and select **"Edit Column Properties."**
    - Ensure the column type is appropriate for the data (e.g., use "Text/Number" for general text or numbers, "Date" for dates, and "Checkbox" for binary choices).

2. **Adjust Alignment:**
    - Highlight the affected cells or column.
    - Use the alignment tools in the toolbar (left, center, or right alignment).

3. **Reset Default Alignment:**
    - If manual adjustments are not working, reset the column or sheet formatting by right-clicking the header and selecting **"Clear Formatting."**

2. Incorrect Date or Number Formats

Problem:

Dates may appear in an incorrect format (e.g., MM/DD/YYYY instead of DD/MM/YYYY), or numbers may show unexpected decimals or symbols (e.g., currency or percentage).

Solution:

1. **Adjust Column Formatting:**
    - Right-click the column header and choose **"Edit Column Properties."**
    - Select the appropriate format under the "Number Format" or "Date Format" options.

2. **Apply Custom Formatting:**

- Highlight the cells or columns with the issue.
- Go to the toolbar and use the number formatting dropdown (e.g., currency, percentage, or plain number).

3. **Check Regional Settings:**
   - Ensure your regional settings in Smartsheet align with your desired format:
     - Go to **Account Settings > Personal Settings > Regional Preferences.**

3. Inconsistent Font Styles or Colors

Problem:

Different rows or columns may have inconsistent fonts, sizes, or colors, leading to a cluttered appearance.

Solution:

1. **Apply Uniform Formatting:**
   - Highlight the entire sheet or affected area.
   - Use the formatting toolbar to set a consistent font, size, and color.

2. **Use Conditional Formatting:**
   - For automated consistency, create rules under **"Conditional Formatting."**
   - Example: Set all overdue tasks to display in red or all completed tasks in green.

3. **Clear Manual Overrides:**
   - Highlight the affected cells, right-click, and select **"Clear Formatting."**

4. Borders and Gridlines Not Displaying Properly

Problem:

Borders may appear uneven or gridlines may not show consistently, making the sheet difficult to read.

Solution:

1. **Add or Adjust Borders:**
    - Highlight the cells where borders are missing or incorrect.
    - Use the border tool in the toolbar to apply or adjust borders.

2. **Toggle Gridlines:**
    - If gridlines are missing, go to **View > Gridlines** and ensure the option is enabled.

3. **Check for Hidden Rows or Columns:**
    - If certain gridlines or borders appear missing, right-click the column/row headers and select **"Unhide Columns"** or **"Unhide Rows."**

5. Overlapping or Merged Cells Issues

Problem:

Merged cells may not display data correctly, or they may disrupt sorting and filtering functionalities.

Solution:

1. **Unmerge Cells:**
    - Highlight the merged cells, right-click, and select **"Unmerge."**

2. **Reorganize Data:**
    - Move or copy data from merged cells to individual rows or columns.

3. **Avoid Future Issues:**
    - Use merged cells sparingly, as they can interfere with sorting, filtering, and formula calculations.

6. Conditional Formatting Not Applying Correctly

Problem:

Conditional formatting rules may not apply as intended, leading to incorrect or missing highlights.

Solution:

1. **Review Conditional Formatting Rules:**
   - Go to **"Conditional Formatting"** in the toolbar.
   - Ensure the rules are set up correctly (e.g., proper criteria and range).
2. **Reapply Rules:**
   - If a rule is not working, delete it and reapply.
3. **Check for Conflicting Rules:**
   - Ensure multiple rules do not overlap or contradict each other.

Pro Tips for Avoiding Formatting Errors

1. **Use Templates:**
   - Start with Smartsheet templates designed for your use case. Templates often include pre-applied formatting that reduces errors.
2. **Plan Formatting in Advance:**
   - Decide on formatting standards (fonts, colors, alignment) before entering data.
3. **Leverage Conditional Formatting:**
   - Use rules to automate formatting rather than applying it manually.
4. **Regularly Audit Your Sheets:**

- Periodically review sheets for inconsistencies or formatting drift.
5. **Train Your Team:**
   - Ensure all collaborators are familiar with Smartsheet formatting best practices to prevent errors from being introduced.

By understanding these common formatting issues and their solutions, you can ensure your Smartsheet projects remain clear, professional, and easy to manage. Following these tips will save time, enhance collaboration, and reduce frustration across your team.

6.2.3 Handling Collaboration Conflicts

Collaboration is one of the key strengths of Smartsheet, enabling teams to work together efficiently on shared projects. However, with multiple people accessing and editing the same sheets, conflicts can arise. These issues often stem from miscommunication, overlapping edits, or unclear permissions. This section will guide you through identifying, preventing, and resolving common collaboration conflicts in Smartsheet.

Understanding Collaboration Conflicts in Smartsheet

Before resolving conflicts, it's important to understand their common causes. Collaboration issues often occur due to:

- **Overlapping Edits**: Two or more collaborators editing the same row or cell simultaneously.
- **Unclear Roles and Permissions**: When users are not sure what they can or cannot do, leading to accidental changes or deletions.
- **Communication Gaps**: Lack of proper communication among team members about changes made in a sheet.
- **Version Control Issues**: Confusion caused by not knowing which version of the sheet is the most recent or accurate.

CHAPTER VI: TIPS AND TRICKS FOR BEGINNERS

Smartsheet offers several features that can help mitigate these issues, but knowing how to troubleshoot them when they arise is essential.

Step 1: Identifying Collaboration Conflicts

The first step in resolving any collaboration conflict is identifying where the issue lies. Here's how you can pinpoint conflicts:

1. **Review the Activity Log**
   - Smartsheet's Activity Log allows you to see who made changes, when, and what was changed.
   - To access the Activity Log:
     - Open the sheet and click on the "Activity Log" button in the toolbar.
     - Filter by user, date, or type of activity to narrow down the changes.
   - Look for conflicting edits or unauthorized changes that might have caused confusion.

2. **Check the Revision History**
   - Revision history helps you identify if multiple users edited the same cells or rows.
   - Smartsheet automatically saves versions of the sheet after major changes. Use this to compare and revert to an earlier version if needed.

3. **Communicate with Collaborators**
   - If the source of the conflict isn't obvious, reach out to team members to discuss recent changes.
   - Ask if anyone encountered issues while editing or if they unintentionally made changes.

Step 2: Resolving Collaboration Conflicts

Once you've identified the issue, follow these steps to resolve it effectively:

1. **Resolve Overlapping Edits**
   - **Use Alerts and Notifications**: Set up notifications to inform collaborators of changes to specific rows or sheets.
   - **Lock Rows or Columns**: If certain rows or columns require exclusive access, lock them to prevent edits by unauthorized users. To lock a row or column:
     - Right-click on the row/column header and select "Lock Row" or "Lock Column."
     - Ensure that only authorized users with Admin permissions can unlock it.
   - **Coordinate Edits**: Use the "Comments" feature to leave notes for collaborators about planned changes.

2. **Revert Changes Using the Activity Log or Revision History**
   - If conflicting edits have already been made, you can revert them:
     - Open the Activity Log, locate the conflicting change, and click "Undo Change."
     - Alternatively, restore an earlier version of the sheet using the Revision History.

3. **Resolve Permission Issues**
   - Verify that each collaborator has appropriate permissions:
     - **Viewer**: Can only view the sheet.
     - **Editor**: Can edit content but cannot change sheet structure.
     - **Admin**: Can edit, delete, and manage permissions.
   - To modify permissions:
     - Click the "Share" button in the top-right corner of the sheet.

- Adjust permissions for each user as needed.

4. **Improve Communication**
   - Use built-in communication tools such as comments, notifications, and email summaries to keep everyone informed.
   - Create a shared workspace or dashboard to centralize updates and reduce miscommunication.

Step 3: Preventing Future Collaboration Conflicts

Prevention is always better than resolution. Follow these best practices to avoid future collaboration issues:

1. **Set Clear Roles and Responsibilities**
   - Define roles for each team member and outline their responsibilities regarding the sheet.
   - Use Smartsheet's "Assigned To" column to clearly indicate task ownership.

2. **Implement Sheet-Level Guidelines**
   - Create and share a document that outlines how the team should use the sheet.
   - Include details on naming conventions, editing rules, and communication protocols.

3. **Use Automation to Streamline Updates**
   - Automate updates to reduce manual input errors:
     - Set up alerts to notify users when tasks are assigned, completed, or overdue.
     - Create automated workflows for approvals or task reminders.

4. **Leverage Smartsheet Features for Collaboration**

- **Comments**: Add comments to rows to communicate changes without editing the data directly.
- **Attachments**: Upload and share relevant files directly within the sheet.
- **Dashboards**: Use dashboards to provide a high-level view of the project for all collaborators.

5. **Regularly Review Permissions and Access**
    - Periodically audit permissions to ensure that only authorized users have access.
    - Remove users who no longer need access to maintain data security.

Real-World Example: Resolving a Collaboration Conflict

Scenario: A marketing team is using Smartsheet to track a product launch. Two team members accidentally overwrite each other's updates in the "Campaign Schedule" column.

Steps Taken:

1. **Review the Activity Log**: The team identifies the conflicting edits and sees who made them.
2. **Communicate**: The team discusses the changes and agrees on the correct version.
3. **Lock the Column**: The team locks the "Campaign Schedule" column and assigns editing rights to only one person.
4. **Automate Notifications**: Alerts are set up to notify the team whenever changes are made to critical columns.
5. **Document Best Practices**: The team updates their guidelines to include communication protocols and editing rules.

Conclusion

Handling collaboration conflicts in Smartsheet is straightforward when you use the platform's tools effectively. By understanding the root causes of conflicts, resolving them systematically, and implementing preventive measures, you can ensure smooth collaboration and maximize team productivity.

With the right approach, Smartsheet becomes not just a tool for managing projects, but a platform for fostering teamwork and achieving shared goals.

6.3 Best Practices for Staying Organized

6.3.1 Naming Conventions for Sheets and Workspaces

Staying organized in Smartsheet starts with a clear and consistent approach to naming your sheets, workspaces, and other resources. Well-thought-out naming conventions are the foundation of efficient collaboration, easy navigation, and long-term success in managing projects. This section explores why naming conventions are essential, key principles to follow, practical tips for creating effective names, and examples to inspire your own system.

Why Naming Conventions Matter

Naming conventions in Smartsheet are not just about aesthetics; they are critical for:

1. **Efficient Navigation**: As your Smartsheet usage grows, it becomes harder to locate specific sheets or workspaces quickly. Clear naming makes finding information fast and intuitive.

2. **Collaboration Clarity**: When working with teams, standardized names ensure that everyone understands the purpose and contents of a sheet or workspace without opening it.

3. **Avoiding Redundancy**: Properly named resources reduce the likelihood of creating duplicate sheets or workspaces.

4. **Long-Term Usability**: Projects evolve, and team members may change. Clear naming ensures your sheets and workspaces remain usable even as circumstances shift.

Key Principles for Effective Naming Conventions

1. **Consistency Is Key**: Use the same format and style for all your sheets and workspaces. Inconsistencies create confusion and make it harder to maintain your system.

2. **Be Descriptive but Concise**: The name should provide enough information to identify the content without being overly long. Strike a balance between detail and simplicity.

3. **Use Standardized Date Formats**: If your sheets or workspaces are time-sensitive, include dates in a consistent format, such as YYYY-MM-DD. This helps with sorting and organizing chronologically.

4. **Avoid Ambiguity**: Use specific terms that clearly indicate the purpose of the resource. For instance, "Project Plan" is vague, while "2025_Product_Launch_Plan" is specific.

5. **Incorporate Team or Department Names**: For team-wide resources, adding the team name (e.g., "Marketing_2025_Strategy") clarifies ownership.

6. **Use Keywords for Searchability**: Think about the terms team members are likely to search for and include them in the name.

7. **Avoid Special Characters**: Stick to letters, numbers, underscores, and hyphens. Special characters can cause issues with some systems or integrations.

Developing a Naming Convention System

Here's a step-by-step process to create a robust naming convention system:

1. Define the Scope of Your System

- Identify the types of resources you use most frequently, such as sheets, reports, dashboards, or workspaces.
- Ensure the naming system works across all these resource types.

2. Determine Key Components

- Break down the information you want to include in names. Common components include:

CHAPTER VI: TIPS AND TRICKS FOR BEGINNERS

- o **Project Name**: e.g., "Website_Redesign"
- o **Date or Timeframe**: e.g., "2025-Q1" or "2025-01-15"
- o **Team or Department**: e.g., "Finance" or "HR"
- o **Resource Type**: e.g., "Plan," "Report," or "Schedule"
- Combine these components in a logical sequence, such as Project_Team_Type_Date.

3. Choose a Format

- Decide how elements will be separated. Common options include underscores (_), hyphens (-), or camelCase (e.g., ProjectPlan2025).
- Example: Marketing_2025-Q1_Campaign_Schedule

4. Create a Reference Guide

- Document your naming conventions and share them with your team. Include examples, rules for abbreviations, and guidelines for updating names as projects evolve.

5. Train Your Team

- Ensure everyone understands and adheres to the naming conventions. Consistency across users is vital for success.

Best Practices for Naming Sheets

1. **Include a Version Number (if applicable)**
   - o If your project requires multiple iterations, include a version indicator in the name, such as v1, v2, or Draft.
   - o Example: Website_Redesign_v1

2. **Group Related Sheets**
   - o Use prefixes or consistent keywords to group related sheets together.
   - o Example: Budget_Marketing_2025 and Budget_Operations_2025

3. **Use Acronyms Sparingly**
    - While acronyms save space, overusing them can confuse team members. Use only well-known or documented acronyms.
    - Example: HR_Policy_2025 is clear, while HRP_2025 might not be.

4. **Update Names as Needed**
    - If a sheet's purpose changes significantly, rename it to reflect its updated role. This avoids confusion over outdated names.

Best Practices for Naming Workspaces

1. **Use Hierarchical Names**
    - If your organization uses nested workspaces, use a hierarchical naming system to indicate relationships.
    - Example: Corporate > Marketing > Campaigns > 2025-Q1

2. **Indicate Ownership**
    - Include the owner's name or department for clarity.
    - Example: Finance_Budgeting_Tools

3. **Avoid Over-Nesting**
    - While nesting workspaces can help with organization, avoid creating excessive layers that make navigation cumbersome.

4. **Include Active vs. Archived Status**
    - Indicate whether a workspace is active or archived to prevent confusion.
    - Example: Archived_2023_Projects

Examples of Effective Naming Conventions

Below are sample naming conventions you can adapt to your needs:

1. **For Sheets**:
   - 2025_Product_Launch_Plan_v1
   - Q1_Marketing_Budget_2025
   - HR_Training_Schedule_2025-01

2. **For Workspaces**:
   - Team_Sales_Reports_2025
   - Archived_Marketing_2024
   - Corporate_Strategy_2025

3. **For Dashboards**:
   - 2025_Q1_Project_Status
   - Finance_Overview_2025

Common Pitfalls to Avoid

1. **Using Vague Names**: Avoid generic names like "Sheet1" or "Untitled Workspace." They provide no context and make navigation difficult.

2. **Failing to Update Names**: Outdated names create confusion. Regularly review and rename resources as needed.

3. **Overloading Names with Details**: While detail is important, overly long names can become cumbersome. Focus on the essentials.

Tips for Long-Term Success

1. **Conduct Regular Audits**
   - Periodically review your sheets and workspaces to ensure they follow naming conventions. Update or archive as necessary.

2. **Create Templates with Predefined Names**

- Use Smartsheet templates with placeholder names to encourage consistency from the start.

3. **Leverage Smartsheet's Search Function**
    - Even with great naming conventions, use the search bar to locate specific sheets quickly.

4. **Solicit Team Feedback**
    - Naming conventions should evolve with your organization's needs. Encourage team input to refine your system over time.

By implementing effective naming conventions, you'll streamline your workflow, foster collaboration, and set a solid foundation for Smartsheet success. With a clear system in place, you and your team can focus more on getting work done and less on hunting for information.

6.3.2 Archiving Old Projects

Archiving old projects in Smartsheet is an essential practice for staying organized, ensuring data security, and maintaining workspace efficiency. Over time, as new projects are created and completed, older projects can clutter your dashboard, reduce productivity, and make it harder to find relevant information. Archiving these old projects doesn't just free up space—it also ensures that your workspace remains a reliable repository of information for historical reference, compliance, or future audits.

This section will walk you through the importance of archiving, the steps involved in doing it efficiently, and the best practices to make this process seamless.

Why Archiving Old Projects Matters

1. **Improved Organization**: Keeping active projects separate from completed ones ensures that your Smartsheet dashboard remains uncluttered and visually organized. This makes it easier to focus on current tasks without distractions.

2. **Faster Navigation**: As your team's workload grows, so does the number of sheets and workspaces. Archiving old projects prevents overcrowding and helps team members quickly locate what they need.

3. **Data Preservation**: Archiving ensures that valuable data from past projects is safely stored and accessible for future reference. This is especially important for organizations that need to comply with regulatory requirements or maintain historical records for audits.

4. **Performance Optimization**: Smartsheet performs best when actively used sheets and dashboards are kept to a manageable number. Archiving reduces the load on your account and ensures smoother operation.

5. **Team Productivity**: A tidy workspace boosts team morale and productivity by reducing the time spent searching for information or managing unnecessary clutter.

How to Archive Old Projects in Smartsheet

Step 1: Identify Projects for Archiving

Start by identifying completed projects that no longer require active collaboration. To do this:

- **Filter by Completion Date**: Use Smartsheet's filtering feature to sort sheets based on their completion dates. Projects older than a specific period (e.g., six months or one year) are good candidates for archiving.

- **Review Project Status**: Check the status of projects to ensure they're marked as "Completed" or "Closed."

- **Consult Your Team**: Before archiving, communicate with your team to confirm that no one needs active access to the project.

Step 2: Export and Backup Project Data

While Smartsheet securely stores your data, it's always a good idea to create backups before archiving. To do this:

- **Export the Sheet**:
    - Open the sheet you wish to archive.
    - Click on **File > Export** and select your preferred format (e.g., Excel, PDF).
    - Save the exported file to a local or cloud storage location.
- **Save Attachments**:
    - Review the project for any attached files or documents.
    - Download these files to ensure they're stored alongside the project data.
- **Backup Automation Rules**: If your sheet has automation rules set up, document or export them to recreate in future projects, if needed.

Step 3: Move Projects to an Archive Folder

Smartsheet allows you to create folders and workspaces for organization. To archive a project:

- **Create an Archive Folder**:
    - Navigate to your workspace.
    - Right-click and select **New Folder**, naming it something like "Archived Projects" or "Completed Work."
- **Move Sheets to the Folder**:
    - Drag and drop the completed sheets into the newly created archive folder.
    - Alternatively, use the **Move to Another Folder** option in the sheet menu.

Step 4: Adjust Permissions (Optional)

Archived projects often don't need to be accessed by everyone. Adjust permissions to limit access:

- Click on the **Sharing** button for the sheet or folder.

- Remove unnecessary collaborators or downgrade their permissions to "Viewer" or "Commenter."
- This ensures archived projects remain secure and don't interfere with active collaboration.

Step 5: Label Archived Projects Clearly

Add tags or naming conventions to make archived projects easy to identify:

- Rename sheets with a prefix like "ARCHIVE_" or "COMP_" (e.g., "ARCHIVE_Marketing Campaign Q1 2023").
- Use color coding or add an "Archived" tag in the sheet properties.

Best Practices for Archiving Old Projects

1. Schedule Regular Archiving Sessions

- Set a quarterly or biannual schedule to review and archive completed projects.
- Assign a team member or administrator to oversee the archiving process.

2. Maintain a Centralized Archive Workspace

- Instead of creating multiple archive folders in different workspaces, maintain a centralized workspace for all archived projects.
- Organize the archive workspace with subfolders based on years, departments, or project types.

3. Document Archiving Policies

- Create a standard operating procedure (SOP) for archiving.
- Include criteria for identifying projects to archive, steps for exporting data, and guidelines for naming conventions.

4. Use Automation for Archiving Notifications

- Set up automation rules to send reminders when a project is marked as "Completed" or hasn't been updated in a specific timeframe.

- For example, create an alert for the admin to archive projects after 90 days of inactivity.

5. Periodically Review Archived Projects

- Every year, review archived projects to determine if any can be deleted permanently.
- Ensure compliance with organizational data retention policies.

Common Mistakes to Avoid

1. **Archiving Too Early**: Make sure all necessary tasks are closed, and no pending follow-ups are left before archiving.
2. **Not Backing Up Data**: Always export critical data to avoid accidental loss during the archiving process.
3. **Ignoring Permissions**: Failing to adjust permissions can lead to unauthorized access to archived projects.
4. **Cluttering Archive Folders**: Organize the archive workspace with a clear structure to prevent it from becoming as cluttered as the active workspace.

Benefits of Following an Effective Archiving Process

By adopting a systematic archiving process in Smartsheet, you'll:

- Save time by quickly finding relevant active projects.
- Preserve valuable historical data for audits, reviews, or future reference.
- Keep your workspace visually clean and easy to navigate.
- Enhance team productivity by reducing distractions.
- Optimize Smartsheet's performance for better usability.

Archiving old projects is not just about decluttering—it's a crucial step in maintaining an efficient and effective Smartsheet workflow. By following these guidelines, you'll create a streamlined, well-organized workspace that supports both your team's current projects and long-term goals.

6.3.3 Maintaining Data Security

Maintaining data security in Smartsheet is a critical best practice, especially as businesses and teams increasingly rely on collaborative cloud-based tools to manage sensitive information. Whether you are managing internal projects, customer data, or financial documents, securing your Smartsheet environment is essential to avoid unauthorized access, data breaches, or accidental data loss. This section will cover the key principles, actionable steps, and practical tips to ensure your data remains safe while utilizing Smartsheet's powerful tools.

Understand the Importance of Data Security

Data breaches can lead to serious consequences, such as financial loss, reputational damage, or legal ramifications. Smartsheet provides a secure platform, but users must actively engage in following security best practices to maximize protection. Maintaining data security ensures:

- **Confidentiality**: Ensuring that only authorized individuals can access sensitive information.
- **Integrity**: Protecting data from unauthorized modification or corruption.
- **Availability**: Ensuring that critical data is accessible to authorized users whenever needed.

Key Features of Smartsheet for Data Security

Smartsheet includes several built-in security features that users can leverage to maintain a secure environment. Familiarizing yourself with these tools will help you strengthen your data protection efforts.

1. **User Permissions and Access Control**
   - Smartsheet allows you to assign specific roles and permissions to users. These include Admin, Editor, Viewer, and more.
   - **Action Step**:
     - Grant access only to those who truly need it. For example, limit editing permissions to project managers while granting read-only access to stakeholders.
     - Regularly audit user permissions to ensure former employees or contractors no longer have access.

2. **Data Encryption**
   - Smartsheet encrypts data both in transit (when being sent to or from Smartsheet) and at rest (when stored in their servers).
   - **Action Step**: Ensure all team members access Smartsheet over secure, private networks to take full advantage of Smartsheet's encryption protocols.

3. **Two-Factor Authentication (2FA)**
   - Two-factor authentication adds an additional layer of security by requiring users to verify their identity using a secondary method, such as a text message code or an authentication app.
   - **Action Step**: Enable 2FA for all accounts to reduce the risk of compromised login credentials.

4. **Audit Logs and Activity Reporting**
   - Smartsheet provides logs that allow you to monitor user activity, such as file access, edits, and deletions.
   - **Action Step**: Periodically review activity reports to identify any suspicious behavior or unauthorized changes.

Best Practices for Securing Your Smartsheet Environment

CHAPTER VI: TIPS AND TRICKS FOR BEGINNERS

To maintain strong data security, follow these best practices:

1. **Use Strong Passwords and Rotate Them Regularly**
   - Passwords are your first line of defense. Ensure that all users create strong, unique passwords and update them regularly.
   - **Tips for Strong Passwords**:
     - Use at least 12 characters, including uppercase, lowercase, numbers, and special symbols.
     - Avoid using easily guessable information like birthdays or names.
   - Encourage the use of password managers to create and store secure passwords.

2. **Restrict Sharing and Set Expiry Dates for Shared Links**
   - Avoid over-sharing sheets or dashboards. When sharing links, set expiration dates or restrict access to specific email domains.
   - **Action Step**:
     - Use the "Viewer" role when sharing with external stakeholders to prevent unintended changes.
     - Disable link sharing when it's no longer necessary.

3. **Implement Access Levels by Workspace or Folder**
   - Organize your sheets into workspaces and assign access permissions at the workspace level to avoid redundant permission management.
   - **Action Step**: Use role-based access control (RBAC) where possible to minimize the risk of accidental access by unauthorized users.

4. **Limit Access to Critical Data Using Filters**
   - Use Smartsheet filters to display only the necessary data to specific users. This way, sensitive information remains hidden from those who do not need it.

- **Action Step**: Create custom views for stakeholders and team members based on their roles and responsibilities.

5. **Monitor and Revoke Inactive Accounts**
    - Dormant accounts pose a security risk if left unchecked. Regularly monitor user activity and deactivate accounts that are no longer in use.
    - **Action Step**: Conduct a quarterly audit of all users and deactivate any account associated with employees who have left the organization.

6. **Backup Critical Data Regularly**
    - While Smartsheet has robust reliability, it's good practice to back up critical data periodically. Export important sheets to Excel, PDF, or other formats and store them securely.
    - **Action Step**: Create a backup schedule and ensure copies are stored in a secure location, such as encrypted external drives or secure cloud storage.

Protecting Against External Threats

1. **Beware of Phishing Attacks**
    - Cybercriminals often use phishing emails to steal credentials or install malicious software.
    - **Action Step**: Train your team to recognize phishing attempts. Encourage them to verify links before clicking and avoid downloading attachments from unknown sources.

2. **Use Secure Connections**
    - Avoid accessing Smartsheet over public Wi-Fi networks, which can be vulnerable to attackers.
    - **Action Step**: Use a VPN (Virtual Private Network) to secure your connection when working remotely.

3. **Limit API Usage**

- Smartsheet's API is powerful, but improperly managed API keys can expose sensitive data.
- **Action Step**: Only generate API keys when necessary, and regularly revoke keys that are no longer needed.

Educating Your Team on Security Protocols

1. **Provide Training on Smartsheet Security Features**
   - Ensure all team members understand Smartsheet's security tools and how to use them effectively.
   - **Action Step**: Schedule regular training sessions to update your team on the latest features and best practices.

2. **Create a Data Security Policy**
   - Draft a clear policy outlining acceptable use of Smartsheet, user responsibilities, and incident response protocols.
   - **Action Step**: Distribute the policy to all users and require acknowledgment of the rules before granting access.

Responding to Security Incidents

Despite your best efforts, security incidents can still occur. Be prepared with a response plan to minimize damage:

1. **Identify and Isolate the Issue**
   - Use Smartsheet's activity logs to identify suspicious behavior and isolate affected sheets or accounts.

2. **Revoke Access**
   - Immediately revoke access for compromised accounts.

3. **Notify Stakeholders**

- Inform your team and management of the breach and outline steps being taken to resolve the issue.

4. **Review and Improve Protocols**
    - After resolving the issue, conduct a post-incident review to identify weaknesses and update your security measures accordingly.

Conclusion

Maintaining data security in Smartsheet is an ongoing process that requires vigilance, proactive planning, and team collaboration. By leveraging Smartsheet's built-in security features, implementing strict access controls, and following best practices, you can confidently use Smartsheet as a secure platform for managing your projects and data. Security is not just a technical responsibility—it's a team effort. Empower your team to prioritize security, and your Smartsheet environment will remain a safe and efficient tool for achieving your goals.

CHAPTER VII
Expanding Your Smartsheet Skills

7.1 Integrating Smartsheet with Other Tools

7.1.1 Smartsheet and Microsoft Office

Smartsheet's integration with Microsoft Office provides users with powerful tools to manage, collaborate, and streamline workflows. This section will guide you through the most effective ways to combine Smartsheet with popular Microsoft Office applications such as Excel, Word, Outlook, and PowerPoint. Whether you're exporting data, embedding Smartsheet links, or automating reporting workflows, these integrations can significantly enhance your productivity.

Why Integrate Smartsheet with Microsoft Office?

Integrating Smartsheet with Microsoft Office enables seamless communication and workflow efficiency. Many teams already rely on Microsoft Office for day-to-day operations, and combining these tools with Smartsheet ensures:

1. **Data Consistency**: Avoid duplication of efforts by syncing data between Smartsheet and Office tools.
2. **Enhanced Collaboration**: Share updates with stakeholders who use Microsoft Office without needing them to learn Smartsheet.
3. **Improved Productivity**: Automate processes and focus on high-value tasks.

Getting Started with Smartsheet and Microsoft Office Integration

Before diving into specific integrations, ensure the following:

- Your Smartsheet account has the necessary permissions to integrate with Microsoft tools.
- You have Microsoft Office applications installed (or access to Office 365 online).
- Your organization's IT policies allow third-party integrations.

Once these prerequisites are in place, you can begin using Smartsheet with Microsoft Office applications.

Integrating Smartsheet with Excel

Excel is one of the most widely used tools for data analysis and reporting. Smartsheet's integration with Excel allows for importing and exporting data seamlessly.

Exporting Data from Smartsheet to Excel

Exporting data from Smartsheet to Excel is useful when:

- You need to perform advanced data analysis using Excel formulas or pivot tables.
- You want to share data with someone who prefers Excel over Smartsheet.

Here's how to export data from Smartsheet to Excel:

1. Open your desired sheet in Smartsheet.
2. Click on the **File** menu and select **Export to Microsoft Excel**.
3. The exported file will be saved as a .xlsx file on your device.
4. Open the file in Excel to make further edits or perform analysis.

Tip: Smartsheet exports include all visible rows and columns. Ensure your data is clean and filtered before exporting to avoid unnecessary clutter.

Importing Data from Excel to Smartsheet

Smartsheet makes it easy to import data from Excel for project management, tracking, or reporting purposes. Follow these steps:

1. In Smartsheet, click on the **+** (Create) button in the left-hand navigation bar.
2. Choose **Import** > **Import from Excel.**
3. Select the Excel file you want to upload.
4. Map the columns in your Excel sheet to the Smartsheet columns.
5. Review the imported data to ensure accuracy.

Pro Tip: Clean your Excel file before importing. Remove unnecessary formatting, merged cells, and empty rows to avoid import errors.

Integrating Smartsheet with Word

Microsoft Word is often used to create formal documents such as reports, proposals, or project plans. Smartsheet helps you embed real-time data from your sheets into Word documents.

Exporting Smartsheet Reports to Word

Smartsheet allows you to create professional Word documents by exporting your data into a readable format.

1. Open a Smartsheet report or sheet.
2. Go to **File** > **Export** > **Export to PDF.**
3. Open the PDF file in Word to edit and customize the document as needed.

Using Smartsheet Data in Mail Merge

You can use Smartsheet data for mail merge in Word to generate bulk letters, labels, or certificates.

1. Export the Smartsheet data as an Excel file.
2. Open Word and go to **Mailings** > **Select Recipients** > **Use an Existing List.**
3. Select the exported Excel file from Smartsheet.
4. Insert merge fields and complete the document.

Example Use Case: Send personalized invitations to team members for a project kickoff event by using Smartsheet data in Word mail merge.

Integrating Smartsheet with Outlook

Smartsheet's integration with Microsoft Outlook enables you to manage tasks and collaborate directly from your email inbox.

Adding Smartsheet to Outlook

Smartsheet offers an add-in for Microsoft Outlook that lets you:

- Add emails as comments in Smartsheet.
- Update Smartsheet tasks directly from Outlook.
- Attach email files to rows in Smartsheet.

To install the add-in:

1. Open Microsoft Outlook and go to **Get Add-Ins.**
2. Search for **Smartsheet for Outlook** and click **Add.**
3. Log in to your Smartsheet account through the add-in.

Creating Smartsheet Tasks from Emails

Once the add-in is installed, you can create tasks from emails:

1. Open the email you want to convert into a task.
2. Click on the Smartsheet add-in icon.
3. Choose the sheet and row where the email should be added.
4. Add details, such as deadlines or assignees, and save.

Use Case: Quickly assign action items from email conversations to your team in Smartsheet without switching applications.

Integrating Smartsheet with PowerPoint

PowerPoint is essential for presenting data to stakeholders. Smartsheet helps you embed live data into PowerPoint slides, ensuring your presentations are always up-to-date.

Exporting Smartsheet Data to PowerPoint

To use Smartsheet data in PowerPoint:

1. Export reports or dashboards from Smartsheet as images or PDFs.
2. Insert these images into your PowerPoint slides.

Embedding Smartsheet Dashboards in PowerPoint

Smartsheet dashboards can be shared as live links:

1. Publish your Smartsheet dashboard.
2. Copy the dashboard URL.
3. In PowerPoint, use the **Insert Hyperlink** feature to link the dashboard to a slide.

Pro Tip: Use this feature for executive presentations to display live project updates directly from Smartsheet.

Best Practices for Smartsheet and Microsoft Office Integration

1. **Standardize Data Formats**: Ensure your Smartsheet and Microsoft Office files use consistent naming conventions, column headers, and formats for easy syncing.
2. **Leverage Templates**: Save time by using Smartsheet templates that integrate seamlessly with Microsoft Office.
3. **Train Your Team**: Ensure all team members understand how to use these integrations to maximize their benefits.

By integrating Smartsheet with Microsoft Office, you can unlock new levels of productivity and collaboration. With the ability to streamline data sharing, automate workflows, and present real-time updates, these integrations will ensure that your team stays aligned and efficient.

7.1.2 Smartsheet and Google Workspace

Integrating Smartsheet with Google Workspace unlocks powerful capabilities to streamline your workflows, enhance collaboration, and simplify project management. By combining the organizational power of Smartsheet with Google's productivity tools, users can manage tasks, share information, and communicate seamlessly across platforms. This section will provide a step-by-step guide to integrating Smartsheet with various Google Workspace applications, including Google Sheets, Google Drive, Google Calendar, and Gmail.

Understanding the Benefits of Integration

Before diving into the details, it's essential to understand why integrating Smartsheet with Google Workspace is valuable:

1. **Centralized Collaboration**: Share Smartsheet data with Google tools to ensure all team members have access to the latest information.

2. **Improved Efficiency**: Automate data transfer and updates between platforms to save time and reduce errors.

3. **Enhanced Communication**: Use Gmail and Google Calendar to set reminders, alerts, and task updates linked to Smartsheet.

4. **Seamless File Management**: Store and manage Smartsheet files in Google Drive, making them accessible from anywhere.

Step 1: Connecting Smartsheet with Google Workspace

Smartsheet offers native integrations with Google Workspace. Follow these steps to connect your Smartsheet account:

1. **Log in to Smartsheet**: Open Smartsheet in your web browser and log in to your account.

2. **Access the Integration Options**: Go to the **Apps and Integrations** section from the account settings or click on the "Integrations" tab on a specific sheet.

3. **Sign in with Google**: Choose "Sign in with Google" if you want to link your Smartsheet account directly to your Google Workspace account. This will enable single sign-on and make it easier to connect both platforms.

4. **Grant Permissions**: Smartsheet will request access to your Google Workspace account. Grant the necessary permissions to enable full functionality.

Once connected, you can start using Smartsheet with Google Workspace tools.

Step 2: Integrating with Google Sheets

Google Sheets and Smartsheet are complementary tools that allow for easy data sharing and synchronization. Here's how to integrate them:

1. **Importing Data from Google Sheets to Smartsheet**:
   - Open your Smartsheet and create a new sheet.
   - Click **File** > **Import** > **Google Sheets**.
   - Select the file you want to import from your Google Drive.
   - The data from your Google Sheet will populate into Smartsheet columns and rows, preserving the formatting where applicable.

2. **Exporting Data from Smartsheet to Google Sheets**:
   - Open the Smartsheet you want to export.
   - Click **File** > **Export** > **Google Sheets**.
   - Smartsheet will create a new Google Sheet in your Google Drive containing the exported data.

3. **Syncing Data Between Smartsheet and Google Sheets**:
   - Use third-party integration tools like Zapier or Coupler.io to set up automatic syncing between Smartsheet and Google Sheets. For example, you can configure a workflow to update your Smartsheet data whenever changes are made in a linked Google Sheet.

Step 3: Using Smartsheet with Google Drive

Google Drive serves as a central repository for your files, making it an ideal tool to integrate with Smartsheet.

1. **Attaching Google Drive Files to Smartsheet Rows**:
   - Open a Smartsheet and select a specific row.

- Click on the attachment icon in the toolbar.
- Choose **Google Drive** and select the file you want to attach.
- The file will now be linked to that row, allowing team members to access it directly from Smartsheet.

2. **Saving Smartsheet Exports to Google Drive**:
    - Export your Smartsheet as a PDF, Excel file, or image.
    - Save the exported file directly to a folder in your Google Drive for easy access and sharing.

3. **Linking Google Drive Folders to Smartsheet Dashboards**:
    - Create a dashboard in Smartsheet and add a widget.
    - Use the "Web Content" widget to embed a Google Drive folder link.
    - Team members can view and access all relevant files from the dashboard.

Step 4: Syncing Smartsheet with Google Calendar

Integrating Smartsheet with Google Calendar ensures deadlines, meetings, and events are synchronized across both platforms.

1. **Exporting Smartsheet Tasks to Google Calendar**:
    - Open your Smartsheet and navigate to the **Calendar View**.
    - Click **Publish** and enable the **iCal** option.
    - Copy the iCal URL and open your Google Calendar.
    - In Google Calendar, click **Add Calendar** > **From URL** and paste the iCal URL.
    - Tasks and events from Smartsheet will now appear on your Google Calendar.

2. **Creating Automated Calendar Events**:
    - Use Smartsheet Automation to create alerts or reminders.

- Configure an automation rule to send an email notification to your Google Calendar email.
- The task will be added to your calendar automatically as an event.

Step 5: Collaborating with Gmail

Integrating Smartsheet with Gmail simplifies communication and task updates.

1. **Sending Smartsheet Notifications via Gmail**:
   - Use Smartsheet's notification and alert features to send task updates, reminders, or approvals directly to Gmail.
   - Customize the message content to include relevant details about the task or project.

2. **Using the Smartsheet Add-On for Gmail**:
   - Install the Smartsheet add-on for Gmail from the Google Workspace Marketplace.
   - Open an email in Gmail and click the Smartsheet icon in the side panel.
   - Create new tasks, update existing rows, or attach emails directly to Smartsheet from Gmail.

Best Practices for Smartsheet and Google Workspace Integration

1. **Leverage Automation**: Automate routine tasks using tools like Zapier to save time.
2. **Keep Permissions Consistent**: Ensure team members have the same access permissions across Smartsheet and Google Workspace to avoid disruptions.
3. **Regularly Sync Data**: Set up periodic updates to ensure data consistency between platforms.
4. **Utilize Training Resources**: Both Smartsheet and Google offer tutorials and guides to help users maximize integrations.

Conclusion

Integrating Smartsheet with Google Workspace is a game-changer for individuals and teams aiming to enhance productivity and collaboration. By connecting Smartsheet with tools like Google Sheets, Drive, Calendar, and Gmail, users can create a cohesive, streamlined workflow that saves time, reduces manual work, and keeps everyone aligned. Whether you're a project manager, team leader, or individual contributor, these integrations are invaluable for achieving your goals efficiently.

7.1.3 Smartsheet and Third-Party Applications

Smartsheet is a versatile tool that becomes even more powerful when integrated with third-party applications. These integrations allow you to automate workflows, simplify data sharing, and enhance your team's productivity. In this section, we'll explore the benefits of integrating Smartsheet with third-party applications, examine popular tools you can connect with, and provide step-by-step instructions for setting up and managing these integrations.

Understanding the Benefits of Integrations with Third-Party Applications

Third-party integrations bridge the gap between Smartsheet and the other tools your team already uses, creating a seamless work environment. Here are some key benefits:

1. **Streamlined Workflows**
   - By integrating third-party apps, you can automate repetitive tasks, such as updating spreadsheets, sending notifications, or generating reports.
   - For example, integrating Smartsheet with a communication tool like Slack can automatically notify your team when changes are made to a shared sheet.

2. **Centralized Data Management**
   - Integrations ensure that data is synchronized across multiple platforms, reducing errors caused by manual data entry.

- For instance, connecting Smartsheet with a CRM like Salesforce allows you to manage client data in one place while updating it in real-time across systems.

3. **Improved Collaboration**
    - When team members can use their preferred tools while staying connected to Smartsheet, collaboration becomes more efficient.
    - Integrations with file-sharing platforms like Dropbox or OneDrive make it easy to attach documents directly to Smartsheet rows without switching between apps.

4. **Enhanced Reporting and Analytics**
    - Tools like Tableau or Power BI can pull data from Smartsheet to create advanced visualizations and dashboards, helping stakeholders make informed decisions.

Popular Third-Party Applications to Integrate with Smartsheet

There are numerous third-party tools that can be connected to Smartsheet, each catering to specific needs. Below are some popular categories and examples:

1. **Communication Tools**
    - **Slack**: Automate notifications for sheet updates or task completions.
    - **Microsoft Teams**: Embed Smartsheet dashboards in Teams channels for real-time collaboration.

2. **File Sharing and Storage**
    - **Google Drive**: Attach files from Drive to rows and manage them directly in Smartsheet.
    - **Dropbox**: Keep your files organized and accessible by linking Dropbox folders to specific projects.

3. **Customer Relationship Management (CRM)**
    - **Salesforce**: Synchronize customer data, track sales pipelines, and automate workflows.

- **HubSpot**: Manage marketing campaigns and monitor performance directly from Smartsheet.

4. **Analytics and Visualization Tools**
    - **Tableau**: Create custom dashboards and detailed reports using Smartsheet data.
    - **Power BI**: Use real-time data from Smartsheet for advanced analytics.

5. **Automation Platforms**
    - **Zapier**: Connect Smartsheet to over 5,000 apps to create custom workflows without coding.
    - **Make (formerly Integromat)**: Build complex automated workflows between Smartsheet and other tools.

6. **Project Management and Development**
    - **Jira**: Sync project tasks and statuses between Smartsheet and Jira for agile development teams.
    - **Trello**: Move tasks between Smartsheet and Trello boards for seamless collaboration.

How to Integrate Smartsheet with Third-Party Applications

While Smartsheet provides native integrations for several apps, many integrations are facilitated through third-party platforms like Zapier or Make. Below is a step-by-step guide to setting up these integrations:

Step 1: Identify Your Integration Needs

- Define your objectives. For instance, do you want to automate notifications, sync data, or generate reports?
- Determine which applications are most relevant to your team's workflow.

Step 2: Check for Native Integrations

- Smartsheet offers direct integrations with apps like Slack, Microsoft Teams, Google Drive, and Salesforce.
- Visit Smartsheet's App Marketplace to see if a native integration exists for your chosen tool.

Step 3: Use Zapier for Custom Workflows: If a native integration is unavailable, Zapier is a powerful option for connecting Smartsheet with thousands of apps. Here's how to set it up:

1. **Sign Up for Zapier**
   - Create an account at Zapier.com and log in.
2. **Create a New Zap**
   - Click on **"Make a Zap"** to start creating a workflow.
3. **Set Smartsheet as the Trigger App**
   - Choose Smartsheet as the trigger app and select a trigger event (e.g., "New Row Added").
4. **Choose the Action App**
   - Select the app you want to integrate with Smartsheet (e.g., Slack, Google Sheets).
   - Specify the action (e.g., "Send a Message" or "Update a Spreadsheet").
5. **Test and Activate Your Zap**
   - Test the integration to ensure it works as expected, then activate the Zap to start automating your workflow.

Step 4: Use Make (Integromat) for Advanced Automations: For more complex workflows, Make allows you to connect Smartsheet with multiple apps. Here's how to get started:

1. **Sign Up for Make**
   - Create an account at Make.com and log in.

2. **Create a Scenario**
   - Click on **"Create a Scenario"** and select Smartsheet as one of the modules.

3. **Add Modules for Other Apps**
   - Drag and drop modules for the apps you want to connect with Smartsheet.
   - Configure the triggers and actions for each module.

4. **Run and Monitor the Workflow**
   - Test the scenario to ensure it functions correctly, then schedule it to run automatically.

Step 5: Monitor and Optimize Your Integrations

- Regularly check the performance of your integrations to ensure they are running smoothly.
- Update your workflows as your team's needs evolve.

Best Practices for Managing Third-Party Integrations

To maximize the benefits of integrating Smartsheet with other tools, follow these best practices:

1. **Maintain Data Security**
   - Ensure that only authorized team members have access to connected applications.
   - Use two-factor authentication to protect sensitive data.

2. **Avoid Overloading with Integrations**
   - Focus on essential tools to prevent clutter and complexity in your workflows.

3. **Document Your Processes**
   - Keep a record of all integrations, including their purposes and configurations, for easy troubleshooting.

4. **Train Your Team**
    - Provide training sessions to help team members understand how to use the integrations effectively.

5. **Evaluate Regularly**
    - Periodically assess whether the integrations are meeting your goals and explore new tools as needed.

By integrating Smartsheet with third-party applications, you can unlock its full potential, streamline your workflows, and keep your team connected across platforms. Experiment with different integrations, and don't hesitate to adapt them to fit your unique requirements. With the right setup, Smartsheet can become the central hub of your organization's productivity.

7.2 Learning from the Smartsheet Community

7.2.1 Accessing Tutorials and Resources

Smartsheet is a robust and versatile tool, but its full potential can only be unlocked with proper guidance and practice. Fortunately, the Smartsheet community offers a wealth of tutorials, resources, and learning opportunities for users at every skill level. Whether you're a complete beginner or an advanced user looking to fine-tune your expertise, leveraging these resources can significantly enhance your experience. This section will explore the various tutorials and resources available and provide detailed steps to access and utilize them effectively.

Understanding the Importance of Tutorials and Resources

Before diving into specific tutorials, it's essential to understand why these resources are so valuable:

- **Step-by-Step Guidance:** Tutorials often break down complex processes into manageable steps, making it easier for beginners to follow along.
- **Visual Learning:** Many resources, such as videos and infographics, provide visual demonstrations that are far more effective than text-only guides.
- **Problem-Specific Solutions:** Tutorials address specific use cases or problems, saving you time and effort in finding tailored solutions.
- **Staying Updated:** The Smartsheet platform is continuously evolving. By following tutorials and resources, you can stay informed about new features, updates, and best practices.

Where to Find Smartsheet Tutorials and Resources

Smartsheet provides a wide range of learning materials through various channels. Below is an overview of the most popular platforms where you can access these resources.

CHAPTER VII: EXPANDING YOUR SMARTSHEET SKILLS

1. Smartsheet Learning Center

The Smartsheet Learning Center is the official hub for all learning materials provided directly by Smartsheet.

How to Access:

- Go to www.smartsheet.com/learning-center.
- Explore categories like "Getting Started," "Templates," "Automation," and more.

Key Features:

- **Interactive Tutorials:** Step-by-step tutorials guide you through basic and advanced Smartsheet functions, from creating sheets to setting up automation.
- **Webinars:** Live and recorded webinars provide in-depth insights into specific topics, often hosted by Smartsheet experts.
- **Help Articles:** These concise articles cover a variety of topics, from troubleshooting issues to mastering advanced techniques.

Pro Tip: Bookmark the Learning Center for quick access whenever you encounter a challenge or want to learn something new.

2. Smartsheet YouTube Channel

The official Smartsheet YouTube channel is a treasure trove of video tutorials, ranging from beginner guides to advanced tips and tricks.

How to Access:

- Visit www.youtube.com/smartsheet.
- Subscribe to the channel to receive notifications about new videos.

Key Features:

- **Playlist Organization:** Videos are grouped into playlists such as "Smartsheet Basics," "Advanced Tips," and "Customer Stories."

- **Quick Tips:** Short videos focus on individual features, making it easy to learn specific functionalities in just a few minutes.
- **Real-World Examples:** Tutorials often use real-world scenarios to demonstrate Smartsheet's capabilities, helping users understand how to apply the tool in their own workflows.

Pro Tip: Use YouTube's "Watch Later" feature to save videos for future viewing.

3. Smartsheet Community Forum

While forums are primarily a place to ask questions and interact with other users, the Smartsheet Community Forum also serves as a valuable resource for tutorials and guides.

How to Access:

- Visit community.smartsheet.com.
- Create a free account to join discussions and access exclusive content.

Key Features:

- **User-Generated Tutorials:** Many experienced users share their own guides and tips, providing fresh perspectives and creative solutions.
- **Pinned Resources:** Moderators often pin high-quality tutorials and best practices at the top of discussions.
- **Search Functionality:** Use keywords to find specific tutorials, such as "conditional formatting tutorial" or "automation guide."

Pro Tip: Engage with the community by asking questions or sharing your own tips. This interaction can lead to faster learning and better connections.

4. Smartsheet Blog

The Smartsheet Blog regularly publishes articles that combine tutorials, tips, and real-world case studies.

How to Access:

- Visit www.smartsheet.com/blog.
- Use the search bar to find articles on specific topics.

Key Features:

- **How-To Guides:** Detailed blog posts walk you through common tasks, such as setting up project plans or using templates.
- **Industry Insights:** Articles often include use cases tailored to different industries, from marketing to construction.
- **Tips for Teams:** Learn how to collaborate more effectively using Smartsheet's features.

Pro Tip: Subscribe to the blog newsletter to receive updates on the latest tutorials and articles.

5. Third-Party Platforms

In addition to Smartsheet's official resources, many third-party platforms offer high-quality tutorials and courses.

Popular Platforms:

- **Udemy:** Offers beginner and advanced Smartsheet courses with video-based lessons.
- **LinkedIn Learning:** Includes Smartsheet training as part of its extensive catalog of professional development courses.
- **YouTube Creators:** Many independent creators post Smartsheet tutorials with unique tips and tricks.

Pro Tip: Look for courses or videos with high ratings and positive reviews to ensure quality content.

Making the Most of Tutorials and Resources

Simply accessing tutorials isn't enough—you need to use them effectively to maximize your learning. Here are some tips for getting the most out of these resources:

1. Set Clear Goals

- Before starting a tutorial, identify what you want to achieve. For example, do you want to learn how to create a dashboard or automate a workflow?
- Focus on one topic at a time to avoid feeling overwhelmed.

2. Practice as You Learn

- Open Smartsheet in a separate window and follow along with the tutorial step by step.
- Create a test sheet or workspace where you can experiment without affecting live data.

3. Take Notes

- Write down key steps or shortcuts for future reference.
- Save links to helpful tutorials in a dedicated folder or document.

4. Ask Questions

- Don't hesitate to ask for clarification in community forums or during live webinars.
- Engage with other users to exchange tips and experiences.

5. Review and Repeat

- Revisit tutorials periodically to reinforce your knowledge.
- Use what you've learned in real projects to build confidence and expertise.

Conclusion

Accessing tutorials and resources is one of the best ways to accelerate your Smartsheet learning journey. Whether you prefer step-by-step videos, written guides, or interactive webinars, the Smartsheet community has something for everyone. By dedicating time to explore these resources and actively practicing what you learn, you'll quickly gain the skills needed to leverage Smartsheet's full potential.

7.2.2 Joining Smartsheet Forums

Joining Smartsheet forums can be a game-changer for beginners and experienced users alike. These forums offer a wealth of knowledge, shared by users, experts, and Smartsheet representatives. Whether you need help troubleshooting an issue, want to explore advanced features, or seek inspiration for optimizing your workflow, forums provide a collaborative environment to enhance your learning. This section will guide you through the steps of joining Smartsheet forums, outline their benefits, and provide practical tips for making the most out of your participation.

1. Why Join Smartsheet Forums?

Smartsheet forums are online communities designed for users to connect, share ideas, and resolve challenges collaboratively. Here's why joining these forums is beneficial:

1. **Access to Collective Knowledge**: Forums are treasure troves of information. By joining, you tap into the collective expertise of Smartsheet users worldwide. From basic troubleshooting to advanced automation ideas, forums have it all.

2. **Solutions to Real-World Problems**: Many users post questions or challenges they've encountered in their Smartsheet journey. Reviewing their solutions can help you tackle similar issues in your projects.

3. **Networking with Professionals**: Forums allow you to interact with like-minded individuals, including professionals from various industries. These connections can lead to partnerships, mentorships, or even career opportunities.

4. **Learning About Updates and Best Practices**: Smartsheet forums are often the first place where users discuss new features, best practices, and industry trends. This keeps you ahead of the curve.

5. **Personal Growth and Contribution**: Sharing your expertise not only helps others but also enhances your understanding of Smartsheet. Over time, contributing to the forums can establish you as a trusted expert within the community.

---

2. How to Join Smartsheet Forums

Becoming a member of Smartsheet forums is straightforward. Follow these steps to get started:

Step 1: Create a Smartsheet Account

Before you can join the forums, you need an active Smartsheet account. If you don't have one, sign up at Smartsheet's official website https://www.smartsheet.com/. A free trial account is sufficient to get started.

Step 2: Access the Smartsheet Community Page

Visit the Smartsheet Community Hub https://community.smartsheet.com/. This is the primary platform for forums and discussions. Bookmark this page for quick access in the future.

Step 3: Register for the Community

Click on the "Sign Up" or "Join the Community" button. You'll be prompted to log in using your Smartsheet credentials. Complete your profile by adding your name, email, and optionally a profile picture. A well-filled profile helps others identify and connect with you.

Step 4: Review the Community Guidelines

Before posting or commenting, familiarize yourself with the forum's guidelines. These outline the dos and don'ts of participation, ensuring respectful and productive discussions.

Step 5: Explore the Forums

Once registered, browse through the available categories and threads. Popular categories include "Formulas and Functions," "Automation," "Templates," and "General Questions." Use the search bar to find topics of interest.

Step 6: Subscribe to Topics and Threads

You can follow specific categories or threads to receive email notifications about new posts or replies. This keeps you updated on discussions you care about.

3. Features of Smartsheet Forums

To fully leverage the forums, it's essential to understand their features. Here are some of the key functionalities:

1. **Categories and Tags**: Discussions are organized into categories like "Getting Started," "API and Developers," and "Tips and Best Practices." Tags further refine topics, making it easy to locate relevant threads.
2. **Search Functionality**: The search bar allows you to find posts using keywords. For example, searching "automation rules" will display all related threads, saving you time.
3. **Posting Questions**: If you encounter an issue, click on the "Ask a Question" button. Provide a clear and concise title, followed by a detailed description of your problem. Attach screenshots or files if needed.
4. **Commenting and Answering**: Engage in discussions by replying to posts. If you know the answer to a question, provide a detailed response. This not only helps others but also builds your reputation in the community.
5. **Upvotes and Accepted Answers**: Users can upvote helpful responses. Marking an answer as "Accepted" highlights it for others facing similar challenges.
6. **Private Messaging**: Some forums allow private messaging between members. Use this feature to connect with specific individuals for detailed discussions.
7. **Badges and Leaderboards**: Active participation earns you badges and places you on the community leaderboard. These rewards motivate users to contribute more.

4. Tips for Making the Most Out of Smartsheet Forums

To maximize your learning and contribution, keep these tips in mind:

Be Specific and Clear

When posting questions, provide all relevant details, including the steps you've taken, the error messages you've received, or the outcome you're expecting. This helps others understand and resolve your issue faster.

Use Tags Effectively

Add relevant tags to your posts to make them more discoverable. For example, if your question is about "conditional formatting," use tags like "formatting" and "rules."

Be Respectful and Constructive

Always maintain a positive and respectful tone. Even if you disagree with someone's suggestion, respond constructively. This fosters a supportive environment.

Engage Regularly

Set aside time each week to browse the forums. Engage with at least a few threads—whether by asking, answering, or providing feedback. Consistent engagement helps you build credibility.

Learn from Experts

Look out for posts or replies from Smartsheet-certified professionals and employees. Their insights are often detailed and backed by experience.

Document Your Learnings

Create a personal knowledge base of the tips and tricks you discover on the forums. This makes it easier to revisit and apply them in your work.

---

5. Smartsheet Forum Success Stories

The power of Smartsheet forums is best illustrated through real-life examples. Here are two success stories:

1. **Streamlining a Team's Workflow**: A small business owner faced challenges in tracking project deadlines. By browsing the "Automation" category, they discovered a workflow rule that automatically sent reminders for overdue tasks. This simple change improved their team's efficiency by 30%.

2. **Building a Custom Dashboard**: A user wanted to create a dashboard to visualize their sales data but didn't know where to start. After posting a question and receiving multiple replies, they successfully built a professional dashboard using chart widgets. The user later shared their experience, inspiring others in similar situations.

6. Moving Forward

Joining Smartsheet forums is not just about solving immediate problems; it's about becoming part of a vibrant community that fosters continuous learning and growth. By actively participating, you'll uncover new ways to optimize your workflows, connect with industry experts, and stay informed about the latest developments in Smartsheet.

Take the first step today—log in, explore the forums, and start engaging with the Smartsheet community. Your journey toward Smartsheet mastery begins here!

7.2.3 Attending Smartsheet Events

Attending Smartsheet events is a powerful way to deepen your understanding of the platform, connect with other users, and stay updated on the latest features and trends. Smartsheet regularly organizes a variety of events, from virtual webinars to large-scale conferences, all aimed at fostering a community of learning and collaboration. In this section, we'll explore the types of events Smartsheet offers, the benefits of participating, how to prepare for these events, and tips for maximizing your experience.

The Types of Smartsheet Events

Smartsheet events are tailored to suit different audiences, whether you are a beginner looking to learn the basics or an advanced user aiming to master complex workflows. Below are some common types of events:

1. **Webinars**: Smartsheet webinars are typically virtual, live-streamed sessions where experts demonstrate features, provide tips, and answer audience questions. These are perfect for users seeking focused guidance on specific topics, such as

automation, integrations, or dashboards. Webinars often range from 30 minutes to an hour and are a great way to learn at your convenience.

2. **User Groups**: Smartsheet user groups bring together local users in a community setting. These events are often informal and allow participants to share real-life use cases, learn from peers, and network with others in their industry.

3. **Workshops and Training Sessions**: These in-depth sessions are designed to provide hands-on learning. Led by certified trainers, workshops focus on skill-building, such as creating advanced reports or using formulas effectively. These sessions can be online or in-person and usually require prior registration.

4. **Annual Conferences (Smartsheet ENGAGE)**: Smartsheet's annual conference, known as **ENGAGE**, is a premier event for users around the world. This large-scale event features keynote speakers, product announcements, breakout sessions, networking opportunities, and more. It's an excellent opportunity to dive deep into the ecosystem and learn directly from Smartsheet's team and partners.

5. **Partner and Industry Events**: Smartsheet also participates in industry conferences and events hosted by their partners. These events focus on how Smartsheet integrates into broader business solutions, providing valuable insights for companies seeking to enhance their workflows.

Benefits of Attending Smartsheet Events

1. **Learning from Experts**: Smartsheet events are led by product experts, trainers, and even the developers who build the platform. This is your chance to learn best practices, gain insights into advanced features, and get answers to technical questions.

2. **Networking Opportunities**: Events provide an opportunity to meet other Smartsheet users, exchange ideas, and collaborate on solutions. You can build valuable professional relationships and find inspiration from how others are using Smartsheet in their industries.

3. **Staying Updated on Features**: Smartsheet regularly releases new features and updates. By attending events, you'll hear about these changes first-hand, learn how they can benefit your work, and stay ahead of the curve.

4. **Hands-On Experience**: Workshops and training sessions offer practical, hands-on experience that you can immediately apply to your work. These sessions are particularly beneficial for building confidence in using Smartsheet effectively.

5. **Professional Development**: Participating in Smartsheet events can be an impressive addition to your professional development. It demonstrates your commitment to learning and staying up-to-date with the latest tools and trends in project management and collaboration.

How to Prepare for Smartsheet Events

To make the most out of your experience, preparation is key. Here are some steps to consider:

1. **Register Early**: Many events, especially workshops and conferences, have limited seats. Early registration ensures you secure your spot and gives you time to plan your schedule around the event.

2. **Review the Agenda**: Most Smartsheet events publish an agenda in advance. Take time to review the topics being covered and prioritize the sessions that are most relevant to your needs.

3. **Set Learning Goals**: Before attending, think about what you hope to gain from the event. Are you looking to improve your reporting skills, learn about automation, or explore integrations? Having clear goals will help you focus your attention.

4. **Bring Questions**: Events are a great opportunity to interact with experts. Prepare a list of questions or challenges you've encountered in Smartsheet to get tailored advice during Q&A sessions.

5. **Familiarize Yourself with the Platform**: If you're attending a workshop or training session, make sure you're familiar with Smartsheet basics. This will help you follow along more effectively during advanced tutorials.

6. **Have the Right Tools**: For virtual events, ensure you have a reliable internet connection and a working device (laptop, tablet, etc.). For in-person events, bring essentials like a notebook, pen, or even your laptop for hands-on activities.

Tips for Maximizing Your Experience

1. **Engage Actively**: Don't be a passive attendee. Ask questions, participate in discussions, and share your experiences. Engaging actively will enhance your understanding and make the event more rewarding.

2. **Network with Attendees**: Smartsheet events are a great place to meet people from various industries and backgrounds. Exchange contact information, join discussions, and connect on professional networks like LinkedIn to build lasting relationships.

3. **Take Notes**: While most events provide recordings or materials post-event, taking your own notes ensures you capture key insights that are most relevant to your needs.

4. **Follow Up**: After the event, take time to follow up with people you've met, review your notes, and implement the new techniques or features you've learned. Share your insights with your team to spread the knowledge.

5. **Participate in Post-Event Surveys**: Many events include surveys to gather feedback. Participating in these surveys helps Smartsheet improve future events and often gives you an opportunity to share suggestions for topics you'd like to see covered.

Recommended Smartsheet Events for Beginners

If you're just starting out, here are some specific events you might consider:

- **"Getting Started with Smartsheet" Webinars**: Focuses on the basics of using the platform effectively.

- **Local User Group Meetups**: A casual environment to learn and share experiences with other beginners.

- **ENGAGE Beginner Tracks**: The annual conference includes dedicated sessions for new users.

- **Workshops on Automation**: Learn how to set up simple automation rules to save time in your workflows.

Conclusion

Attending Smartsheet events is an invaluable opportunity for personal and professional growth. Whether you're a beginner or an experienced user, these events offer a wealth of knowledge, networking opportunities, and practical tips to help you excel with Smartsheet. By preparing thoughtfully, engaging actively, and following up afterward, you can make the most of these experiences and bring meaningful improvements to your workflow.

7.3 Planning for Advanced Features

7.3.1 Exploring Premium Add-Ons

Smartsheet offers a wide range of premium add-ons that significantly enhance its capabilities, allowing users to automate processes, gain deeper insights, and manage projects more efficiently. These add-ons cater to diverse business needs, from project portfolio management to resource allocation, workflow automation, and advanced reporting. In this section, we'll explore some of the most powerful Smartsheet premium add-ons and how they can benefit your workflows.

What Are Smartsheet Premium Add-Ons?

Premium add-ons are advanced tools and integrations available to Smartsheet users as part of paid upgrades. While the core Smartsheet platform provides robust project and task management functionality, premium add-ons extend this functionality to tackle complex workflows, enterprise-scale projects, and industry-specific challenges. These tools are particularly useful for businesses looking to standardize processes, improve collaboration, or scale operations.

Smartsheet's premium add-ons are ideal for:

- Organizations managing multiple projects simultaneously.
- Teams requiring detailed reporting and analytics.
- Workflows that demand automation and customization.
- Businesses with specific compliance or resource management needs.

Key Smartsheet Premium Add-Ons

1. Smartsheet Advance

Smartsheet Advance is a comprehensive package of tools designed for large-scale, enterprise-level workflows. It includes powerful features such as:

- **Control Center:** Centralizes project creation and management, ensuring consistency across your organization.
- **Dynamic View:** Allows users to securely share specific data views with collaborators based on their role.
- **Data Shuttle:** Automates data imports and exports between Smartsheet and other systems (e.g., CRM or ERP tools).

How It Helps: Smartsheet Advance is perfect for organizations managing portfolios of projects or dealing with complex data integrations. For instance, Control Center standardizes project creation processes, saving hours of manual effort. Dynamic View, on the other hand, enables teams to securely share sensitive data without exposing unnecessary details to external stakeholders.

Practical Use Case: A marketing agency uses Smartsheet Advance to manage campaigns for multiple clients. With Control Center, they can create project templates for campaigns, ensuring uniformity. Data Shuttle automatically updates campaign performance metrics from a CRM into Smartsheet, reducing manual data entry.

2. Resource Management by Smartsheet

This add-on focuses on resource planning and tracking, making it easier to allocate people, time, and budgets to specific tasks or projects. It includes:

- **Capacity Planning:** Provides visibility into team availability and workload distribution.
- **Time Tracking:** Tracks actual time spent on tasks versus estimates.
- **Forecasting Tools:** Predicts resource needs for future projects.

How It Helps: Resource Management is essential for teams working with limited resources or tight deadlines. It prevents overbooking team members and ensures that all resources are utilized effectively.

Practical Use Case: An IT consulting firm uses Resource Management to assign consultants to client projects based on their availability and skills. The tool's forecasting feature helps the firm anticipate future hiring needs as they scale up operations.

3. Bridge by Smartsheet

Bridge is an automation platform that connects Smartsheet with other apps and services. It allows users to create complex, automated workflows without any coding. Key features include:

- **Pre-built Connectors:** Integrates Smartsheet with popular tools like Salesforce, Jira, and Slack.
- **Custom Workflows:** Automates multi-step processes across platforms.
- **Error Notifications:** Monitors workflows and alerts users when errors occur.

How It Helps: Bridge eliminates the need for manual task transfers between Smartsheet and other tools. It's ideal for organizations seeking to reduce human error and improve efficiency.

Practical Use Case: A customer support team integrates Smartsheet with Salesforce using Bridge. When a new support ticket is created in Salesforce, Bridge automatically updates a task in Smartsheet, ensuring that the team follows up promptly.

4. WorkApps

WorkApps lets you create custom apps using Smartsheet data without requiring any programming knowledge. Features include:

- **Custom Branding:** Design apps with your organization's branding.
- **Role-Based Views:** Display different data and workflows to users based on their roles.
- **Mobile Compatibility:** Accessible on mobile devices for on-the-go collaboration.

How It Helps: WorkApps is perfect for teams that rely on mobile collaboration or need tailored user experiences. It ensures that team members see only the information relevant to their tasks, reducing distractions.

Practical Use Case:
A construction company creates a custom WorkApp for site managers. The app includes project schedules, task assignments, and safety checklists, allowing managers to access everything they need in one place.

5. Calendar App

The Calendar App transforms Smartsheet data into visual, interactive calendars. It's particularly useful for scheduling and timeline-based workflows. Key features include:

- **Customizable Views:** Display calendars by day, week, month, or custom timelines.
- **Color Coding:** Highlight different types of tasks using color-coded labels.
- **Dynamic Updates:** Automatically syncs with updates in Smartsheet.

How It Helps: The Calendar App is invaluable for teams managing events, deadlines, or project timelines. It provides a clear overview of upcoming tasks and helps teams stay on track.

Practical Use Case: An event planning team uses the Calendar App to track venue bookings, vendor deadlines, and event dates. The color-coded view helps them quickly differentiate between internal tasks and external deadlines.

Benefits of Premium Add-Ons

Premium add-ons provide the following benefits to Smartsheet users:

1. **Enhanced Productivity:** Automating tasks and integrating with other tools saves time and reduces manual effort.
2. **Improved Collaboration:** Features like WorkApps and Dynamic View make collaboration smoother by tailoring data access to user roles.

3. **Scalability:** Premium tools like Resource Management and Control Center support enterprise-level workflows, enabling teams to handle large-scale projects efficiently.

4. **Better Decision-Making:** Advanced reporting and visualization tools provide actionable insights for managers and stakeholders.

How to Get Started with Premium Add-Ons

To start using Smartsheet's premium add-ons:

1. **Identify Your Needs:** Assess your current workflows and identify areas where premium add-ons could improve efficiency.

2. **Explore Smartsheet Plans:** Check Smartsheet's pricing and feature availability to ensure compatibility with your organization's budget and goals.

3. **Request a Demo:** Smartsheet offers demonstrations for many premium features. Take advantage of these to see how the tools can fit your workflows.

4. **Train Your Team:** Once implemented, provide training sessions or tutorials to ensure team members can use the add-ons effectively.

Conclusion

Exploring premium add-ons is an excellent way to unlock the full potential of Smartsheet. By leveraging these advanced tools, you can streamline operations, automate repetitive tasks, and gain deeper insights into your projects. Whether you're managing resources, integrating with third-party apps, or building custom workflows, Smartsheet's premium add-ons are designed to help your team work smarter, not harder.

7.3.2 Introducing Advanced Integrations

Smartsheet is a versatile platform, but its true power lies in its ability to integrate seamlessly with a wide range of tools and systems. Advanced integrations allow you to streamline processes, enhance collaboration, and create a unified digital workspace. This section explores some of the most impactful ways to integrate Smartsheet with other tools to take your workflow to the next level.

1. Understanding the Importance of Integrations

Integrations are the bridge that connects Smartsheet with other tools, ensuring your data flows smoothly across platforms. Whether you want to automate data syncing, reduce manual tasks, or centralize reporting, integrations make it possible.

Benefits of Advanced Integrations:

- **Increased Efficiency:** Eliminate repetitive tasks like double data entry by automating data sharing between tools.
- **Improved Collaboration:** Enable teams using different platforms to work together seamlessly.
- **Enhanced Decision-Making:** Access real-time data across systems for better insights and faster decisions.
- **Scalability:** As your business grows, advanced integrations allow Smartsheet to adapt to your expanding ecosystem.

Before diving into specific integrations, it's crucial to assess your workflows to identify areas that can benefit from enhanced connectivity.

2. Preparing for Advanced Integrations

Before implementing integrations, follow these preparation steps to ensure a smooth setup:

1. **Audit Your Current Tools and Processes:** List all the tools your organization currently uses (e.g., CRMs, ERPs, communication apps) and evaluate how they interact with Smartsheet. Look for inefficiencies or areas where manual work can be automated.
2. **Define Integration Goals:**

- Do you want to sync data automatically?
- Are you looking to centralize reporting?
- Do you need to trigger actions in other tools based on updates in Smartsheet?

Clear goals will guide your integration strategy.

3. **Understand Smartsheet's Integration Options:** Smartsheet offers multiple ways to integrate with other tools:
    - **Native Integrations:** Prebuilt connectors for popular platforms like Microsoft Office and Google Workspace.
    - **Zapier and Integromat:** Middleware solutions that create automated workflows between Smartsheet and hundreds of apps.
    - **Smartsheet API:** A powerful option for developers to create custom integrations tailored to specific needs.

3. Key Advanced Integrations to Consider

Here are some of the most impactful advanced integrations for Smartsheet users:

3.1 CRM Tools (Salesforce, HubSpot, etc.)

Integrating Smartsheet with CRM tools like Salesforce or HubSpot helps sales and marketing teams stay aligned.

Use Cases:

- Automatically update sales pipelines in Smartsheet when deals are closed in Salesforce.
- Sync customer data across platforms for accurate reporting.
- Trigger follow-up tasks in Smartsheet based on CRM activity, such as new lead entries or updated customer information.

How to Integrate:

- Use Smartsheet's Salesforce Connector for a direct integration.
- Explore middleware tools like Zapier to connect Smartsheet with other CRMs.

Pro Tips:

- Map out your CRM fields and Smartsheet columns to ensure seamless syncing.
- Set up notification alerts in Smartsheet for changes in your CRM system.

3.2 Communication Tools (Slack, Microsoft Teams, etc.)

Communication is key to effective collaboration, and integrating Smartsheet with tools like Slack or Microsoft Teams can streamline team discussions.

Use Cases:

- Send automatic updates to a Slack channel when a task is completed in Smartsheet.
- Allow team members to create Smartsheet tasks directly from a Microsoft Teams chat.
- Use Smartsheet as a centralized dashboard while using Teams or Slack for day-to-day communication.

How to Integrate:

- Use the Smartsheet integration app for Slack or Teams, available in their respective app marketplaces.
- Configure workflows to push updates or alerts from Smartsheet to communication platforms.

Pro Tips:

- Keep notifications specific to avoid overwhelming your team with unnecessary alerts.
- Use Smartsheet links in your messages to provide direct access to sheets or dashboards.

3.3 BI and Reporting Tools (Tableau, Power BI, etc.)

Advanced reporting tools like Tableau or Power BI can enhance your ability to visualize and analyze Smartsheet data.

Use Cases:

- Create interactive dashboards in Power BI using Smartsheet data.
- Combine Smartsheet data with other data sources in Tableau for cross-functional insights.
- Automate reporting updates by syncing Smartsheet with your BI tool.

How to Integrate:

- Use Smartsheet's live data connectors for Tableau or Power BI.
- Configure data pipelines to update dashboards in real-time.

Pro Tips:

- Ensure your Smartsheet data is clean and well-structured for accurate visualization.
- Use filters in Smartsheet to display only the relevant data in your BI tool.

3.4 Automation Tools (Zapier, Integromat, etc.)

Automation tools like Zapier and Integromat open up endless possibilities for connecting Smartsheet with virtually any app.

Use Cases:

- Trigger email alerts when tasks in Smartsheet meet specific criteria.
- Automatically create new rows in Smartsheet from form submissions in Google Forms.
- Sync Smartsheet with project management tools like Trello or Asana.

How to Integrate:

- Create "Zaps" in Zapier or "Scenarios" in Integromat to link Smartsheet with other apps.
- Use conditional logic to set up sophisticated workflows.

Pro Tips:

- Test your automation workflows thoroughly before deploying them.
- Monitor your automation logs to ensure everything is running smoothly.

---

4. Best Practices for Implementing Advanced Integrations

1. **Start Small:** Begin with one or two integrations to ensure a smooth transition and avoid overwhelming your team.
2. **Train Your Team:** Provide training on how the integrations work and how they can benefit daily workflows.
3. **Monitor Performance:** Regularly check the performance of your integrations to ensure they are functioning as expected.
4. **Document Your Workflows:** Create a reference guide outlining how your integrations work and who to contact for support.
5. **Leverage Support Resources:** Use Smartsheet's help center, community forums, and customer support for troubleshooting and guidance.

---

5. Conclusion: Unlocking the Full Potential of Smartsheet

Advanced integrations empower you to transform Smartsheet from a standalone tool into a central hub for your organization's workflows. By connecting Smartsheet with your most critical tools, you can reduce inefficiencies, improve collaboration, and drive better results.

Remember, the key to successful integrations is planning, testing, and continuous improvement. With the right approach, you'll unlock Smartsheet's full potential and elevate your productivity to new heights.

7.3.3 Preparing for Enterprise-Scale Use

As your organization grows, so do the demands on your tools, workflows, and systems. Smartsheet offers powerful capabilities that can support enterprises at scale, but preparing to use it effectively in a large-scale environment requires careful planning, configuration, and strategy. This section explores how to get your organization ready for enterprise-scale use of Smartsheet, focusing on best practices, advanced features, governance, and team enablement.

1. Understanding the Requirements of an Enterprise Environment

Before scaling Smartsheet for enterprise use, it's essential to assess the needs of your organization and understand how Smartsheet can address them. Consider the following factors:

- **Number of Users**: Large enterprises may require access for hundreds or thousands of employees across departments.
- **Complexity of Workflows**: Enterprise workflows often involve multiple teams, interconnected processes, and cross-functional projects.
- **Data Security and Compliance**: Enterprises often have strict requirements around data security, privacy, and compliance with regulations like GDPR or HIPAA.
- **Integration Needs**: Large organizations rely on numerous software systems, such as CRM, ERP, and HRIS platforms. Smartsheet must integrate seamlessly with these tools.
- **Scalability and Performance**: Ensure that Smartsheet can handle large datasets, heavy automation, and high levels of activity without performance issues.

By clearly understanding your enterprise's needs, you can tailor Smartsheet to meet them effectively.

2. Leveraging Enterprise Features in Smartsheet

Smartsheet offers several features designed for enterprise use. Here are some key tools and capabilities to explore:

2.1 Workspaces for Departmental Collaboration

Workspaces allow you to organize sheets, reports, and dashboards by department, team, or project.

- Create separate workspaces for each department (e.g., Marketing, HR, IT).
- Set permissions to control access to sensitive information.
- Use consistent templates and folder structures across workspaces for standardization.

2.2 Control Center for Portfolio Management

The Smartsheet Control Center is a premium add-on designed for enterprise-scale portfolio and program management.

- Automate the creation of new projects and workspaces using templates.
- Centralize reporting and dashboards for real-time visibility into portfolio performance.
- Ensure consistency across projects with automated governance and standardized processes.

2.3 Advanced Automations

Enterprise-scale workflows often involve complex automation needs.

- Use multiple triggers and conditions to streamline approvals, task assignments, and notifications.
- Combine automation rules with data linking across sheets to ensure real-time updates.
- Utilize integrations with third-party tools (e.g., Zapier or Workato) for custom automation workflows.

2.4 Governance Tools

Smartsheet Enterprise plans include governance and control features to ensure compliance.

- **Global Account Settings**: Define organization-wide settings for security, sharing, and integrations.
- **Activity Log**: Monitor changes, access logs, and user activity for better oversight.
- **Data Retention Policies**: Configure how long data should be stored and how deleted data is handled.

3. Planning for User Adoption and Enablement

Scaling Smartsheet to an enterprise level isn't just about the technical setup—it also requires a focus on user adoption and training. A successful rollout depends on your team understanding and embracing the platform.

3.1 Developing a Training Plan

- **Basic Training for New Users**: Cover Smartsheet essentials, such as creating sheets, sharing files, and using templates.
- **Advanced Training for Power Users**: Focus on complex formulas, automation, and dashboards.
- **Custom Training for Departments**: Tailor sessions to specific teams, highlighting features relevant to their workflows.

3.2 Identifying Champions

Recruit a group of Smartsheet champions—power users within the organization who can:

- Act as local experts in their teams.
- Provide support and guidance to their colleagues.
- Advocate for best practices and efficient use of Smartsheet.

3.3 Communicating the Benefits

- Highlight how Smartsheet will reduce manual work, improve collaboration, and streamline processes.
- Share success stories from early adopters or pilot projects to build enthusiasm.
- Address concerns and resistance by showing how Smartsheet integrates with existing workflows.

4. Scaling Integrations with Other Tools

Enterprises often rely on a network of software applications to support operations. Preparing Smartsheet for enterprise-scale use involves integrating it seamlessly with other tools.

4.1 Using Smartsheet's Integration Capabilities

- **Direct Integrations**: Smartsheet integrates natively with tools like Microsoft Teams, Salesforce, and Jira.
- **API Access**: Use Smartsheet's API to build custom integrations tailored to your organization's unique needs.
- **Third-Party Connectors**: Explore integration platforms like Zapier and Workato for additional automation.

4.2 Connecting Data Across Systems

- Establish bi-directional data flows between Smartsheet and systems like ERP or CRM.
- Automate data updates across platforms to ensure consistency.
- Use Smartsheet's Data Shuttle for bulk data import/export and data synchronization.

4.3 Ensuring Integration Security

- Work with your IT team to configure secure API connections.
- Regularly audit integrations to ensure they comply with organizational security standards.

- Monitor usage and access logs for anomalies.

5. Establishing Governance and Best Practices

To maintain consistency and control across a large organization, governance is key.

5.1 Setting Organizational Standards

- **Templates and Naming Conventions**: Create standardized templates and naming conventions for sheets, reports, and dashboards.
- **Guidelines for Sharing**: Define policies for internal and external sharing of Smartsheet data.
- **Automation Rules**: Standardize automation rules to ensure consistency across teams.

5.2 Monitoring and Auditing Usage

- Regularly review user activity and sheet performance.
- Identify unused sheets, redundant workflows, or compliance risks.
- Use the Activity Log and Admin Center to maintain oversight.

5.3 Ensuring Compliance

- Work with legal and compliance teams to configure Smartsheet settings in line with regulations.
- Utilize Smartsheet's security features, such as two-factor authentication and single sign-on (SSO).
- Prepare for audits by documenting workflows and access policies.

6. Continuous Improvement and Feedback

Scaling Smartsheet for enterprise use is an ongoing process. Regularly gather feedback from users and refine your processes.

6.1 Conducting User Surveys

- Identify pain points and opportunities for improvement.
- Assess how well Smartsheet is meeting the organization's needs.
- Use feedback to shape future training and updates.

6.2 Staying Updated on New Features

- Monitor Smartsheet's updates and feature releases.
- Attend webinars or training sessions to stay ahead.
- Incorporate new features into your workflows to maximize efficiency.

6.3 Expanding Use Cases

- Explore new ways to use Smartsheet across different departments.
- Pilot advanced features, such as Smartsheet Control Center or Dynamic View, in new teams.
- Continuously innovate and optimize processes using Smartsheet's capabilities.

By following these steps, your organization can unlock the full potential of Smartsheet and scale its use effectively across an enterprise environment. From governance and training to advanced automation and integrations, Smartsheet can be a powerful tool to support your business goals.

CHAPTER VIII
Conclusion

Recap of Key Concepts

As we conclude this guide, let's revisit the core concepts and skills we've covered throughout the book. These ideas form the foundation of your Smartsheet knowledge and will help you build confidence as you work on your projects. Whether you're managing data, collaborating with teammates, or visualizing workflows, these key takeaways will guide you toward greater efficiency and success.

1. Understanding the Basics of Smartsheet

What Smartsheet Is and Why It Matters

Smartsheet is a powerful tool that combines the functionality of spreadsheets with the flexibility of project management software. It enables individuals and teams to collaborate, automate processes, and visualize data seamlessly. By understanding its potential, you can better streamline your workflows and increase productivity.

Core Components of Smartsheet

- **Sheets**: The foundation of your work in Smartsheet, where you can input, organize, and manage your data.
- **Dashboards**: A way to visualize critical metrics and data in an easily digestible format.
- **Reports**: A tool to pull information from multiple sheets into one place for better insights.
- **Workspaces**: A shared environment for managing sheets, reports, and dashboards collaboratively.

2. Setting Up and Navigating Smartsheet

Creating Your Account and Choosing a Plan

Getting started with Smartsheet begins with setting up an account. Depending on your needs, you can start with a free trial or select a plan that fits your goals, whether you're an individual user or part of a larger team.

Key Features of the Interface

The Smartsheet interface is designed to be user-friendly, but understanding the main sections is crucial:

- **Toolbar**: For accessing key functions like creating new sheets, importing data, or sharing files.
- **Navigation Pane**: For managing your workspaces and locating your sheets and dashboards.
- **Sheet View Options**: Includes Grid, Gantt, Card, and Calendar views for flexible data presentation.

3. Managing Data in Sheets

Inputting and Organizing Data

One of Smartsheet's greatest strengths is its ability to manage data effectively. You've learned how to:

- Add data manually by typing into cells or importing from external sources like Excel or Google Sheets.
- Organize data using **columns** such as text, date, dropdowns, checkboxes, and contact lists.

Sorting and Filtering

Sorting and filtering allow you to view your data in meaningful ways. For example:

- Sort by column headers to organize rows alphabetically, numerically, or chronologically.

- Use filters to display only the data that matches specific criteria, such as tasks assigned to a specific team member.

Using Conditional Formatting

You can highlight key data with conditional formatting rules, such as:

- Coloring overdue tasks in red.
- Highlighting completed tasks in green.

4. Collaborating with Team Members

Sharing Sheets and Workspaces

Smartsheet excels at team collaboration. Sharing your sheets with teammates is easy, whether by inviting collaborators directly, generating shareable links, or embedding sheets in external platforms. Key sharing options include:

- Setting permissions as **Viewer**, **Editor**, or **Admin** to control access levels.
- Sharing entire workspaces to allow seamless collaboration on multiple projects.

Communicating Within Smartsheet

The **Comments** feature is an excellent way to centralize communication:

- Add comments to specific rows to provide context or updates.
- Use @mentions to notify team members directly.

Notifications and Alerts

Stay informed with automated alerts. For example:

- Receive notifications when someone assigns you a task.
- Get updates when changes are made to high-priority items.

5. Automating Workflows

Creating Automation Rules

Automation is a game-changer for saving time and reducing manual work. You've learned to:

- Set up rules for recurring tasks or regular reminders.
- Create alerts for deadlines or when new rows are added.

Using Approval Workflows

Approval workflows streamline decision-making processes by:

- Notifying the right people for task approvals.
- Automatically updating sheet statuses after approvals are completed.

Best Practices for Automation

- Start small: Focus on automating simple tasks first, like sending reminders for overdue items.
- Monitor performance: Regularly check if automation rules are working as intended.

6. Visualizing Data

Dashboards for Real-Time Insights

Dashboards are a great way to monitor progress and display critical data. The steps to create an effective dashboard include:

- Adding **Widgets** such as charts, metric displays, and reports.
- Customizing visuals to match your organization's branding or goals.

Reports for Consolidated Views

Reports pull information from multiple sheets into one place. You've learned how to:

- Build a new report from scratch or using a template.
- Filter and group data to highlight trends or key points.

Exporting and Presenting Data

Presenting your Smartsheet data is straightforward:

- Export to Excel or PDF for offline use.
- Integrate with presentation tools like PowerPoint or Google Slides to share your findings.

7. Staying Organized and Secure

Naming Conventions

Using consistent naming conventions for your sheets, reports, and workspaces ensures:

- Ease of navigation.
- Faster identification of relevant files.

Archiving and Maintaining Data

To avoid clutter:

- Archive old sheets and dashboards that are no longer in use.
- Delete unnecessary or duplicate files to maintain clarity.

Data Security Best Practices

- Enable two-factor authentication (2FA) for enhanced security.
- Regularly review access permissions to ensure the right people have access.

8. Expanding Your Smartsheet Skills

Exploring Integrations

Smartsheet integrates with many third-party tools, including:

- Microsoft Office (Excel, Word).
- Google Workspace (Docs, Sheets).
- Other platforms like Salesforce, Slack, and Jira.

Joining the Smartsheet Community

Take advantage of Smartsheet's robust user community by:

- Participating in forums to share tips and ask questions.
- Accessing tutorials, webinars, and knowledge bases for continuous learning.

Final Thoughts

Smartsheet is an incredibly versatile tool, and mastering its foundational concepts will set you on the path to efficient project and data management. By understanding how to set up sheets, manage workflows, and collaborate effectively, you're now equipped to tackle real-world challenges with confidence.

Your journey doesn't end here—explore advanced features, experiment with integrations, and continue growing your skills. Smartsheet is more than a tool; it's a gateway to smarter and more productive work.

CONCLUSION

Next Steps for Beginners

After exploring the basics of Smartsheet, you are now equipped with the foundational knowledge to manage tasks, collaborate effectively, and create workflows that improve productivity. However, becoming proficient with Smartsheet is an ongoing journey. In this chapter, we will outline detailed steps to help you build on your newfound knowledge and develop advanced Smartsheet skills over time. These steps are designed to guide beginners through real-world applications, best practices, and additional resources to help you maximize Smartsheet's potential.

Step 1: Practice and Experiment with Basic Features

The best way to solidify your understanding of Smartsheet is by using it regularly. Practice with real projects or create mock sheets to simulate common tasks.

1. **Create Sample Projects**: Start by setting up a few sample projects. For instance, create a personal to-do list, a small project management sheet, or a simple task tracker. This hands-on practice will help you become comfortable with:
    - Creating and editing columns (e.g., text, dropdown, date).
    - Inputting and organizing data.
    - Applying basic formulas, such as SUM or COUNT.

2. **Explore Templates**: Smartsheet offers a wide range of pre-built templates for various use cases, such as project management, marketing calendars, or event planning. Use these templates as a starting point to understand best practices in sheet design.

3. **Experiment with Automation**: Test simple automation workflows, such as setting up alerts for task deadlines or creating approval workflows. This will give you a better understanding of how automation can save time.

Step 2: Develop a Routine for Using Smartsheet

To integrate Smartsheet into your daily workflow, establish habits and routines that ensure consistent use of the platform.

1. **Daily Check-Ins**: Make it a habit to review your Smartsheet projects every morning. Use the built-in notification system to stay updated on tasks, approvals, or changes made by collaborators.

2. **Update Tasks Regularly**: Keep your sheets up-to-date by marking tasks as complete, updating due dates, or adding comments. Consistent updates ensure the accuracy of your data and improve team collaboration.

3. **Set Weekly Goals**: At the start of each week, use Smartsheet to outline key priorities and goals. For example:
   - Create a "Weekly Overview" sheet to track your top objectives.
   - Use conditional formatting to highlight overdue tasks or priorities.

Step 3: Explore Collaboration Features

Collaboration is one of Smartsheet's core strengths. Start leveraging its collaboration tools to work more effectively with your team.

1. **Assigning Tasks**: Assign tasks to team members and ensure they have the necessary permissions to view or edit the sheet. For example:
   - Use the "Assigned To" column to designate responsibilities.
   - Add comments to clarify instructions or provide updates.

2. **Use Comments Effectively**: Smartsheet's comment feature is a powerful tool for communication. Some best practices include:
   - Keeping comments concise and specific.
   - Tagging team members (@username) to ensure they receive notifications.
   - Using comments for updates or approvals rather than cluttering the sheet with extra rows.

3. **Leverage Shared Workspaces**: If you're working on multiple projects with a team, consider creating shared workspaces. This allows you to centralize all related sheets, dashboards, and reports in one location.

Step 4: Learn Advanced Features Gradually

Once you're comfortable with the basics, start exploring more advanced features that can streamline your workflows.

1. **Master Conditional Formatting**: Use conditional formatting to highlight important data automatically. For example:
    - Highlight tasks with approaching deadlines in red.
    - Use color coding to categorize tasks by priority level.

2. **Dive into Reporting**: Learn to create custom reports to consolidate data from multiple sheets. Reports are especially useful for:
    - Tracking overdue tasks across projects.
    - Generating summary views for stakeholders.
    - Combining data for weekly or monthly reviews.

3. **Explore Dashboards**: Dashboards are a visual way to present project progress or key metrics. Start by creating a simple dashboard with:
    - A pie chart showing task status (completed, in progress, overdue).
    - A summary of upcoming deadlines.
    - Key performance indicators (KPIs) for your team.

Step 5: Integrate Smartsheet with Other Tools

Smartsheet integrates seamlessly with many popular tools, enabling you to expand its capabilities and streamline workflows.

1. **Connect Smartsheet to Google Workspace or Microsoft Office**

CONCLUSION

- Import data from Google Sheets or Excel directly into Smartsheet.
- Export Smartsheet reports to Excel for offline sharing or advanced calculations.

2. **Use Smartsheet's Automation Integrations**
    - Integrate with Slack or Microsoft Teams to receive task notifications directly in your messaging app.
    - Automate task updates with platforms like Zapier.

3. **Leverage Calendar Syncing**: Sync Smartsheet with your Google Calendar or Outlook Calendar to keep track of project deadlines and milestones.

Step 6: Engage with the Smartsheet Community

Smartsheet has a vibrant community of users and resources. Engaging with the community can provide you with inspiration, solutions, and tips for using the platform more effectively.

1. **Join the Smartsheet Community Forum**
    - Ask questions, share solutions, and learn from experienced users.
    - Participate in discussions to discover innovative ways to use Smartsheet.

2. **Access Tutorials and Webinars**
    - Explore the official Smartsheet learning center, which includes video tutorials and live webinars.
    - Watch recorded sessions on topics such as project management or automation.

3. **Attend Smartsheet Events**
    - Smartsheet hosts virtual and in-person events where you can learn from experts and network with other users.

Step 7: Develop Your Smartsheet Expertise

To become proficient in Smartsheet, you can aim to achieve certifications or specialize in specific use cases.

1. **Complete the Smartsheet Certification Program**
    - Smartsheet offers certification courses for users at different levels. Completing these certifications can validate your skills and enhance your resume.
2. **Specialize in Specific Use Cases**
    - Identify a niche area where you can use Smartsheet extensively, such as project management, marketing campaigns, or resource allocation.
3. **Share Your Knowledge**
    - Teach others in your organization how to use Smartsheet. Creating internal training resources or hosting workshops can also deepen your own understanding.

Step 8: Plan for Long-Term Use

Finally, think about how you can integrate Smartsheet into your long-term workflows and career growth.

1. **Create a Personal Smartsheet Roadmap**: Set goals for what you want to achieve with Smartsheet. For instance:
    - Improve your team's project completion rate.
    - Automate 80% of recurring tasks.
2. **Review and Optimize Regularly**
    - Schedule regular reviews of your sheets and workflows to identify areas for improvement.
    - Update automation rules or templates as your needs evolve.

CONCLUSION

3. **Expand Your Use of Smartsheet**: Over time, consider exploring premium Smartsheet features, such as Control Center, Dynamic View, or premium integrations, to handle complex projects and enterprise-scale requirements.

By following these steps, you will continue to grow your Smartsheet skills and build confidence in using the platform for personal and professional success. Remember, the key to mastery is practice, exploration, and consistent learning. Let Smartsheet evolve with you as your needs expand, and you'll unlock its full potential in no time.

Made in the USA
Thornton, CO
01/23/25 20:23:15

394d7833-535e-4613-b31a-bd23894a8294R03

Acknowledgments

I would like to extend my heartfelt gratitude to you, the reader, for choosing **"Smartsheet for Beginners: The Quick-Start Guide"**. *Your decision to purchase this book marks the beginning of your journey toward mastering Smartsheet, and I truly hope that it provides you with valuable insights and tools to optimize your work processes.*

Creating this book has been a rewarding experience, and I couldn't have completed it without the support of the Smartsheet community and the countless individuals who shared their experiences and knowledge. Special thanks to the Smartsheet team for developing such an intuitive platform that has inspired so many people worldwide.

I also want to acknowledge the readers, professionals, and experts in the field of project management and collaboration tools. Your feedback, suggestions, and shared experiences have helped shape this book into something practical and useful for beginners and seasoned users alike.

To my family, friends, and mentors, thank you for your unwavering support throughout this project. Your encouragement and belief in my work have made this possible.

Lastly, to you, the reader—thank you for investing your time and trust in this book. I hope it serves as a valuable resource in your Smartsheet journey and beyond. Keep exploring, learning, and making the most out of Smartsheet!

Best wishes,